IMAGES
of America

CAMERON TRADING POST

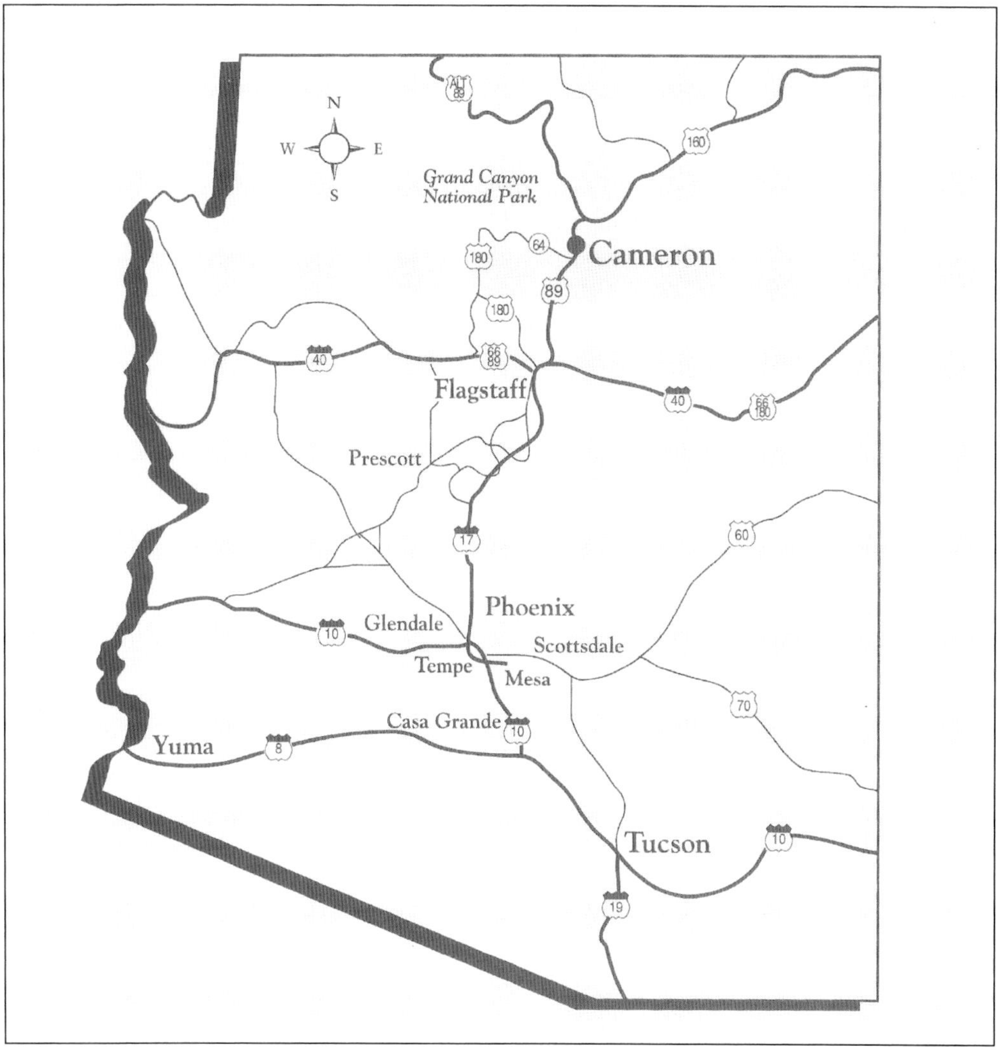

Cameron, Arizona, is located 50 miles north of Flagstaff on Highway 89 and just a mile north of Highway 64 heading west to the Grand Canyon. Hubert Richardson and his brother Claude Dick, or "C.D.," established the Little Colorado Trading Post in 1916 but renamed it Cameron in 1924 after territorial senator Ralph Cameron, who was instrumental in obtaining congressional funding for the bridge over the Little Colorado River. (Courtesy of Atkinson Trading Company.)

ON THE COVER: A group of local residents gathers for a photograph in front of Cameron Trading Post in the 1940s. From left to right are (first row) Norman Cody, Betty Ann Huskon, Jean Cody, Jean Mann, Sally Littlesmith, and Kee Cody; (second row) Evans Huskon, Max Huskon, Roy Huskon, Charlie Huskon, Harrison Sloan, Joe Kerley, Haskall Means, and Moody Semallie. Roy Huskon, whose portrait is above the door of the store, worked at the trading post. (Courtesy of Tom Collins.)

IMAGES
of America

CAMERON TRADING POST

Carolyn O'Bagy Davis

ARCADIA
PUBLISHING

ISBN 978-1-4671-1697-8

Published by Arcadia Publishing
Charleston, South Carolina

Printed in the United States of America

Library of Congress Control Number: 2015960687

For all general information, please contact Arcadia Publishing:
Telephone 843-853-2070
Fax 843-853-0044
E-mail sales@arcadiapublishing.com
For customer service and orders:
Toll-Free 1-888-313-2665

Visit us on the Internet at www.arcadiapublishing.com

To the people of Cameron and to the Atkinson family for their stewardship and care in preserving the beauty and traditions of Cameron Trading Post on the joyous centennial celebration of their first 100 years.

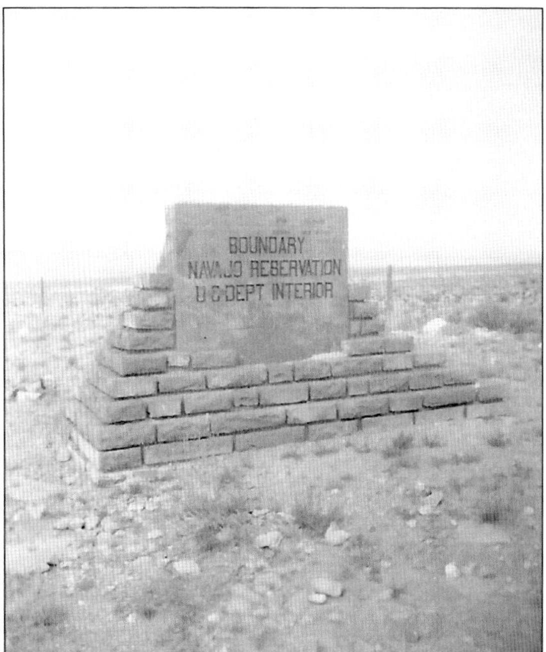

The Navajo Indian Nation, with a population of 300,000, covers 27,000 square miles across northern Arizona, southern Utah, and northwestern New Mexico. This 1940s image of the Navajo Reservation boundary marker is near Gray Mountain Trading Post on Highway 89, north of Flagstaff, Arizona. (Courtesy of Editha Watson.)

Contents

ACKNOWLEDGMENTS

For their generous help and support, I would like to thank Robert Arnold, Jim Babbitt, Lisa Baldwin, Brian Barker, Kim Besom, Virgil Bigsinger, Luana Boyd, Dan Cassidy, Tom Collins, Steven Curtis, Al Dart, Joan DeVine, Diane Drobka, Al Ferg, Gwen M. Gallenstein, David Gillette, Jamie Gould, Ann Empie Groves, Kayla Hawthorne, Anne Hillerman, Jimmy Jensen, Leland Jones, Peter L. Kresan, Harvey Leake, Ann-Mary Lutzick and Old Trails Museum, Richard and Sherry Mangum, Joe McNeill, Abraham Mohler, Lana O'Brien, Gayle Ortega, Alan Pratt, Sally Preston, Jonathan Marc Pringle, Bill Richardson, Frances Richardson, Joe Rodgers, Wilma Rodgers Seeley, May Stevens, Mark Sublette and Medicine Man Gallery, Paul and Mae Talker, Emerald Tanner, Joe E. Tanner, Scott Thybony, Margaret Van Cleve, Linda Vanderwagon, Ryan Jess Vogelsang, Angel Walker, Tex and Helyn Walker, Janelle Weakley, John S. Westerlund, Caroline Wilson, and Betty Rodgers Worthey.

Unless otherwise noted, all photographs are from the collection of the author.

Please note that Navajo text that appears next to a personal name is the Navajo translation of that name.

INTRODUCTION

Cameron is the heart of northern Arizona, the crossroads for all travel, the hub for trails and roads leading north and east. Before the 1911 construction of a suspension bridge across the Little Colorado River at the western edge of the Painted Desert, historic and prehistoric trails crossed the river near the site that later became known as Cameron. Nearby Tanner's Crossing was considered the safest crossing for wagons and horses. Native people, Spanish explorers, mountain men, government surveyors, Mormons, and other pioneers all crossed the Little Colorado River near present-day Cameron. And even at that historic site, the quicksand-bottomed river nearly swallowed wagons, animals, and equipment or swept them away in the muddy, torrential flash floods that raced along the generally dry riverbed. Mormon historian James H. McClintock writes that "the Little Colorado River is a treacherous stream at best with a broad channel that wanders at will through the alluvial country that melts like sugar or salt at the touch of water." Author Zane Grey first journeyed north of Flagstaff in 1907 on a trip to the Grand Canyon's north rim. In a letter to his wife, Grey writes that he was dreading the Little Colorado River crossing. The river was rising, and "there was sure to be trouble."

On a 1908 trip, Grey wrote of "hot flying sand. Stifling, blistering heat," in the valley of the Little Colorado. A crossing of the Painted Desert was a long and arduous journey. In 1911, Arizona historian Sharlot Hall recorded that "the country looked like it has just come out of the oven."

To the west of Cameron, the impassible Little Colorado River Gorge opened dramatically on its way to meet the Colorado River at the bottom of the Grand Canyon. From Tanner's Crossing, deep wagon ruts led north through the trackless Painted Desert to the dangerous raft crossing at Lee's Ferry on the Colorado River. In between, there was nothing.

A few Navajo families lived in hogans scattered across the Painted Desert, herding sheep in search of grass in the barren landscape. Then, in 1916, Hubert and C.D. Richardson claimed 112 acres and built a trading post on the south side of the river, just five years after construction of the narrow suspension bridge. In the early years, almost all of the customers were Navajos. Hubert, who took over Cameron from his brother, traded with them for wool, skins, livestock, and rugs, and very soon, travelers began to patronize Cameron, stopping for food as well as lodging. Cameron became the crossroads, the jumping-off point for travelers journeying through Arizona in all the compass directions. A century later, Hubert Richardson's trading post is an Arizona institution. Cameron is seen by guests from all over the world who visit the curio shop, market, a restaurant with two full kitchens that seats 240 guests, a 66-room motel, art gallery, US post office, gas station, convenience store, gardens, online store, and an RV park. Tour groups are often booked up to two years in advance, and it is not unusual to see 8 to 12 tour buses in the large parking area. The tiny community of Cameron is surrounded by the Navajo Indian Reservation, and local Navajo people form the competent staff that operates this huge enterprise.

Joe Atkinson, C.D. Richardson's grandnephew, took over the lease for Cameron Trading Post in 1977, finalizing the purchase in 1983. Atkinson recalled that at the time of the purchase, he had no money and had to borrow the down payment, using "creative financing." Although Cameron Trading Post is surrounded by the Navajo Reservation, it is an independent business enterprise; therefore, the store and business do not fall under Navajo tribal law. When the Richardson brothers established Cameron Trading Post in 1916, the reservation boundary ended at the Little Colorado River. In 1934, the boundary was moved several miles to the south, and in 1940, Congress deeded Richardson the land in a special act.

The list of famous people who have visited Cameron Trading Post over the decades could fill pages. Oliver La Farge, Pulitzer Prize winner for *Laughing Boy,* visited Cameron in 1921 and writes an account of his visit in *Raw Material.* Western writer Dane Coolidge stayed at Cameron in 1925, where he wrote the first outline for a book he titled *Talking Rock.* The hero of his story is named Blue Eyes, very likely a reference to Hubert Richardson, whose Navajo name was Naa' Dootlizhii, or Blue Eyes. Author Zane Grey used Cameron as a setting in several of his books, and almost a dozen movie adaptations of Grey's stories were filmed at and around Cameron. Contemporary author Tony Hillerman knew local Cameron residents and set several scenes from his mysteries at the trading post.

In 1929, astronomer Edwin Hubble, who proved the existence of other galaxies, stayed at Cameron with his wife, Grace, and went out to nearby Dinosaur Canyon searching for petrified wood and fossils. Sports stars and movie stars visited Cameron. Errol Flynn, Randolph Scott, Humphrey Bogart, and John Wayne stayed at Cameron while filming westerns in northern Arizona. One former store manager recalled that on one occasion, Wayne was briefly locked in the men's lavatory when the handle fell off the door. Everyone was amazed when, after some pounding and yelling—and locating a maintenance worker—Wayne strode out of the men's room.

Lenny Mora, store manager in the 1980s, related that Goldie Hawn and Jeff Bridges visited and shopped at the store in 1985. Many employees and visitors were impressed, but Mora did not know who they were because television service had only come to Cameron the previous year; plus, he always worked such long hours, he never had time to watch the programs. The comedian Red Skelton was a repeat customer who came to the trading post to purchase Navajo rug weavings.

Barry Goldwater visited Cameron in the early 1920s and recalled that it was a small post, a "handful of tents and huts." Another politician, Richard Nixon, was marooned at Cameron during a snowstorm in the early 1930s when he was a law student. In later years, as US president, Nixon held secret meetings at Cameron with his notorious associate Bebe Rebozo, and a last visit, also with Rebozo, took place in the 1970s, shortly after Nixon resigned from office.

Cameron Trading Post is one of the last remaining authentic trading posts in the Southwest. The store blends modern commerce with traditional Indian trading customs and continues to serve as the active trade and cultural center of the area.

Over the last 100 years, Cameron Trading Post has become a favorite stopping place for travelers. As Arizona author Scott Thybony note, Cameron Trading Post is the main event for 100 miles. "Tour buses, trucks pulling boats down from Lake Powell, rental cars returning from the Grand Canyon, and pickups in from the sheep camps all end up here."

One

A Treacherous Stream at Best

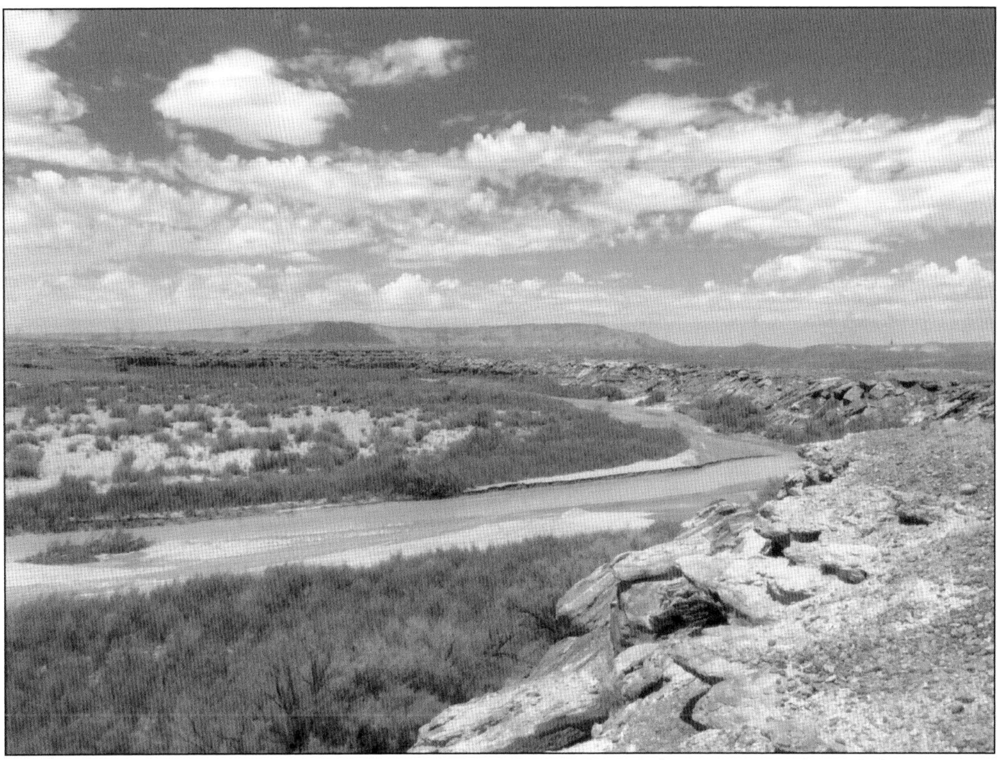

The Little Colorado River posed the threat of raging floods and dangerous quicksand that claimed wagons, freight, horses, and travelers. When it flooded, the river was too dangerous to attempt a crossing; at other times, the riverbed could be dry. As one traveler wrote, the river was too thick to drink and too thin to plow.

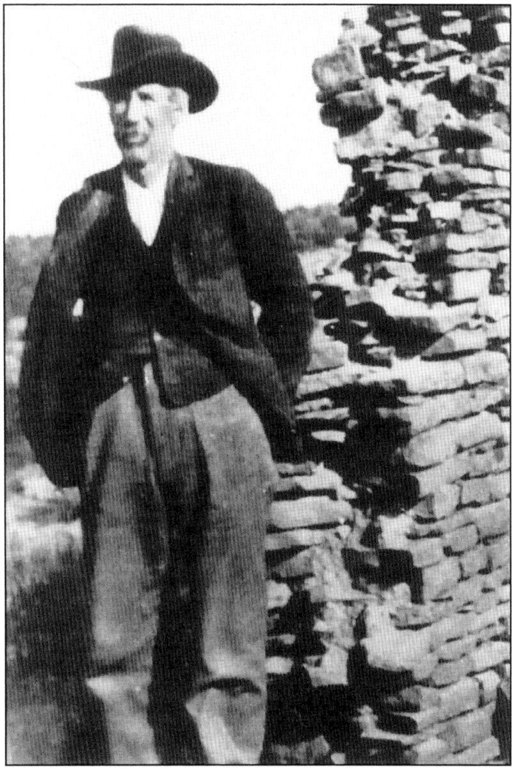

A member of a Mormon exploration party from Utah, Seth Tanner first came to Arizona Territory in 1875. Tanner later returned to Arizona Territory, where he built an isolated cabin on the Little Colorado River just east of Cameron. The site, known as Tanner's Crossing, was one of the safest places to cross the river. Tanner knew the areas that had the firmest footing and when it would be safe to venture across the water and avoid quicksand. In addition to being a river crossing guide, Tanner prospected in the Grand Canyon. Besides Tanner's Crossing, there is also a Tanner's Spring and Tanner Wash, and in the Grand Canyon, there is a Tanner Mine and a Tanner Trail. Tanner's name to local Navajo people was Hosteen Shush, or Mister Bear. (Left, courtesy of Joe E. Tanner.)

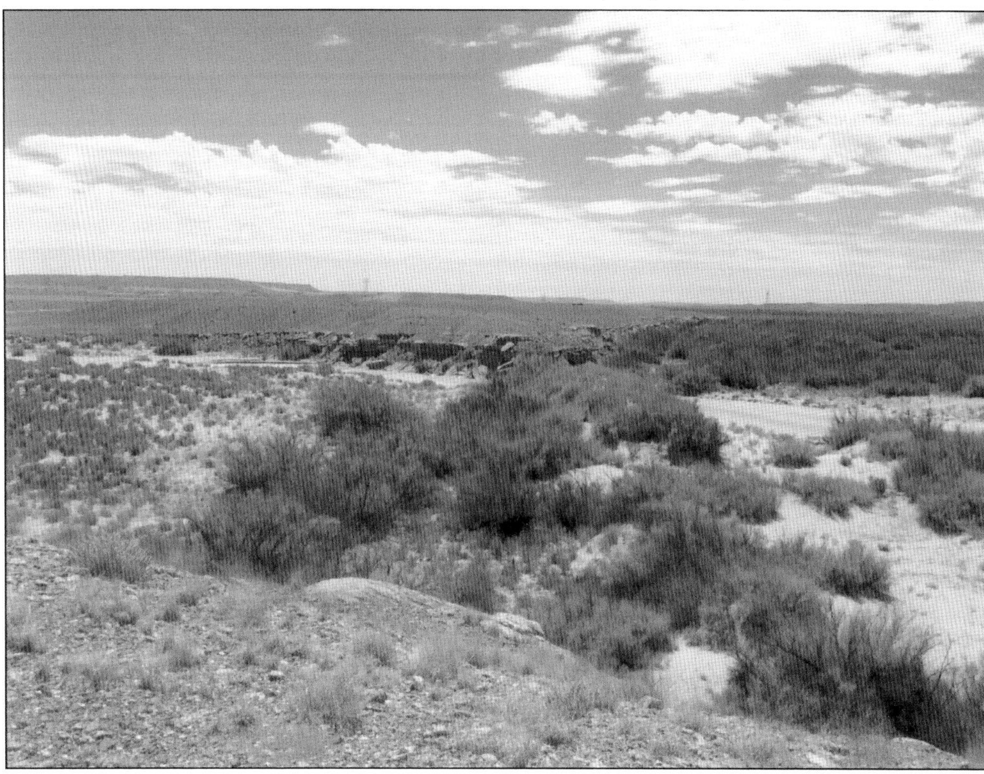

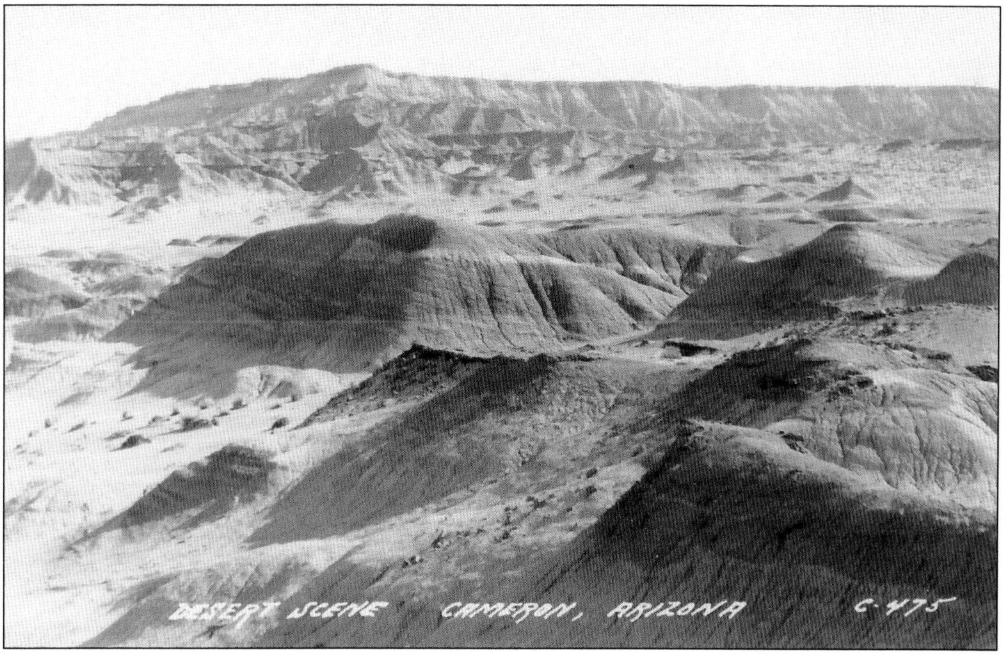

The Painted Desert extends east from Cameron to Holbrook and the Petrified Forest, encompassing 7,500 square miles. It is sometimes known as the Blue Desert, and the colors are striking, even with the nearly total lack of vegetation. In 1927, writer William Hamilton Nelson speculated that the desert must be "the earthly palate of some celestial angels," and that "a chameleon would naturally explode in this desert trying to change to all of these colors." (Courtesy of Lisa Amaral.)

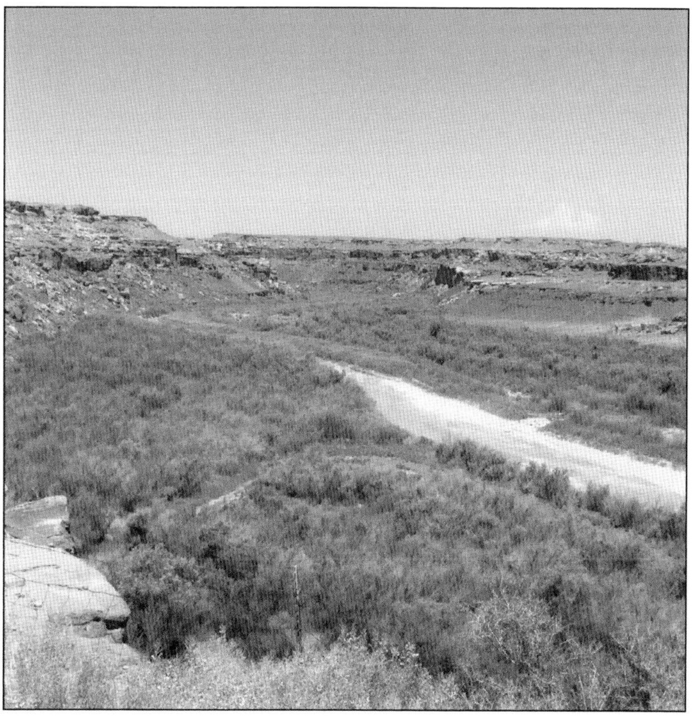

The Little Colorado River drains the Painted Desert, running 340 miles from western New Mexico and eastern Arizona to the Colorado River. Except for the headwaters and lower end of the river, it is dry most of the year. In 1873, Norwegian missionary Andrew Amundsen wrote: "The little Colorado . . . it is . . . no plase fit for a human being to dwell upon. The moste desert lukking plase that I ever saw, Amen."

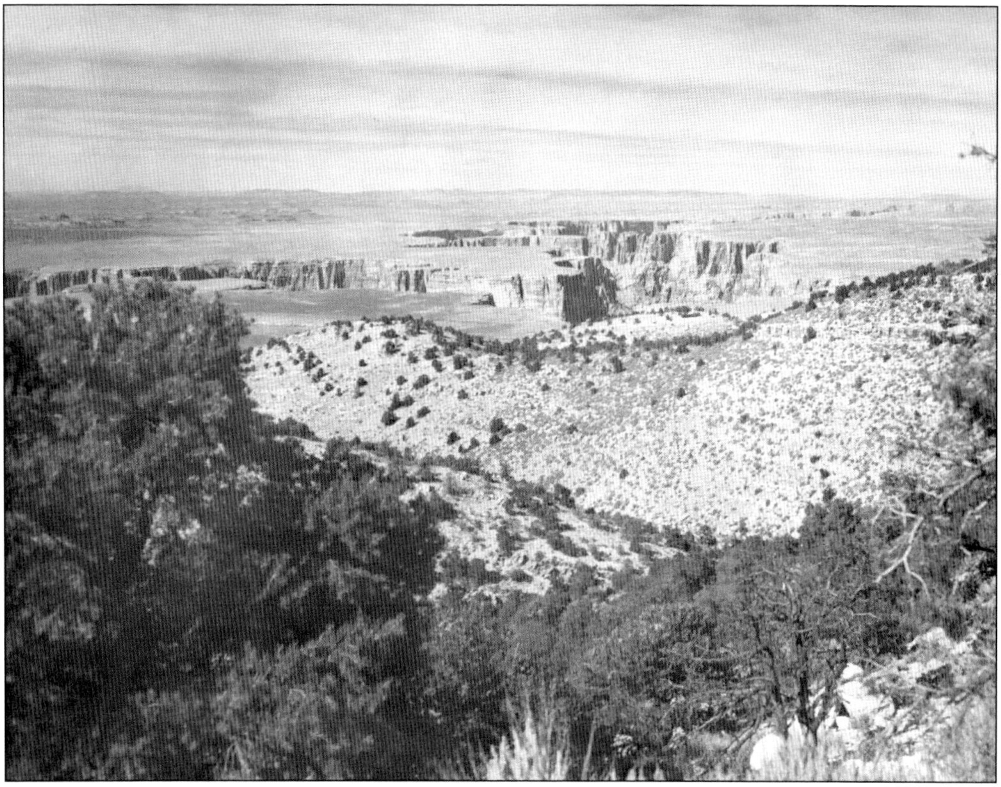

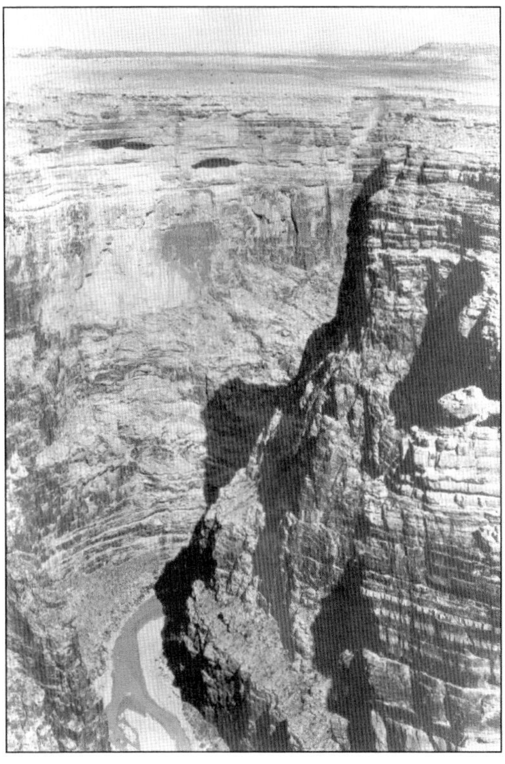

At Cameron, the broad, mostly dry riverbed of the Little Colorado flows west, dropping into an ever-deepening gorge, falling 2,000 feet in 30 miles as it runs to the Colorado River. Sheer rock walls frame the river, making it impassable for most of its length. (Above, courtesy of Grand Canyon Museum Collection, No. 02353; left, photograph by George Grant, courtesy of Grand Canyon Museum Collection, No. 12628.)

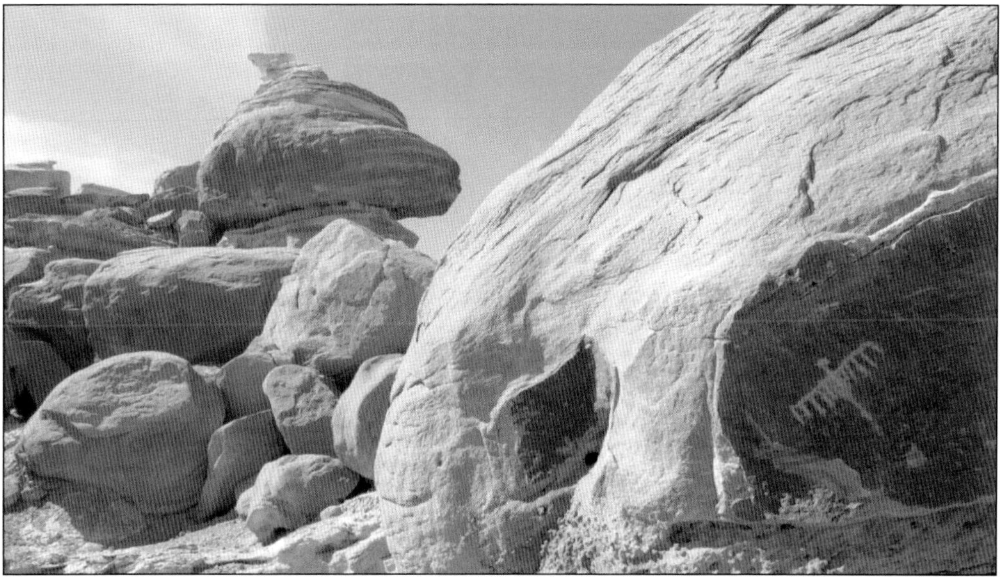

Ancient trails traverse the Painted Desert. At the confluence of the Colorado and the Little Colorado Rivers is the Sipapu, revered by the Hopi as the place of emergence into this world. An Archaic traveler carved the thunderbird petroglyph, seen above, a spirit guide through the ages. Spanish explorers also passed this way. In 1540, Francisco Vázquez de Coronado sent Don García López de Cárdenas to find a river to the west. On the eastern edge of the Grand Canyon, the words "Monte Video" are carved on a sandstone ledge, possibly recording the first sighting of the canyon. Recent research has mostly discounted the 1540 inscription; however, it is certain that the Spanish exploration party would have passed near the future site of Cameron. (Above, courtesy of Scott Thybony; below, courtesy of Grand Canyon Museum Collection.)

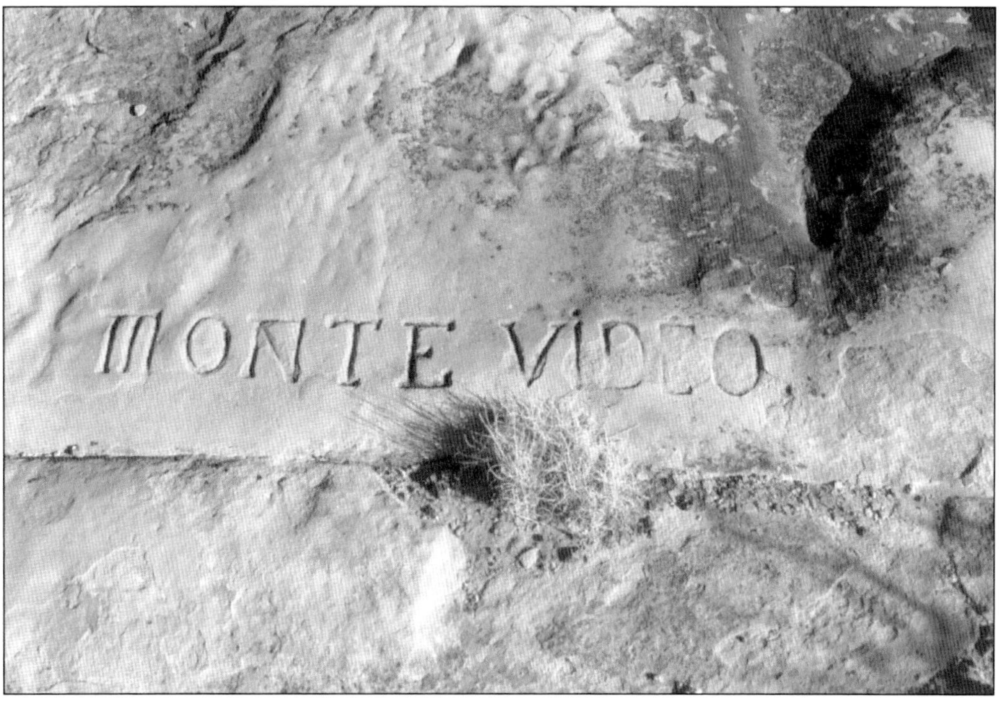

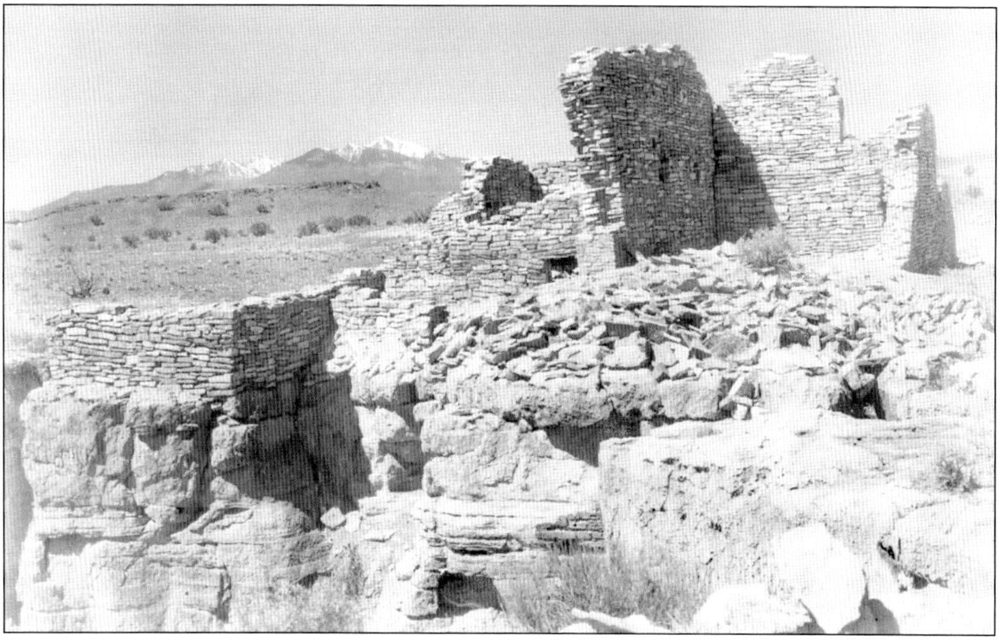

Capt. Lorenzo Sitgreaves, a government topographical engineer, led the first scientific expedition across Arizona in the fall of 1851; later, the Sitgreaves National Forest in eastern-central Arizona was named in his honor. Leaving Zuni Pueblo in western New Mexico, the expedition followed the Zuni River to the Little Colorado River hoping to discover a navigable river in the Southwest. But Sitgreaves learned that the river dropped into a deep gorge near Cameron. The expedition then traveled south and discovered the prehistoric ruins at Wupatki. Sitgreaves recorded that the ground was strewn with pottery. Lomaki Pueblo, pictured above, was built on the edge of a vertical-walled canyon. In the distance, the snowcapped San Francisco Peaks rise above the ruin. Crack-in-the-Rock, seen below, was a defensive site accessible through a narrow chimney that opens into the pueblo. (Above, courtesy of the National Park Service, WUPA 13470; below, courtesy of the National Park Service, WUPA 13400.)

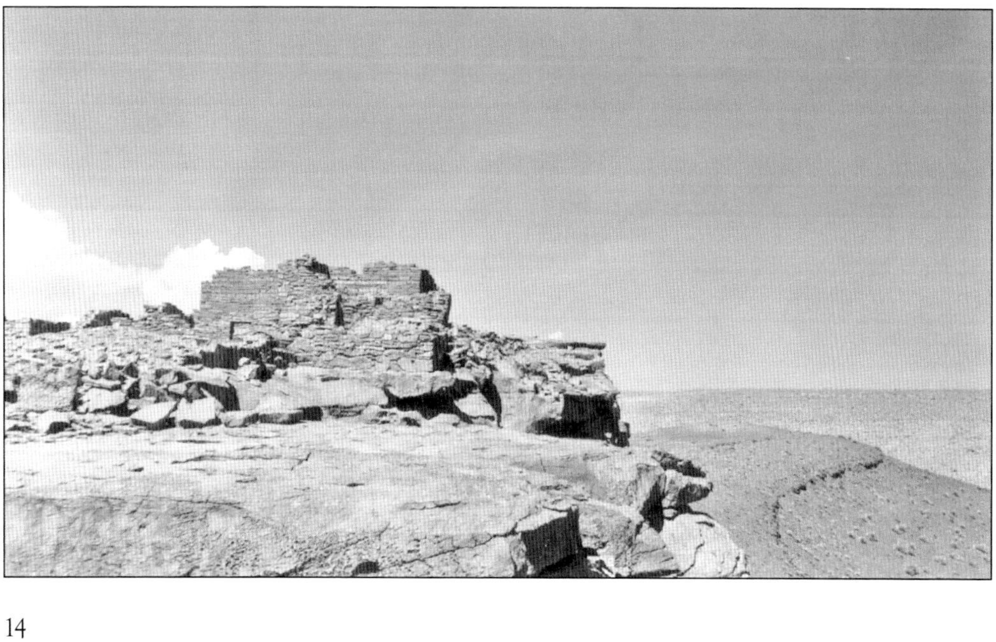

Water for Cameron Trading Post was obtained from Tappan Spring, just downriver from the store. In 1883, John W. Young established the Arizona Cattle Company, known as the A One Bar outfit. The range covered 875 square miles and was one of the largest cattle operations in the west. Because of the reliable water source at Tappan Spring, a winter camp was established, and due to its remote and nearly hidden location below the rim, the site was also popular with rustlers. Unknown numbers of stolen cattle were branded in the corrals near the spring. (Right, photograph by Art Metzger, courtesy of Grand Canyon Museum Collection, No. 18730.)

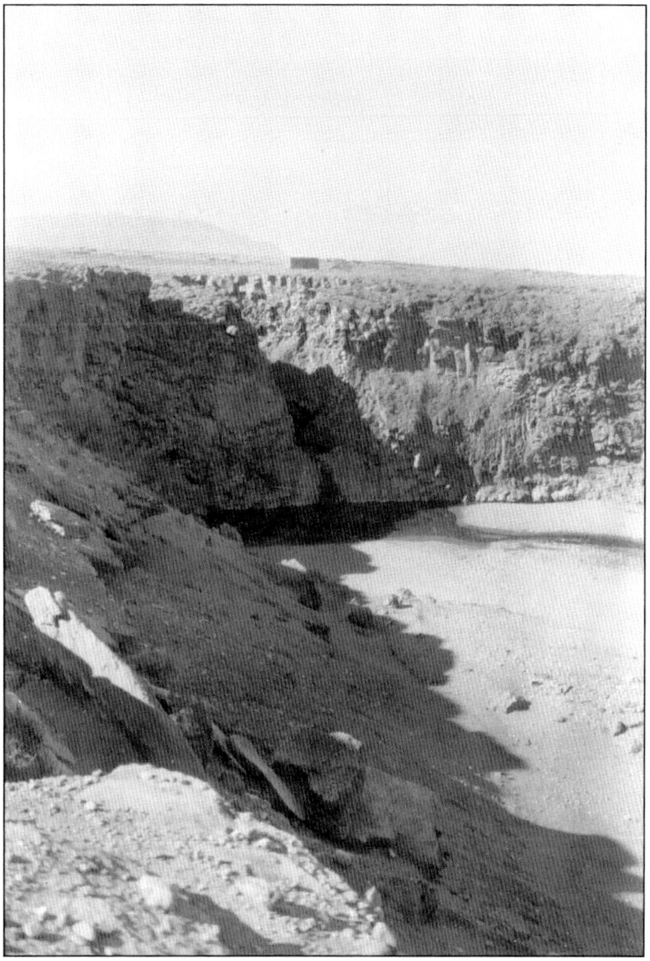

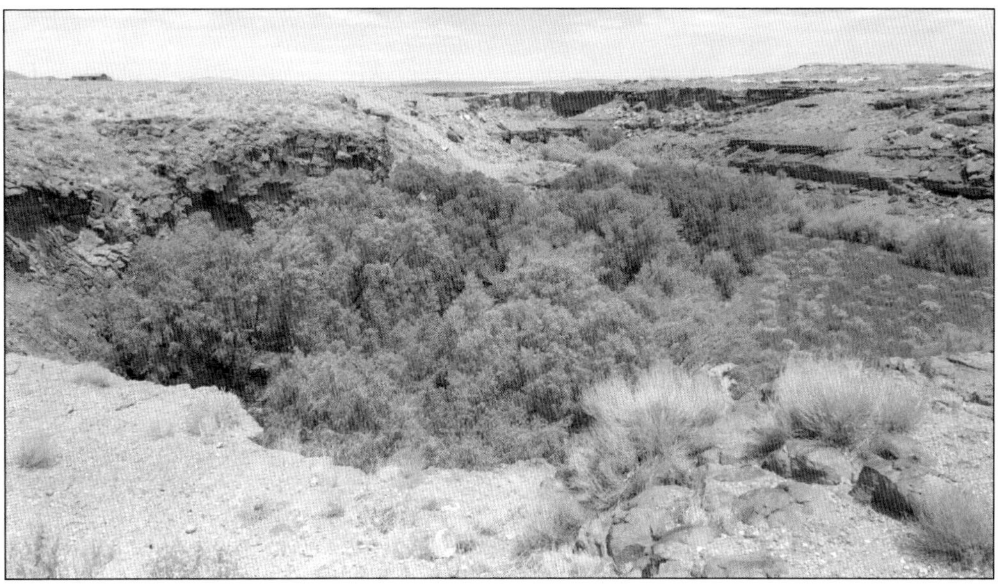

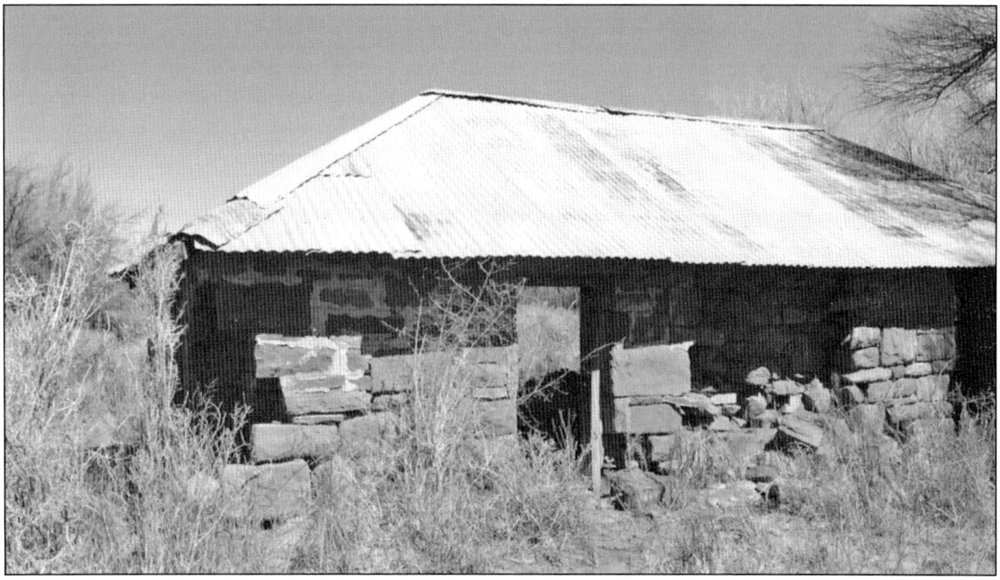

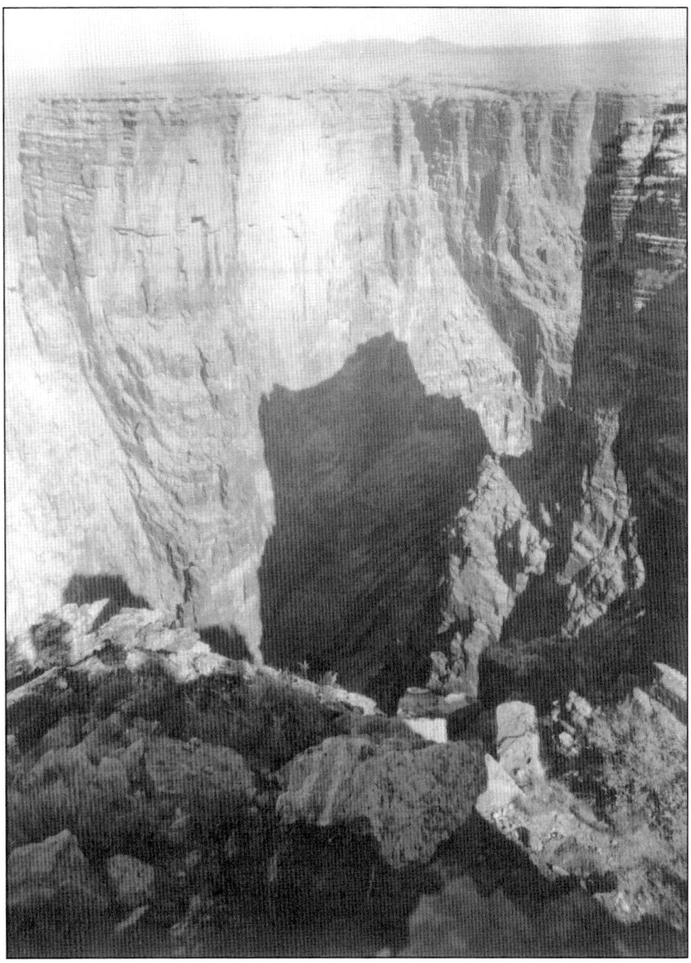

The stone, tin-roofed building was a line camp from the A One Bar Ranch. Pictographs near Tappan Spring Canyon indicate that this area has been traversed by people since ancient times. Below Tappan Spring, the river dropped deeper into the Little Colorado River Gorge. Cowboys called this part of the Gorge "Poison Canyon," because one drop meant death. This photograph was taken in 1924 by a member of the Doheny Scientific Expedition. (Above, courtesy of Scott Thybony; left, courtesy of Grand Canyon Museum Collection, No. 18739.)

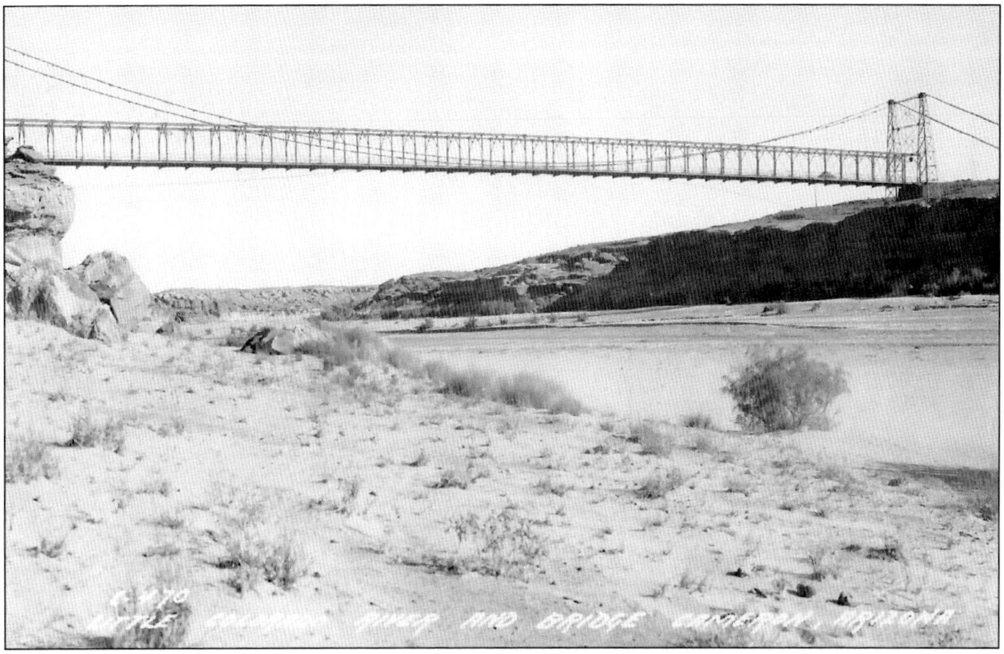

Built in 1911, the Cameron Bridge, at 660 feet, was the longest suspension bridge west of the Mississippi River. It is located at the point of the Little Colorado River where it plunges into a sheer-walled gorge. Constructed by the Kansas City Midland Bridge Company, the lightweight bridge had a 14-foot roadway. During construction, Tuba City trader Samuel Preston erected a temporary tin shack to serve as a trading post and supply site. Materials used in the construction of the bridge had to be hauled by wagon from Flagstaff, located 50 miles south. Preston had the freighting contract, and his wife operated the trading post. At right, a very early horseless carriage vehicle has stopped on the bridge. The automobile has right-hand drive and tall wheels, like those used on wagons. (Both, courtesy of Lisa Amaral.)

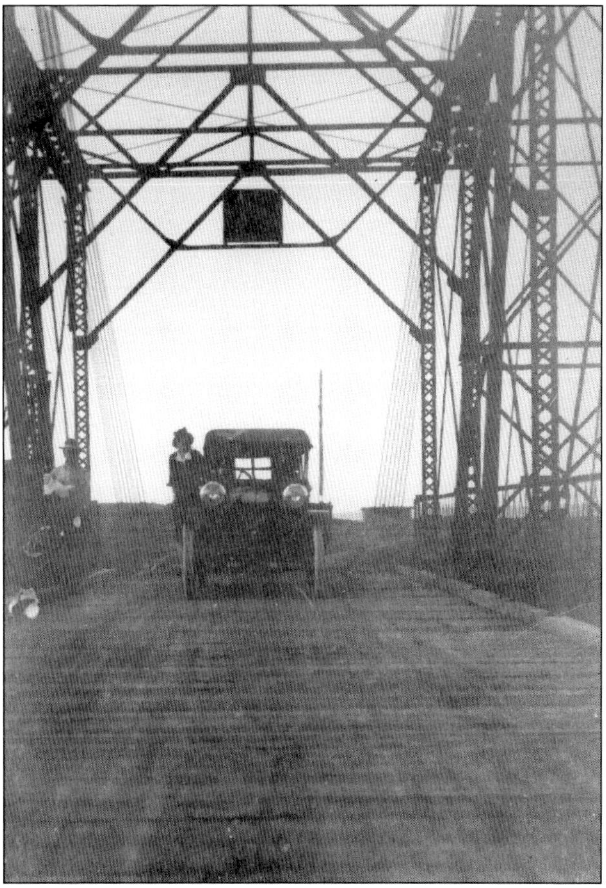

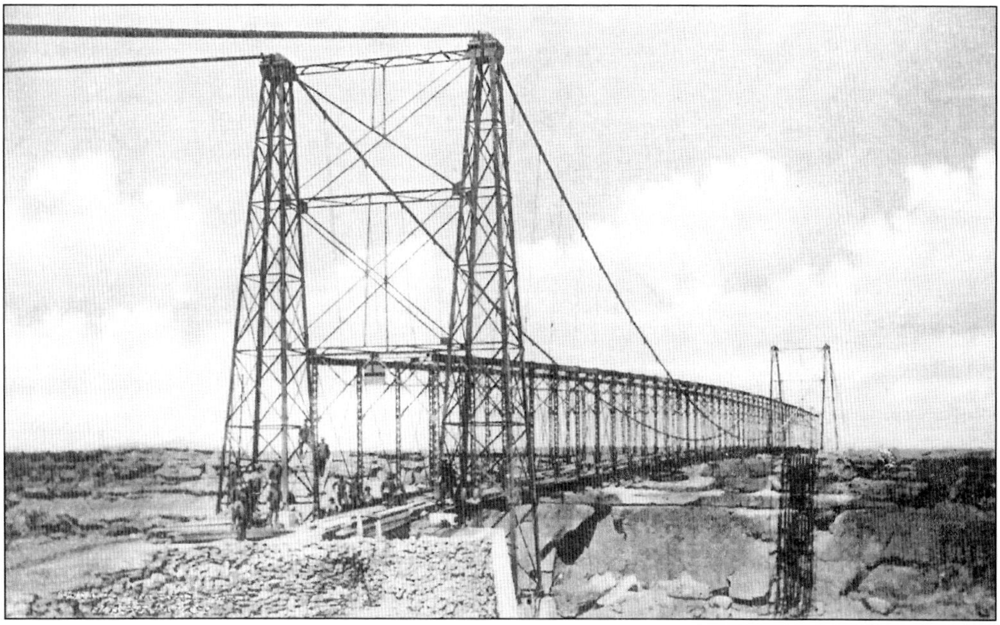

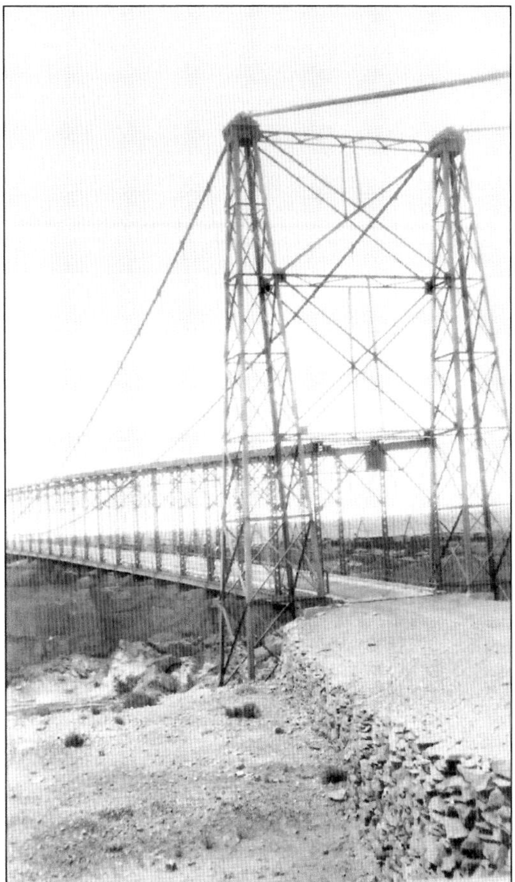

Several Navajos came from the Shonto area to work on construction of the bridge. Some names and initials of the workmen can still be seen inscribed in the concrete supports under the bridge. Many of the workmen and their families stayed, establishing the small community that came to be known as Cameron. Above, workmen lay a new wooden bed on the bridge about 1919. After the bridge was built, Sam Preston abandoned his small trading post and returned to Tuba City. (Above, courtesy of Tom Collins; left, courtesy of Lisa Amaral.)

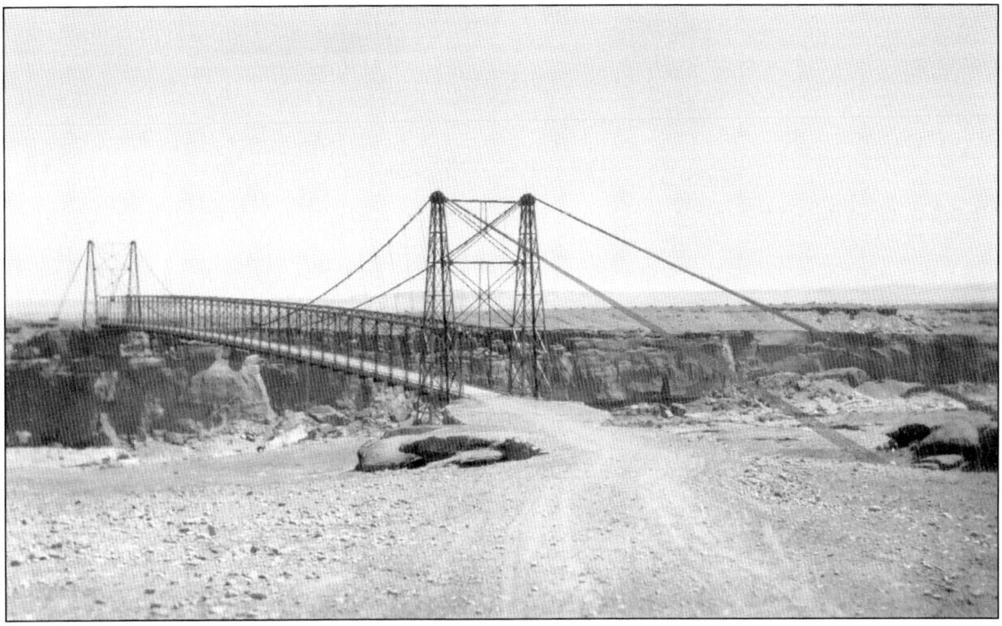

In 1913, four years after serving as the 26th president of the United States, Theodore Roosevelt visited northern Arizona, crossing the Little Colorado River at Cameron on the two-year-old bridge. Roosevelt and his party traveled to the North Rim, where he hunted at "Uncle" Jimmy Owens's cabin. Roosevelt later attended a snake dance on the Hopi Mesas and took a horse-packing trip to Rainbow Bridge with guide John Wetherill. Members of the hunting party, from left to right, are Archibald B. Roosevelt, Nicholas Roosevelt, Theodore Roosevelt, Uncle Jimmy Owens, Quinten Roosevelt, and Jesse Cummins. (Above, courtesy of Grand Canyon Museum Collection, No. 10706; below, courtesy of Grand Canyon Museum Collection, No. 10455.)

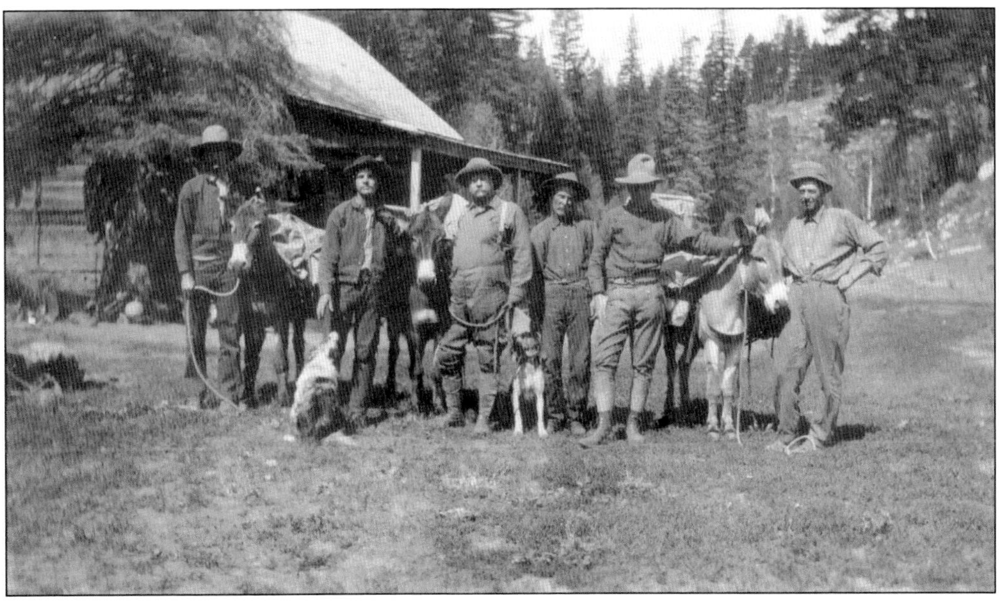

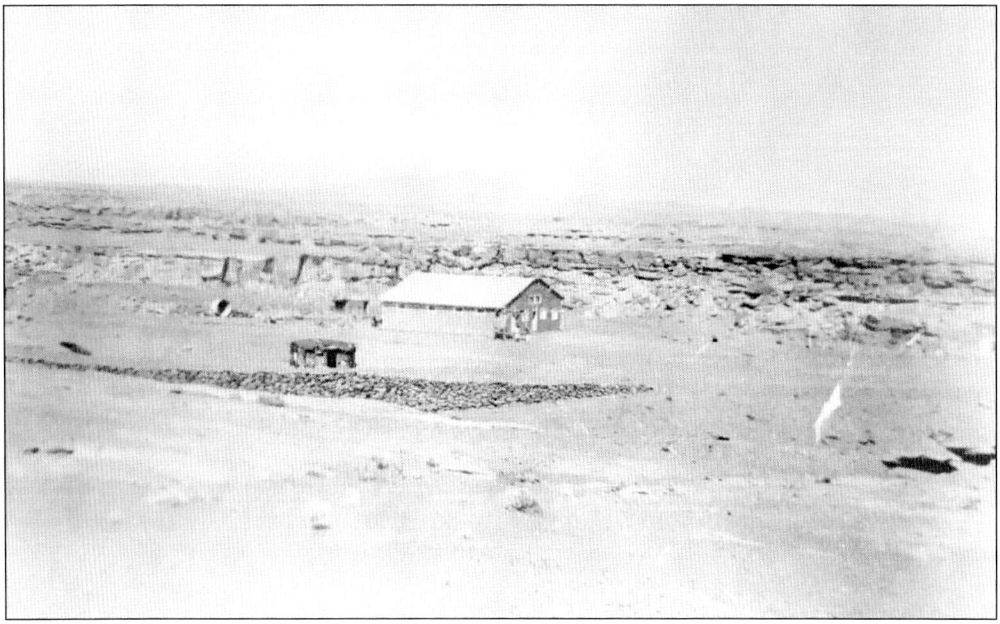

After completion of the steel suspension bridge across the Little Colorado River in 1911, Hubert Richardson looked at the site for a potential trading post but decided it would not be a profitable area. Five years later, he returned after learning that cattle buyers had purchased 3,000 head of cattle from Navajo ranchers in nearby Gray Mountain. In 1916, Richardson built an east-facing store on the south side of the bridge. It was originally called Little Colorado Trading Post but was later renamed Cameron after Ralph Henry Cameron. Richardson recalled that local Navajo families owned huge herds of sheep and cattle, 600 or 800 sheep was common, and it was not unusual to have 1,200 to 1,700 sheep at the post for shipment to Flagstaff or Winslow. (Above, courtesy of Atkinson Trading Company.)

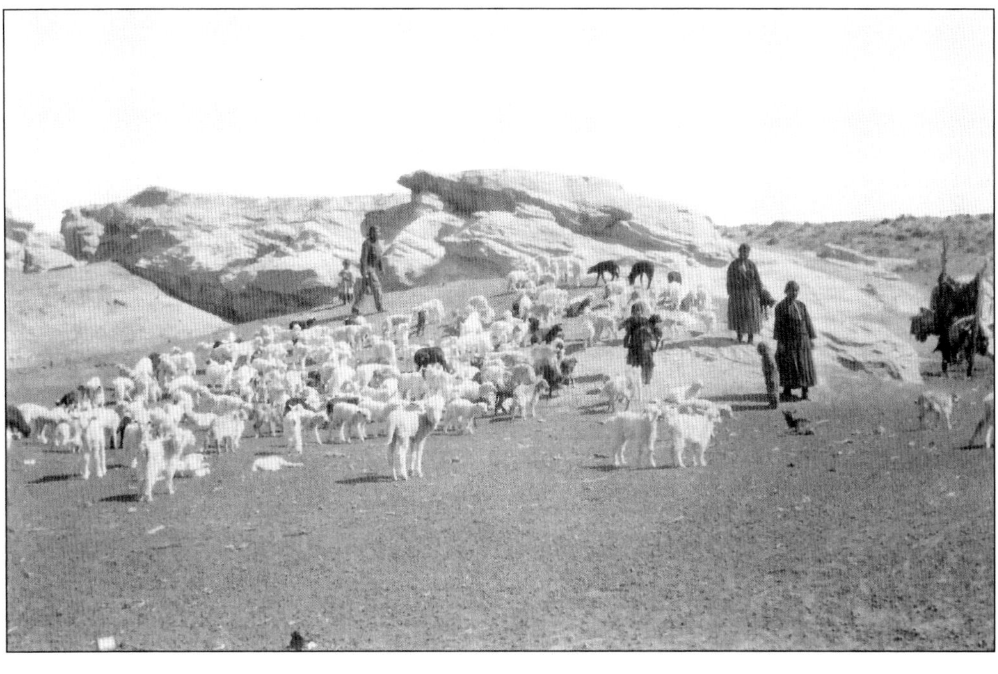

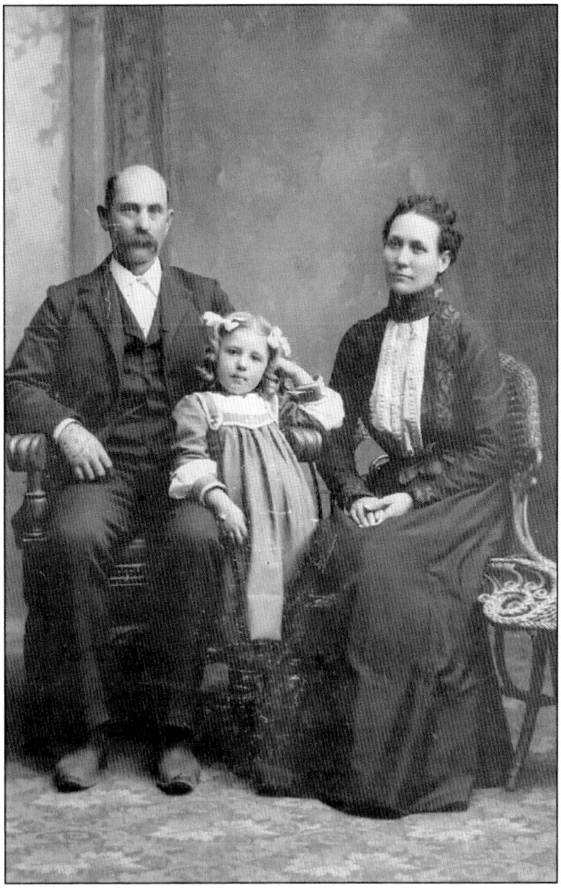

John W. Richardson (1851–1937) had seven children—sons Julius, Samuel Irby, Virgil, Claude Dick, and Hubert and daughters Ethel and Mary Jane—before he was widowed. He subsequently married Mattie Keys, with whom he had another daughter, Freeda. The boys became traders, and the girls married men who also were traders. Below, from left to right, C.D. partnered with his brother Hubert at Blue Canyon and operated Shonto, Kaibeto, the Gap, Tuba City, and Sunrise Trading Posts; Samuel "S.I." Irby had Wolf Post, Rainbow Lodge, Inscription House, and Two Guns Trading Posts; Mary Jane is pictured in the middle; Julius died as a young man; and Hubert owned Sunrise Springs, Indian Wells, Blue Canyon, Leupp, and Cameron Trading Posts. (The brothers bought and sold trading posts fairly frequently.) (Both, courtesy of Lana O'Brien.)

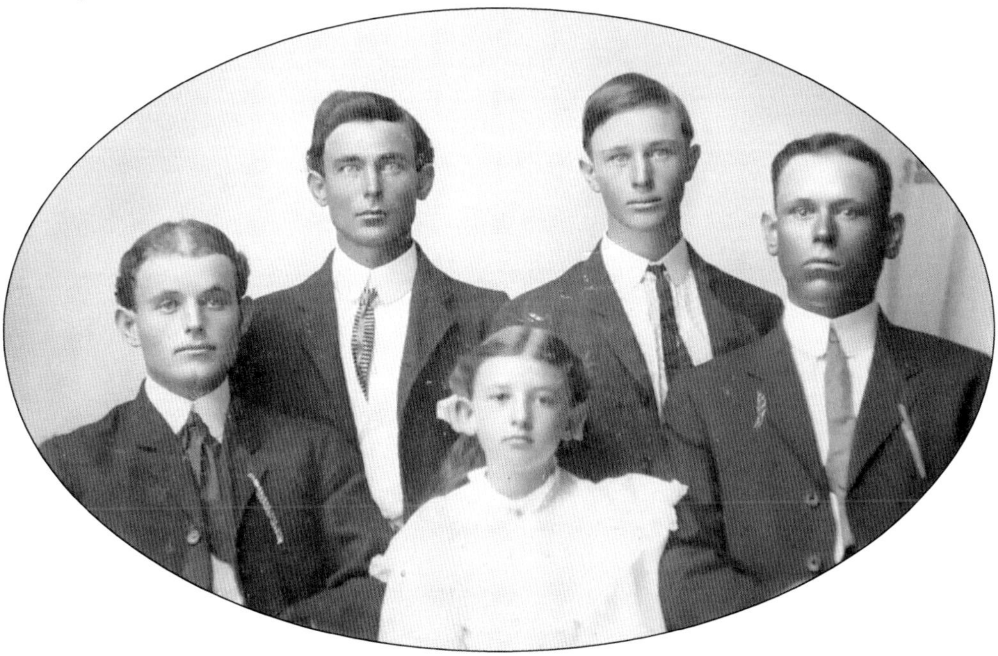

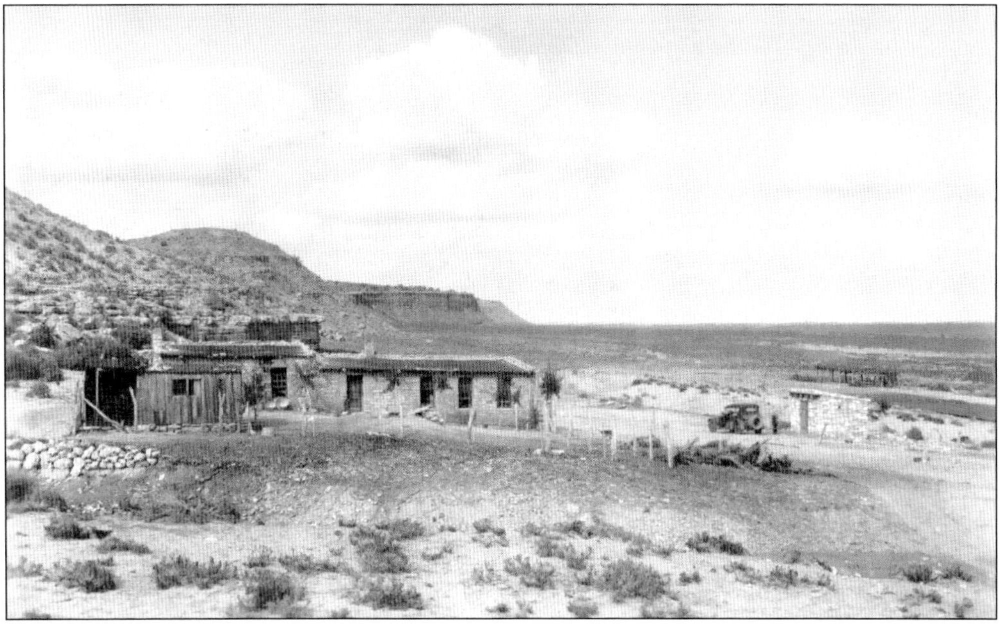

Hubert Richardson came from a trading family. In 1909, at age 19, he acquired Sunrise Springs Trading Post from his uncle Joel Higgins "J.H." McAdams. The following year, he bought Indian Wells Trading Post from his nephew Gladwell "Toney" Richardson. In the 1911 photograph below, Hubert's uncle George "Pink" McAdams visited Indian Wells Trading Post. McAdams is second from the right, and others are unidentified. McAdams opened his first trading post about 1879; it was a stockade cabin on Rabbit Mesa just north of Tuba City. Two years later, he moved northeast to Redlake, and later had other trading posts: Willow Springs, Tuba City, Wolf Post, and Houck. His first wife was a Navajo lady, Chischillígie Bitce, the daughter of a Navajo headman from the Redlake area. Their daughter was Assan Nahtahni, or Headman's Daughter. (Above, courtesy of Harvey Leake; below, courtesy of Lana O'Brien.)

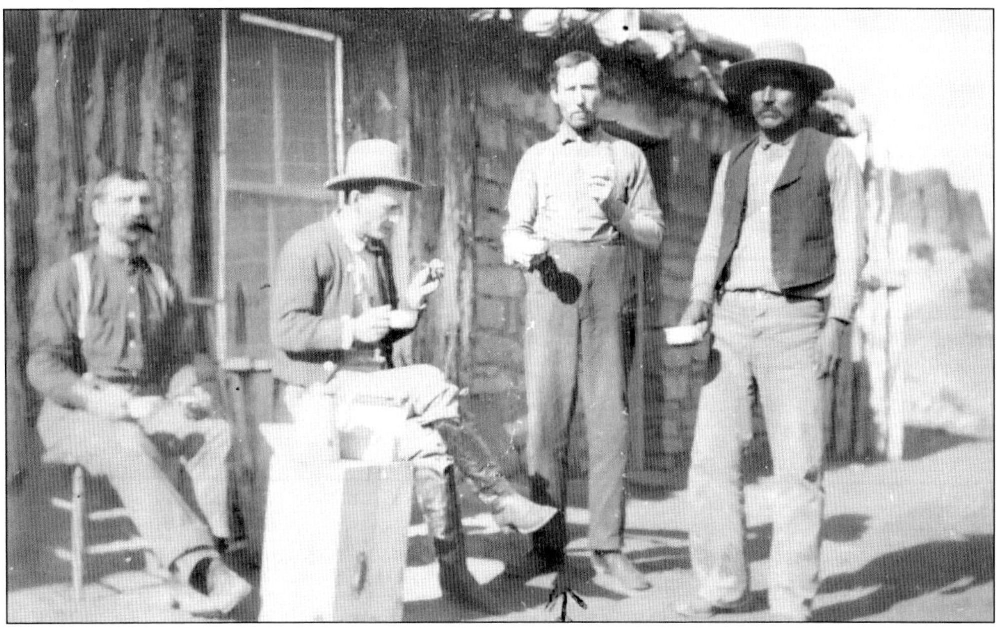

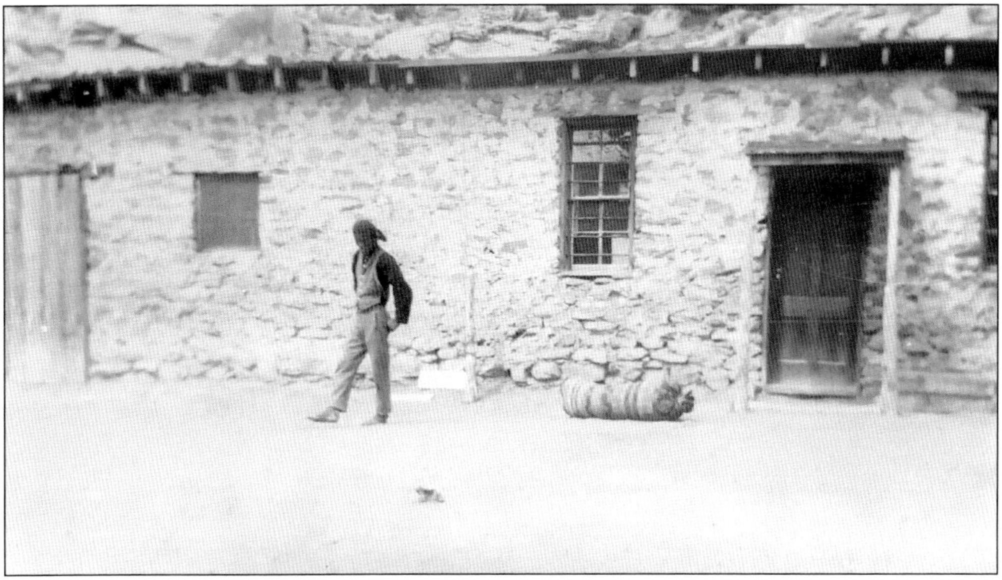

In 1913, Hubert and his brother C.D. opened Blue Canyon Trading Post, seen above. In the fall of 1912, Maybel Wilson came from Bay City, Michigan, to teach at Indian Wells. She and Hubert were married the following summer on July 9, 1913. Their first son, John "Jack" Hubert, was born the next summer. During Christmas 1914, Hubert and C.D. were stranded in a snowstorm when their automobile broke down 75 miles away, leaving Maybel and C.D.'s wife, Trula, alone at Blue Canyon. In the double-exposure image below, C.D.'s daughter Helen holds Hubert's baby son Jack. Trula wrote on the back of the photograph that their husbands were away, it was storming, and their nearest neighbors were 25 miles away. The young mothers were nervous, and they "hardly realized it was xmas." (Both, courtesy of Lana O'Brien.)

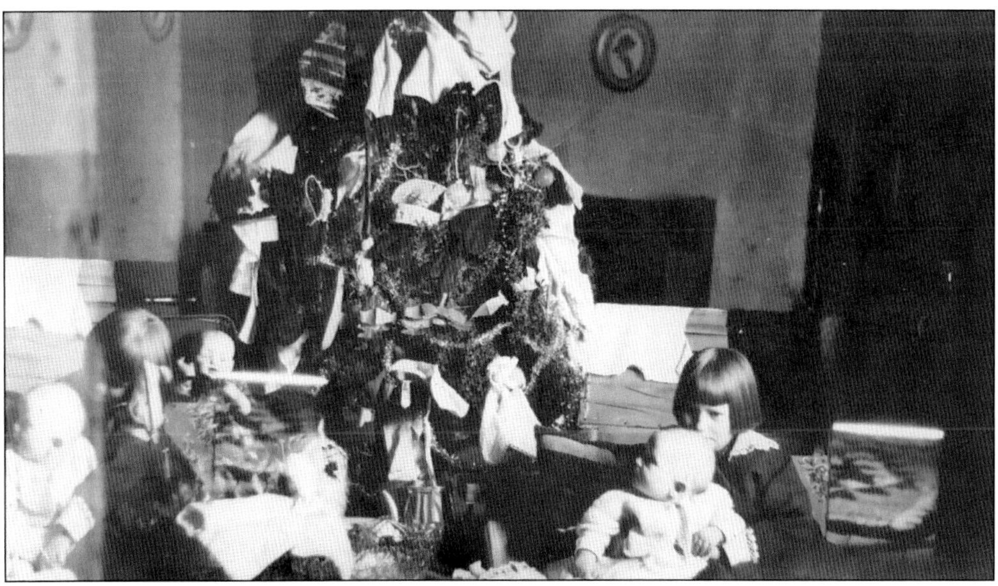

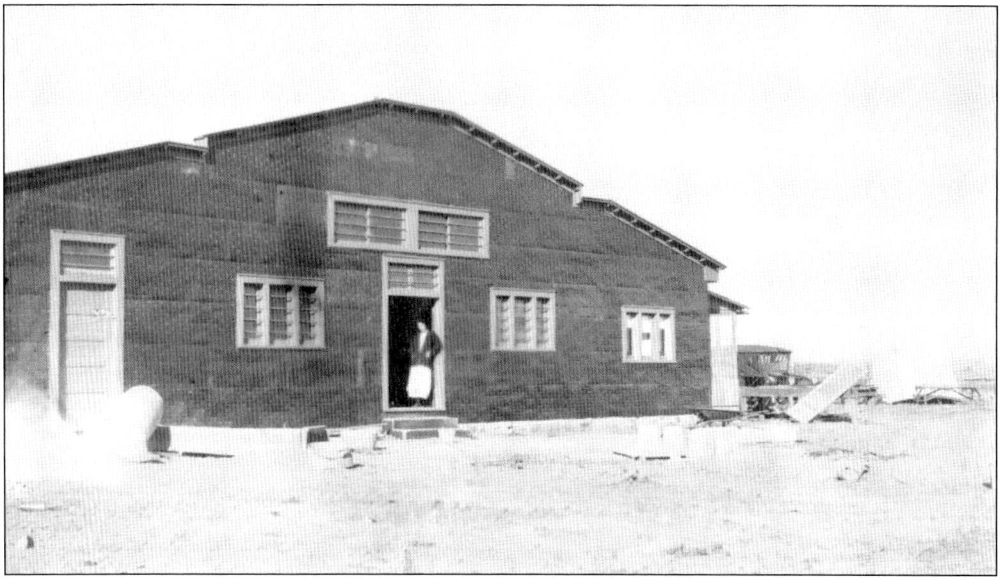

In the early years at Cameron Trading Post, it was remote and desolate. Hubert's nephew Gladwell Richardson recalled that in addition to the drafty wooden store, there were four flimsy "shack" cabins that were very uncomfortable because the wind blew downriver all through the night. According to him, "Especially did Talking Wind shake the flimsy cabin walls while conversing with himself around sharp corners." When Gladwell took his wife, Millie, to Cameron, they endured "bone-chilling cold sweeping through the thin wooden walls." The cold did not bother Gladwell, but Millie hated the place. Cameron at that time was typical of most trading posts, with no running water or electricity, but to Millie it was the "most desolate and barren place on the river." (Above, courtesy of Lana O'Brien; below, photograph by Edward H. Kemp, courtesy of Grand Canyon Museum Collection, No. 15975.)

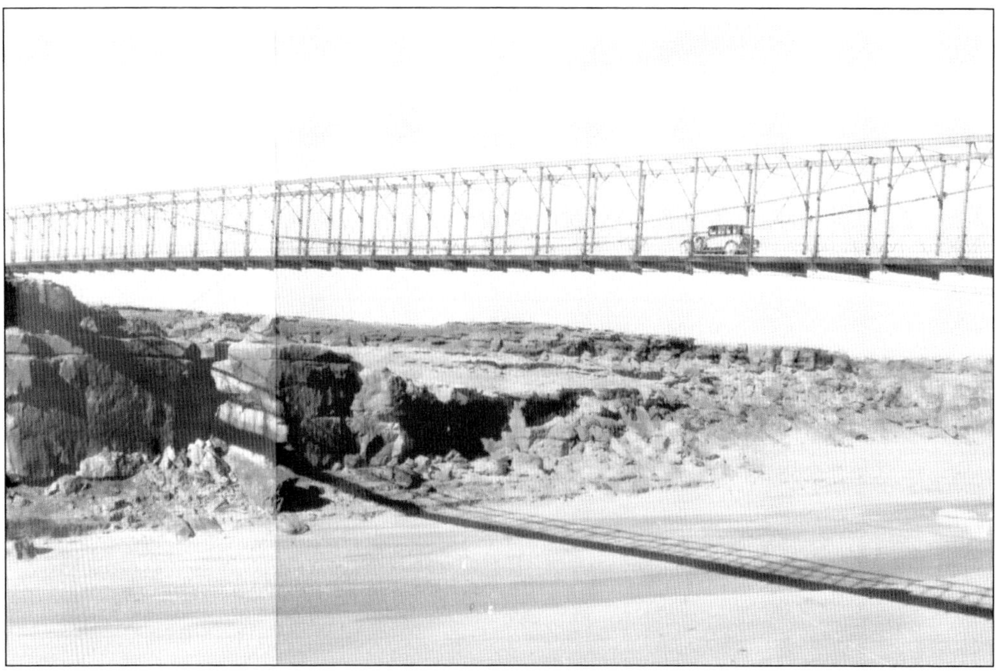

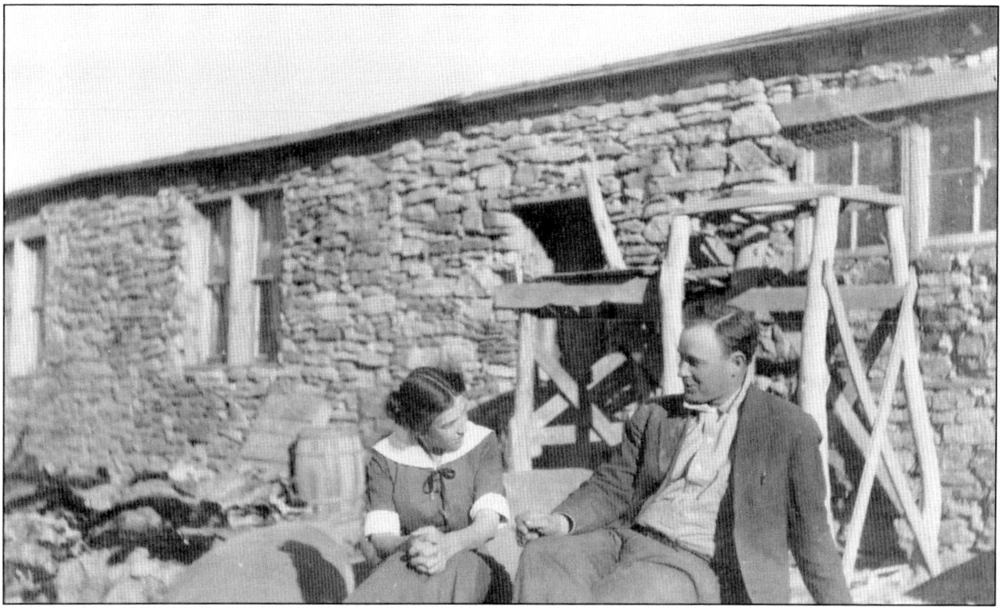

The charming, early photograph above of Maybel and Hubert was taken in front of one of his trading posts. They are sitting on 300-pound wool bags piled in front of the store. The wooden structure behind Hubert held the bags upright while they were being filled with wool. Below, Maybel and Hubert stand in front of Cameron Trading Post at the front of the automobile; the others in this photograph are unidentified. The round portrait of Roy Huskon can be seen above the store's doorway. Huskon worked for Hubert, managing the trading post when Hubert was away on buying trips. The Huskon family originally came from the Gray Mountain area and have lived at Cameron for many generations. (Both, courtesy of Lisa Amaral.)

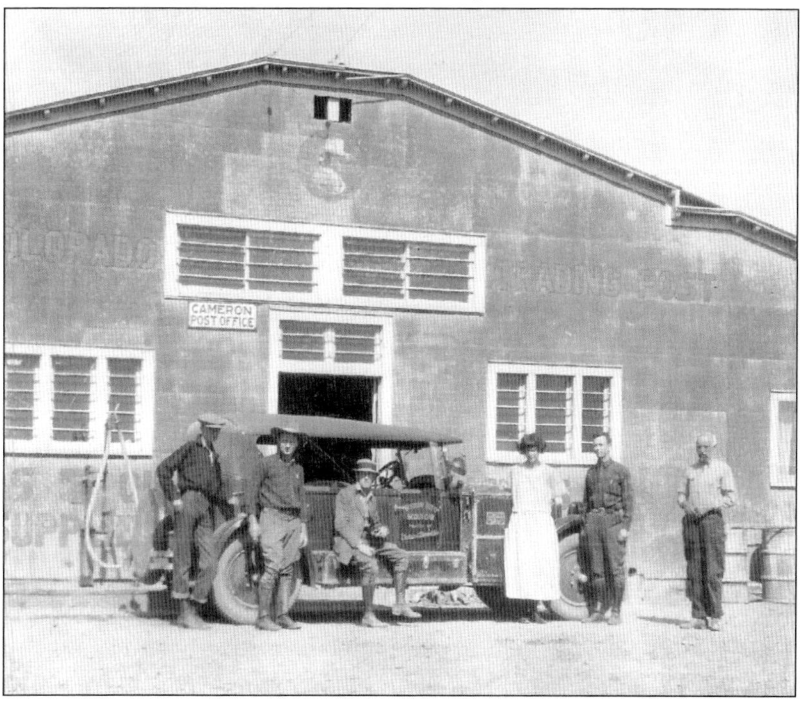

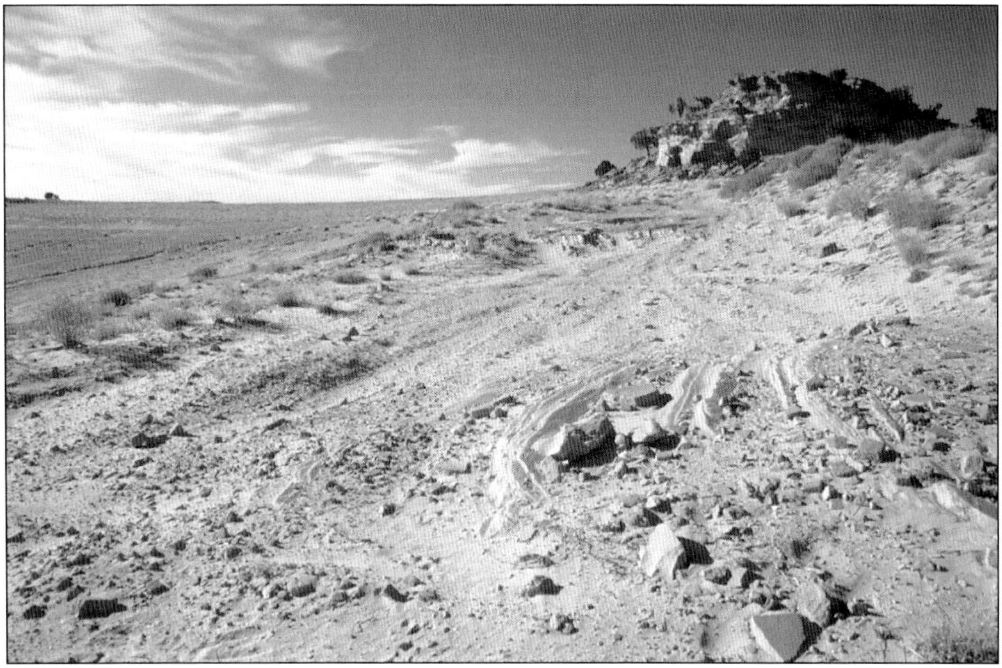

In 1916, the trading post was not the only structure at Cameron. Copper was discovered on the east side of the Echo Cliffs north of Cameron (note the copper nuggets on the ground pictured above), but deep sand and lack of roads made any mining operations impossible. During World War I, the price of copper doubled and the Holt Company developed a tank based on a Caterpillar tractor. In addition to wartime use, as seen below, the Navajo Copper Company set up an office in Flagstaff in 1916 and ordered 12 Caterpillars. The company had three camps—one at Greenlaw near Flagstaff; a second camp at Cameron, which consisted of a huge warehouse and barn; and a third camp at the Gap—as well as the mine at Bobsburg. (Above, courtesy of Sherry Mangum; below, courtesy of the Library of Congress.)

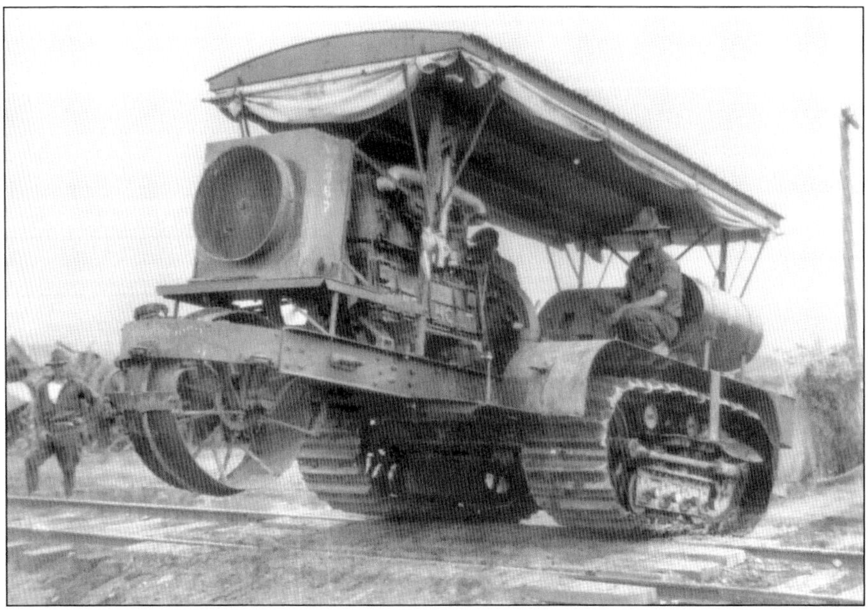

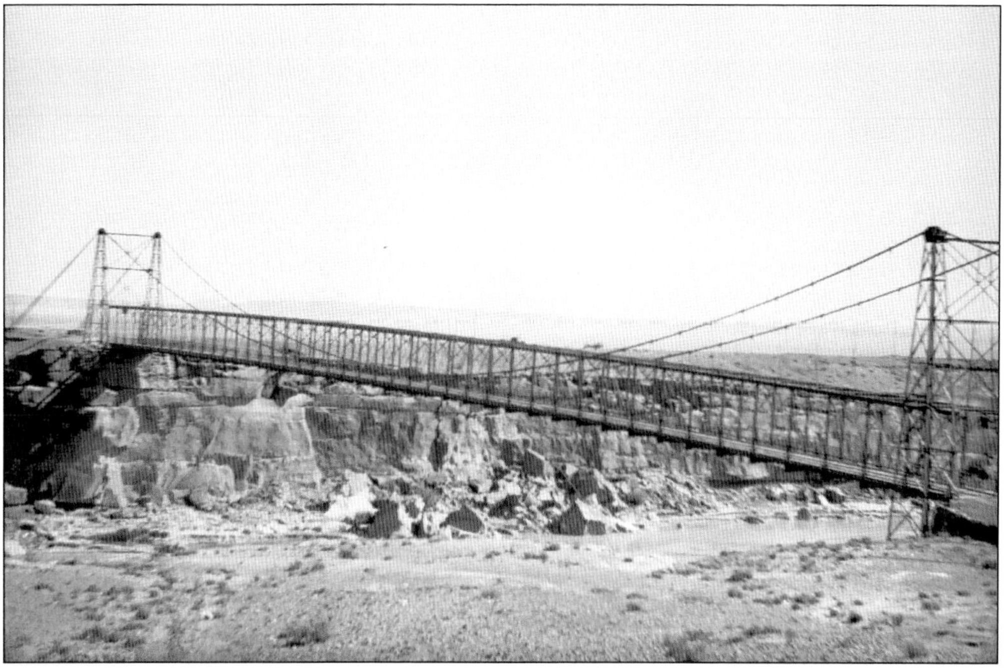

The Holts pulled 10 ore-cars with wide, solid metal wheels that would roll through the sand—a trackless train, running 100 miles from Greenlaw to the mine—at five miles per hour. By 1918, the war had ended and the price of copper plunged. The company went bankrupt and three remaining Holts were sold. The new owner decided to bring the Holts back to Flagstaff, but the suspension bridge at Cameron was too light to support the weight of the 10-ton Holts. The alternative was Tanner's Crossing, but as the Caterpillars went across the river, they began sinking. Two were saved, but the third one was never recovered from the quicksand. The Coppermine Trading Post at Bobsburg was eventually closed, and the abandoned stone building is all that is left of the Navajo Copper Company. (Above, photograph by Dudley Scott, courtesy of Grand Canyon Museum Collection, No. 06768.)

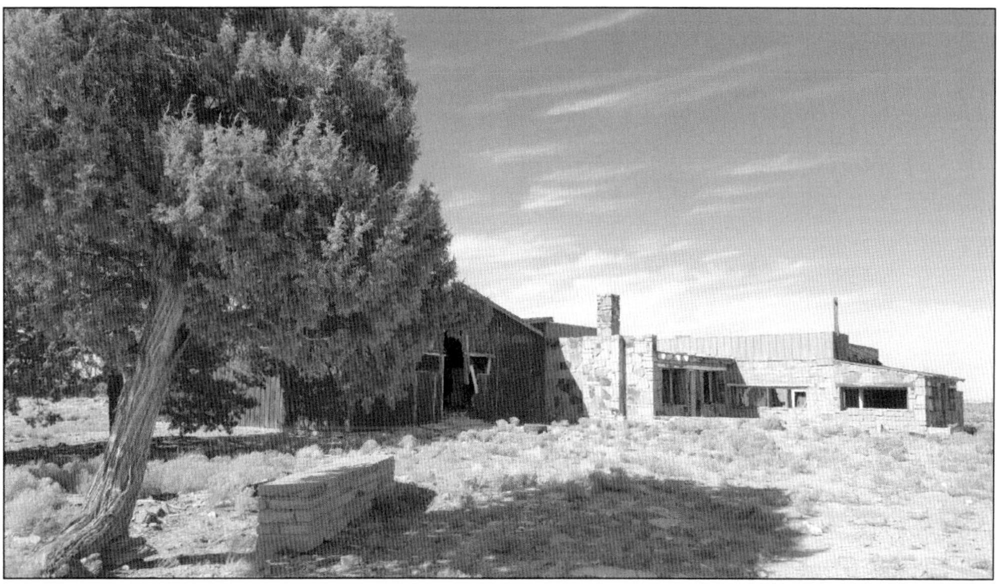

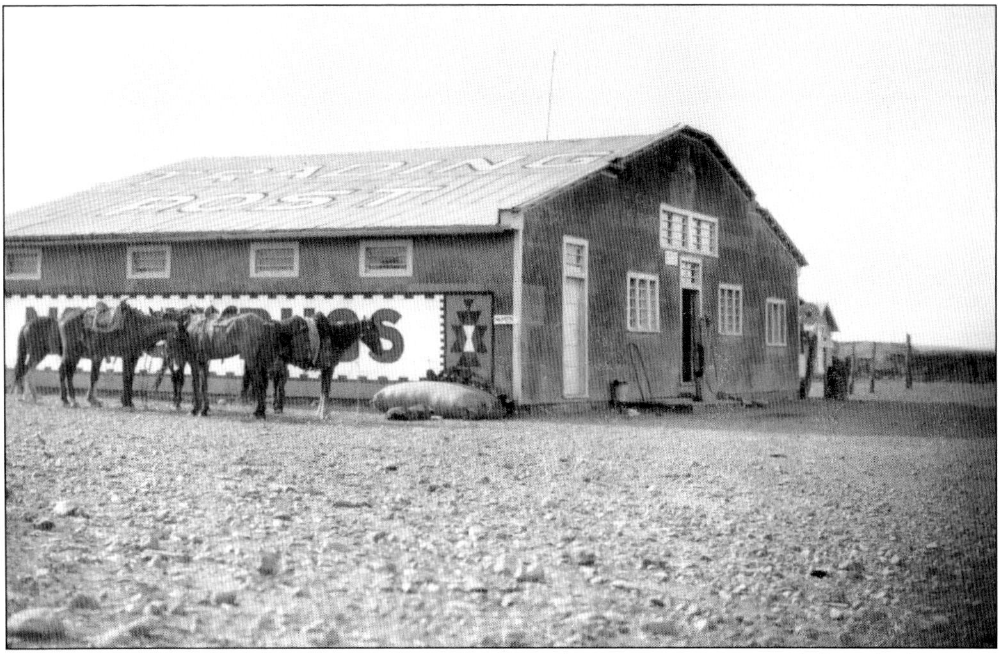

Pulitzer Prize–winning author Oliver La Farge visited Cameron in 1921 and described coming upon the store with a rusty tin roof. There was a windmill and a hitching rack for horses. La Farge realized he had discovered the meaning of the word *remote*. He was fascinated with the Navajo customers wearing tall hats or a headband, turquoise earrings, and hair knotted in back. (Courtesy of Lisa Amaral.)

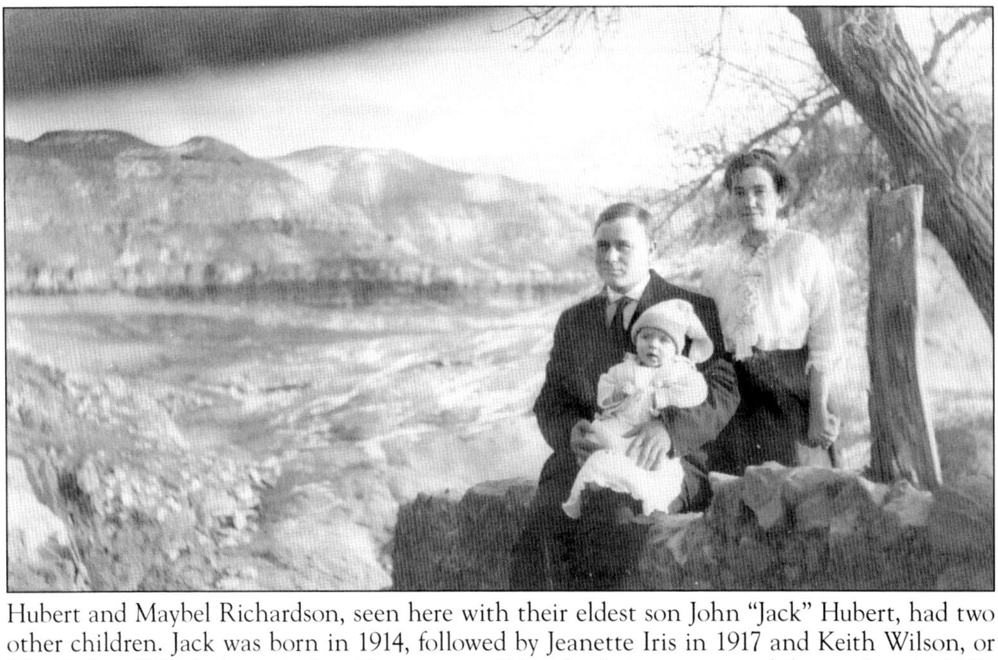

Hubert and Maybel Richardson, seen here with their eldest son John "Jack" Hubert, had two other children. Jack was born in 1914, followed by Jeanette Iris in 1917 and Keith Wilson, or "Buddy," in 1919. Jack worked at Cameron until his death in an automobile accident in 1955; Jeanette married and moved to Colorado; Buddy managed Kaibito Trading Post, situated north of Cameron. (Courtesy of Lana O'Brien.)

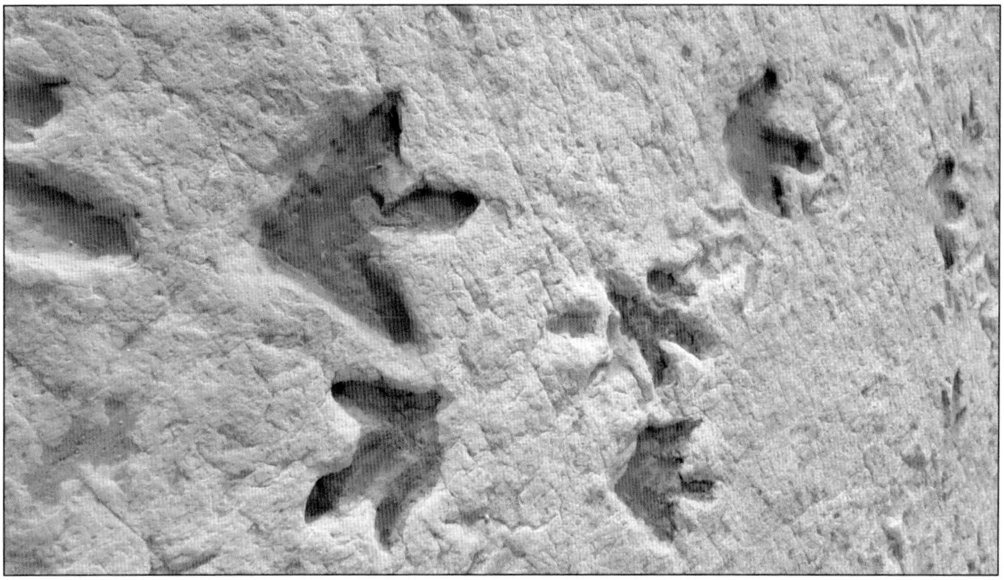

The landscape in the Cameron area displays fascinating geological variety and is known for the evidence of prehistoric life forms; 180 million years ago, a diverse group of ancient animals roamed the area, including meat-eating dinosaurs. A four-footed reptile weighing up to 200 pounds from the early Triassic period left behind hundreds of footprints in the mudflats that have turned to stone, as seen above. Because the tracks of the five-fingered quadruped, some as large as 13 feet, resemble a human hand, there was speculation in earlier times that the tracks of the Chirotherium, or "Hand Beast," pictured at right, may have been made by people who did not survive one of the biblical floods. Slabs of stone containing these tracks were used in building the hotel at Cameron in 1928. (Right, courtesy of Tom Collins.)

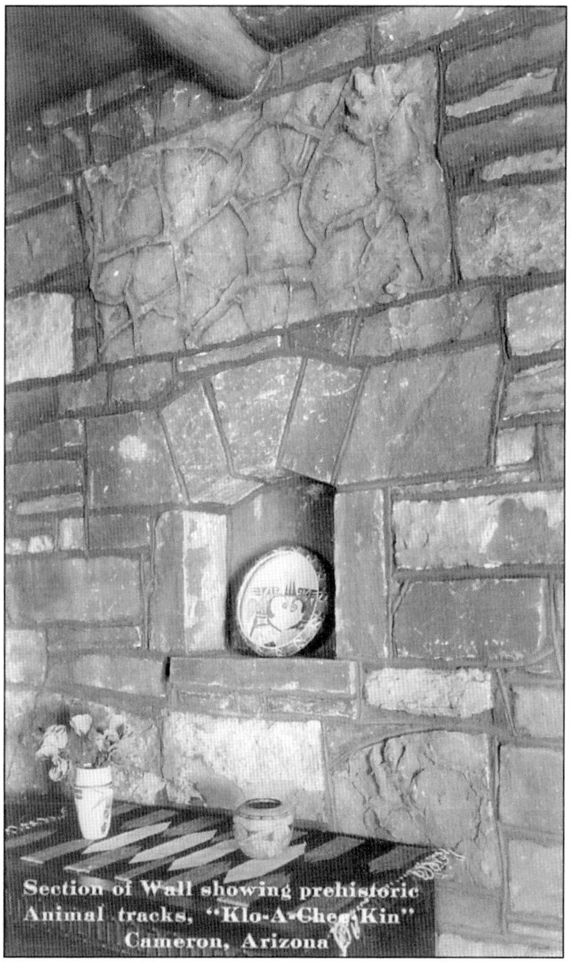

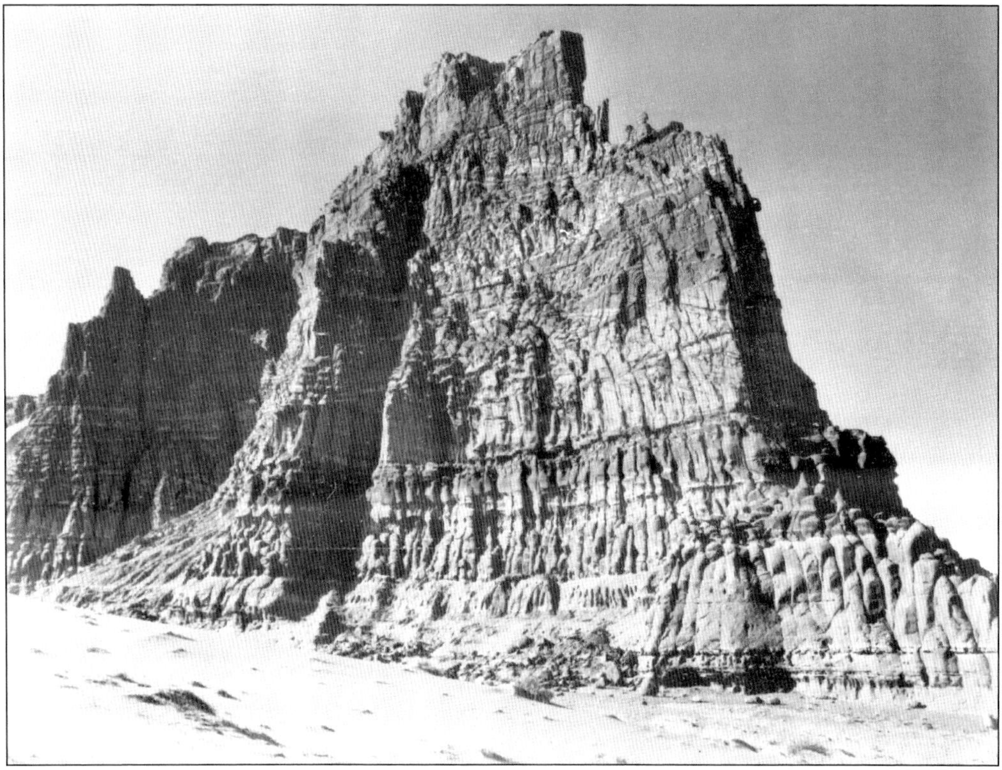

Two million years ago, large reptiles walked the land that later came to be known as the Painted Desert. Hundreds of their footprints, as well as fossilized plants and bones were discovered in the hardened mud in Dinosaur Canyon, seen above. Some trackways were created by running dinosaurs, indicating that the small, meat-eating reptiles could run up to 14 miles per hour. Remains from other prehistoric creatures were discovered in the mud and tidal flats. Fossilized bones, trees, and pinecones lay buried, sleeping under hardening layers of mud and sand, only giving up their secrets millions of years in the future. (Above, courtesy of US Geological Survey; below, photograph by George Grant, courtesy of Grand Canyon Museum Collection, No. 05949.)

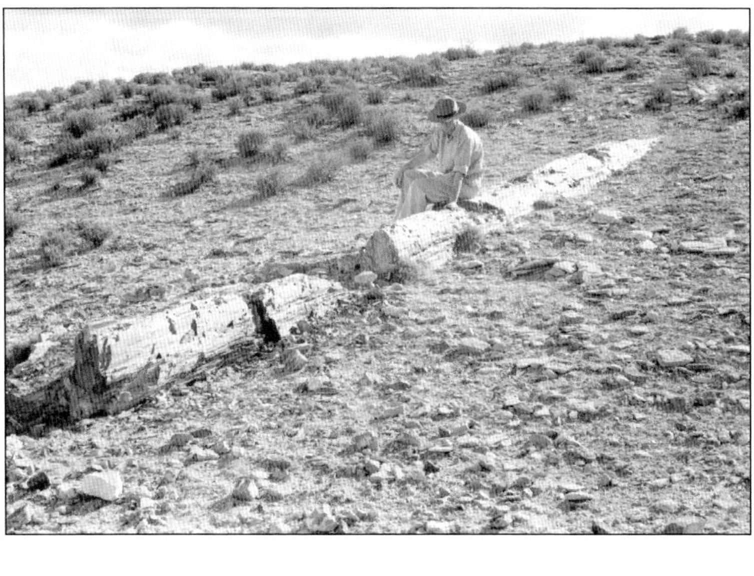

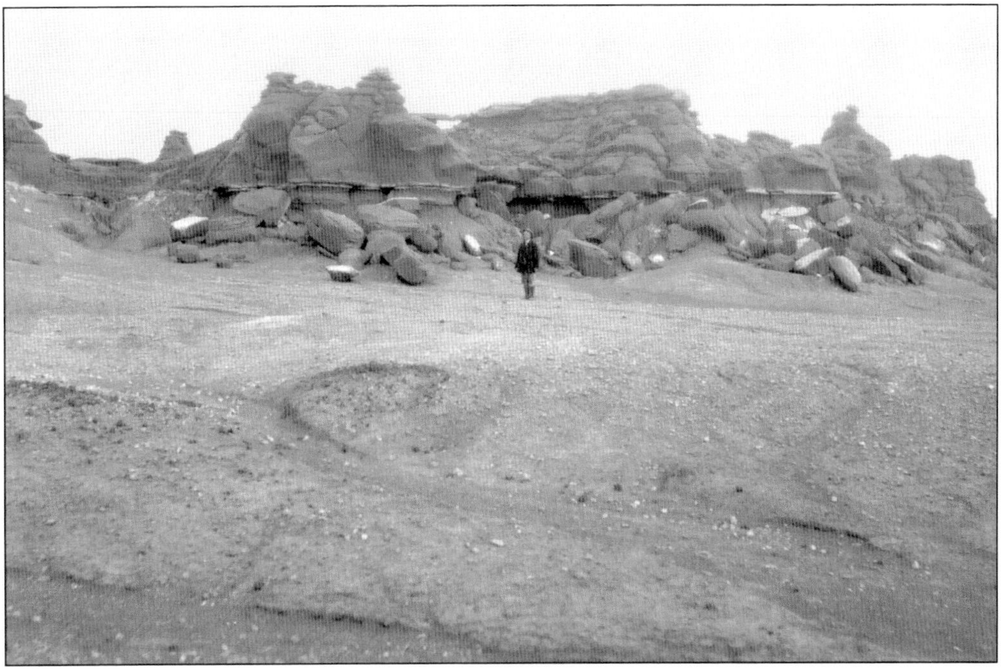

In the fall of 1924, oil tycoon Edward Doheny, who was implicated in the Teapot Dome Scandal about the same time, sponsored a scientific expedition to northern Arizona, seeking to prove the theory that a race of gigantic humans once lived on the earth. Prominent vertebrate paleontologist Charles Gilmore was a part of the group that explored Dinosaur Canyon east of Cameron (the member of the expedition in Dinosaur Canyon seen above is unidentified). The group then traveled to the Grand Canyon. Among its controversial discoveries was a petroglyph of a "standing dinosaur," pictured at right—proof, the expedition members argued, that ancient man had coexisted with the giant reptiles. (Above, courtesy of Grand Canyon Museum Collection, No. 18747; right, photograph by Walter Herriman, courtesy of Grand Canyon Museum Collection, No. 4680A.)

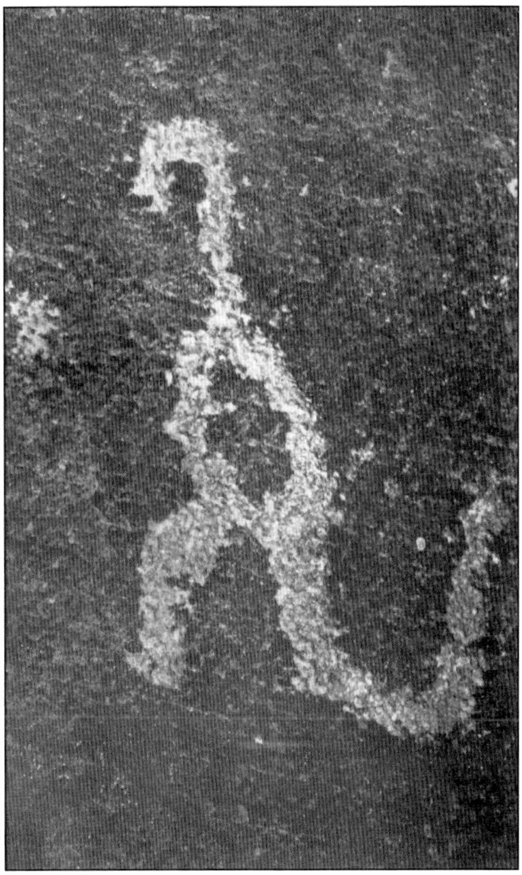

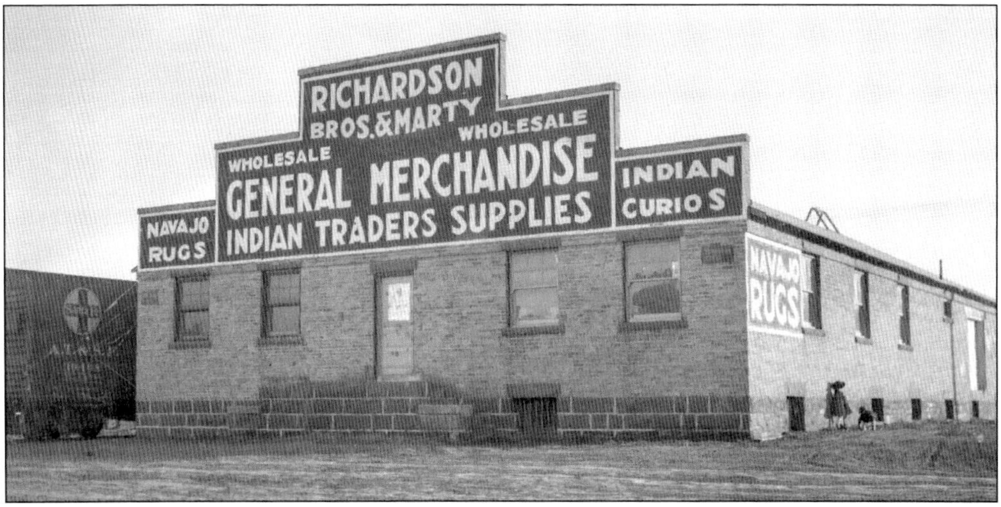

Hubert Richardson, brother C.D., and partner Edwin Jacob "E.J." Marty established a trading post and wholesale store in Winslow, Arizona, in 1916. The huge warehouse-sized building, pictured above, which backed onto the Atchison, Topeka & Santa Fe Railway, served as a distribution point for the brothers' many trading posts. It was also convenient for Hubert and Maybel, who had a house in Winslow. As their children grew older, Maybel, seen below with her youngest son, Buddy, spent much of the school year with her children in Winslow. The brothers sold the building in 1924 to Lorenzo Hubbell Jr., and after changing hands several times, it was purchased by the City of Winslow. It is now the Winslow Chamber of Commerce and Visitor's Center. (Above, courtesy of Lana O'Brien; below, courtesy of Lisa Amaral.)

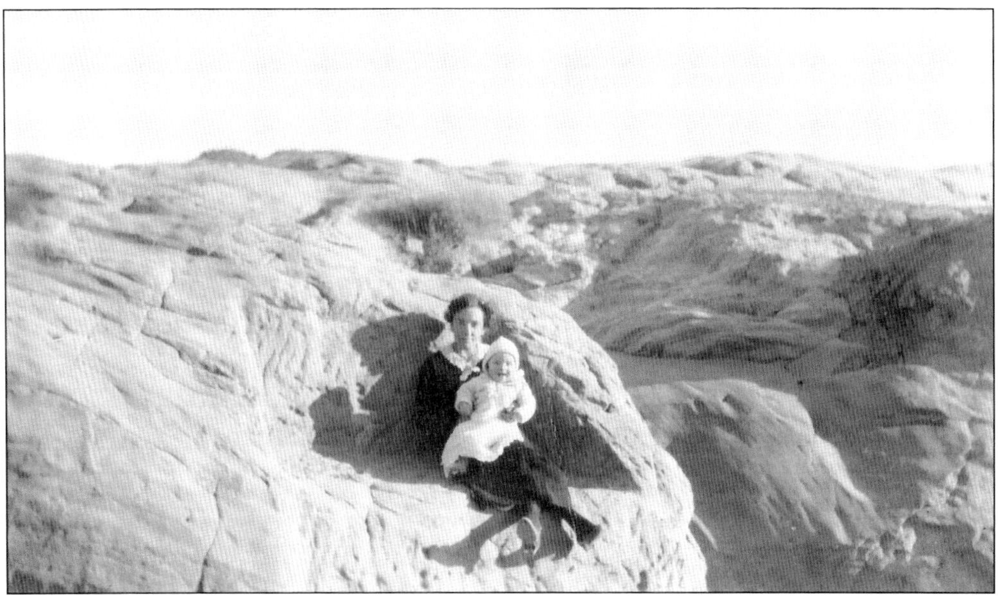

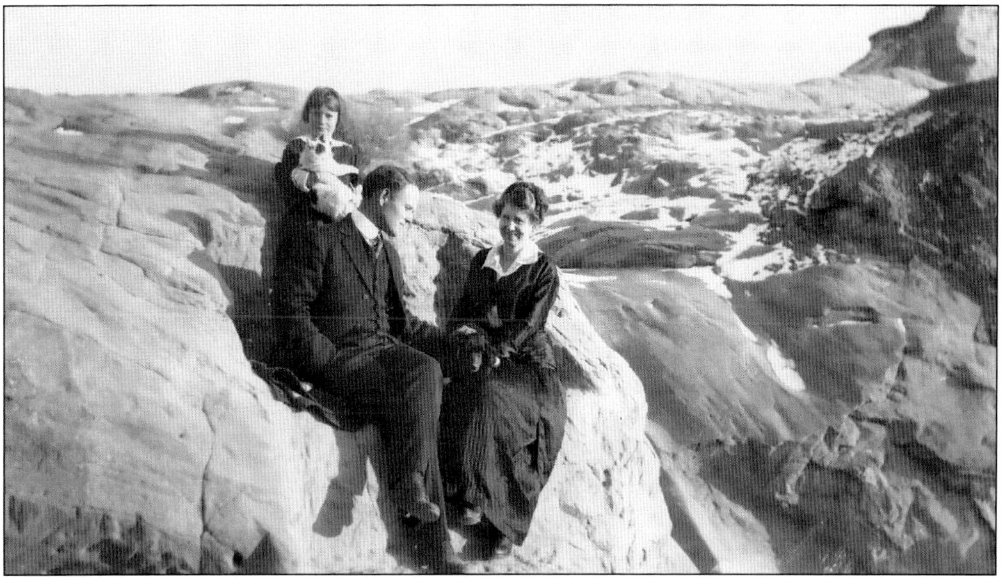

Hubert and his older brother, C.D., were partners in many trading posts. C.D. built Kaibito Trading Post near White Horse Mesa in 1914. He sold it in 1921 to Earl Morris, who then sold it two years later to Hubert, who ran the post with his son Buddy until 1966. C.D. married Trula Turpen, who was also a member of an old-time trading family, and they had three children. C.D. and Trula are pictured above with their daughter Helen, as well as their pet cat and dog, about 1918. C.D. also owned the Hopi Navajo Trading Post in Tuba City. According to historian Jim Babbitt, the post was likely built by Buck Lowrey. C.D. owned the store until 1928, when it was purchased by Babbitt Brothers and renamed the Bell Trading Post. The store closed in 1930, and today, there are no traces of the building. (Both, courtesy of Lana O'Brien.)

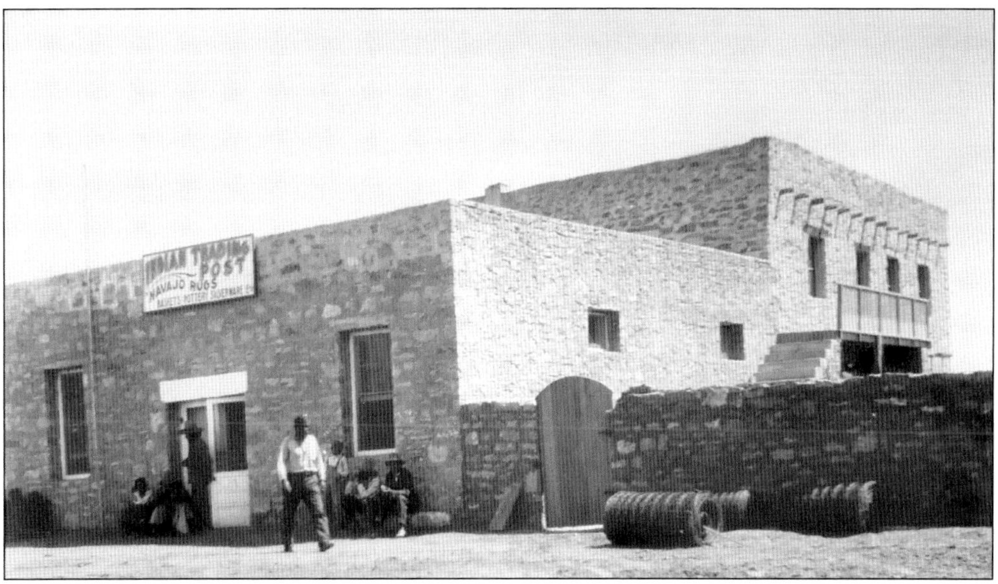

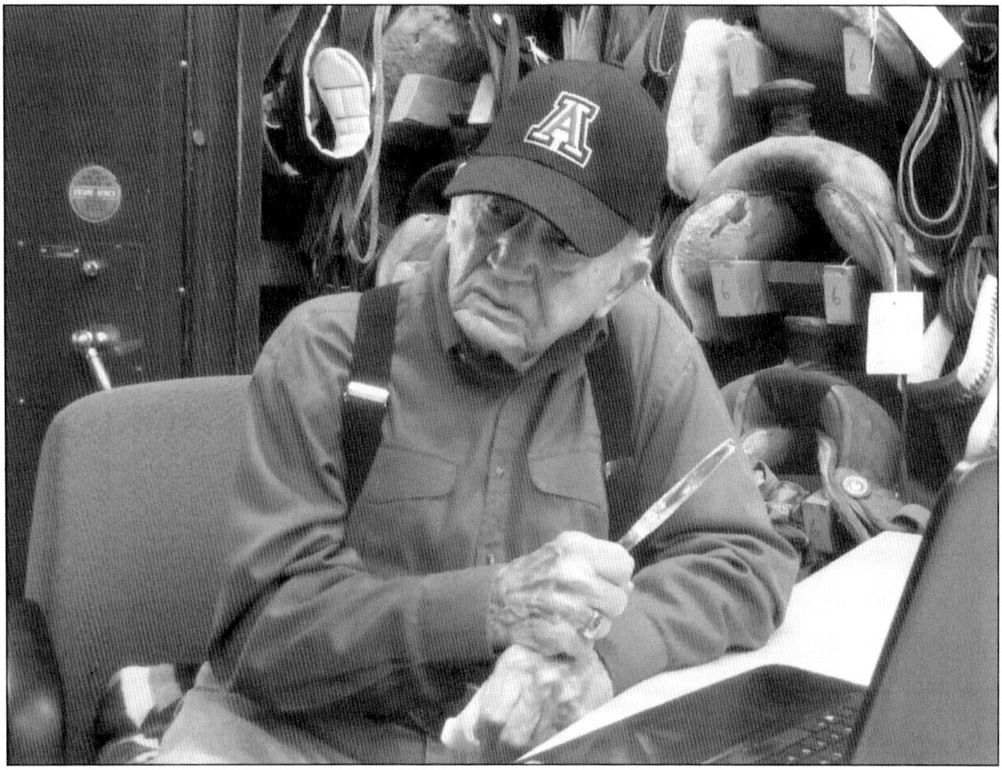

C.D.'s son William Thomas "Bill" Richardson is now 97 years old. He owns Richardson's Trading in Gallup, New Mexico, and visits the store most afternoons. Bill recalls visiting Cameron as a boy, where he would play with Hubert's son Jack. When bags of wool were piled along the side of the store in the springtime, they would slide off the tin roof and land on the huge wool bags. As young men, they both attended the University of Arizona. Bill remembered a sheep corral that was always full of sheep at Cameron behind the store. He also remarked that his father and Hubert were both quiet men; they talked in low voices, never shouting, and Bill recalls that he "never heard them fuss at anybody."

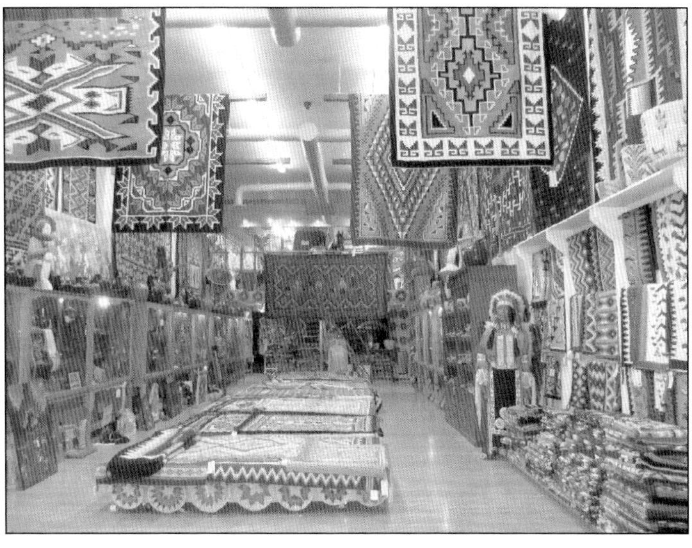

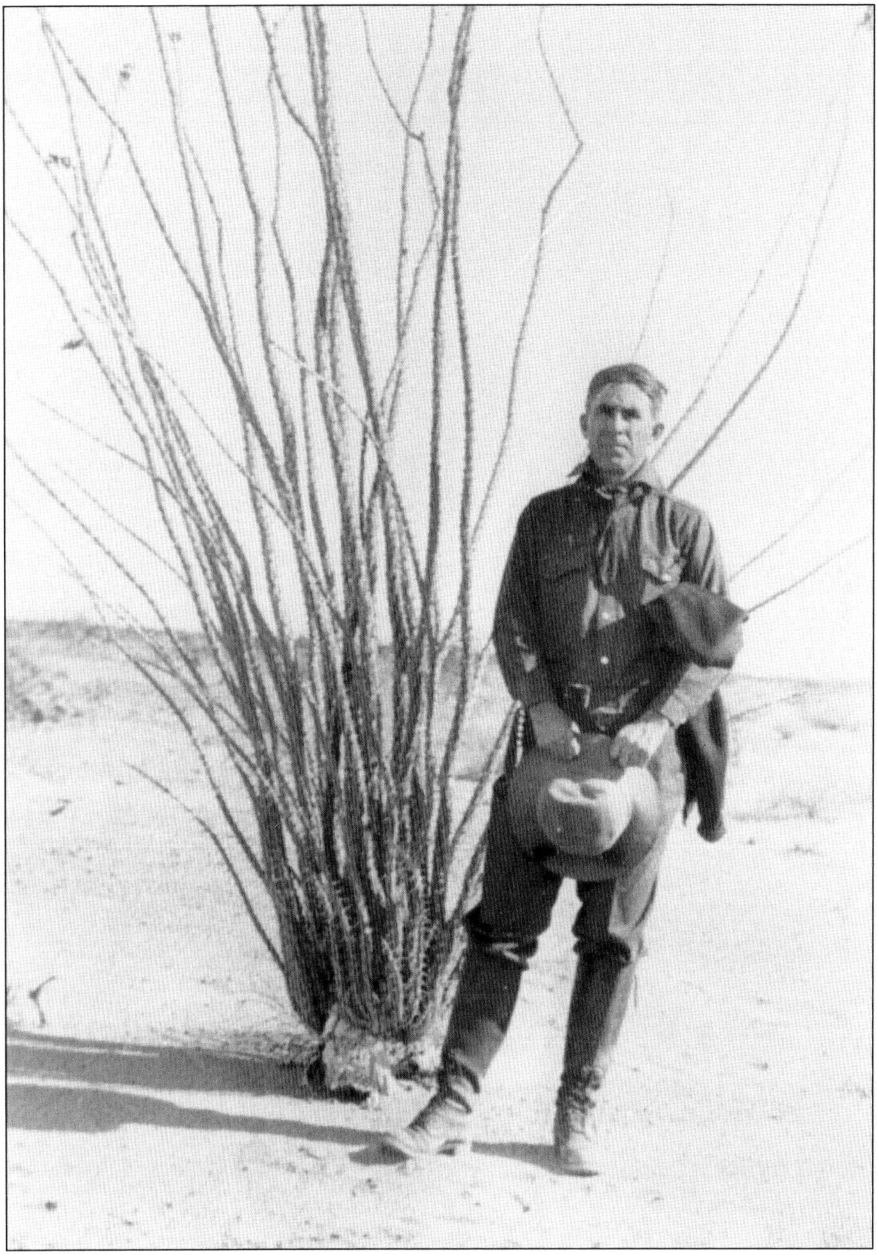

Many authors visited Cameron over the decades and often used the area for settings in their books. Zane Grey made several trips through Cameron, beginning in 1907. The journey to the Painted Desert is described in *Lost Pueblo*: "Yellow and red, and . . . a great hollow of many hues, out of which dim purple shapes climbed." In 1907, traveling by wagon at about two-and-a-half miles an hour through the deep sand, Grey wrote about "the gray and ghastly skeleton of the earth," and noted that the winds blew so hard, sand was everywhere—even their meals were gritty. Grey stayed at Cameron Trading Post and incorporated the landscape and people into his novels, almost a dozen of which were made into movies filmed near Cameron, including *Heritage of the Desert*, *To the Last Man*, *The Light of Western Stars*, *The Vanishing American*, *Drums of the Desert*, *Under the Tonto Rim*, *The Water Hole*, and *Sunset Pass*. (Courtesy of Zane Grey West Society.)

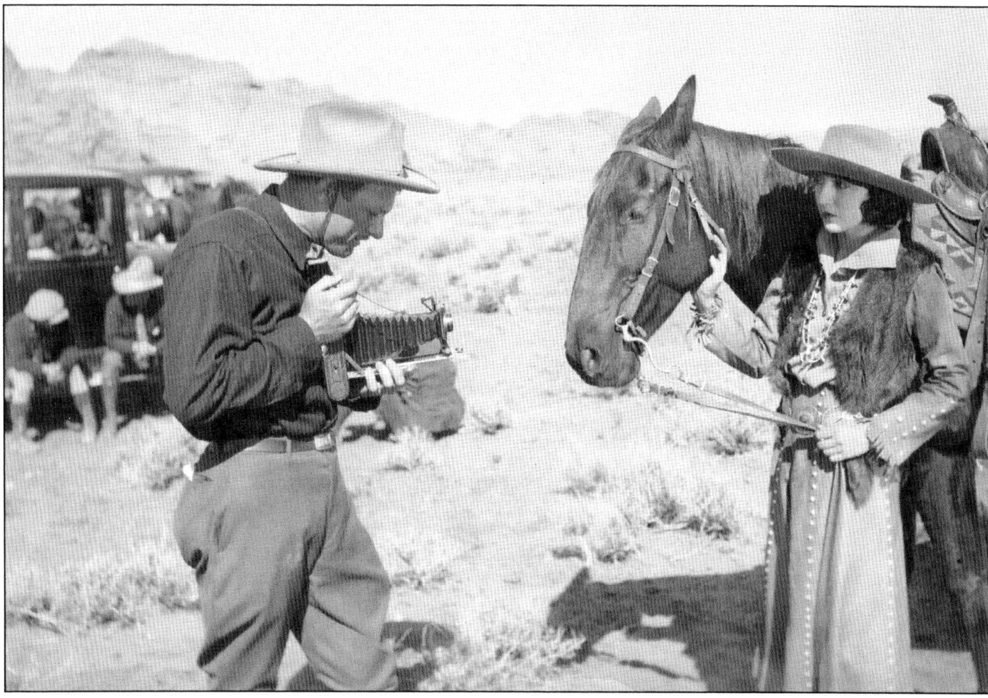

Zane Grey's *Heritage of the Desert* was filmed by the Famous Players-Lasky Corporation (now Paramount Pictures) in the Cameron area in 1923. The film starred 22-year-old Bebe Daniels, seen above being photographed by another actor in the movie, Lloyd Hughes. The group picture below was likely taken as a souvenir for the cast and crew of the movie. Daniels sits on a horse in the center of the group, and costar Noah Beery, the bearded man in black, is to her right. At her left is Ernest Torrence wearing the black hat. All three were big stars in silent films but are mostly forgotten today, and the silent version of this film unfortunately no longer exists. (Above, courtesy of Northern Arizona University, Cline Library, NAU.PH.2003.15.4.5; below, courtesy of Northern Arizona University, Cline Library, NAU.PH.2003.15.4.6.)

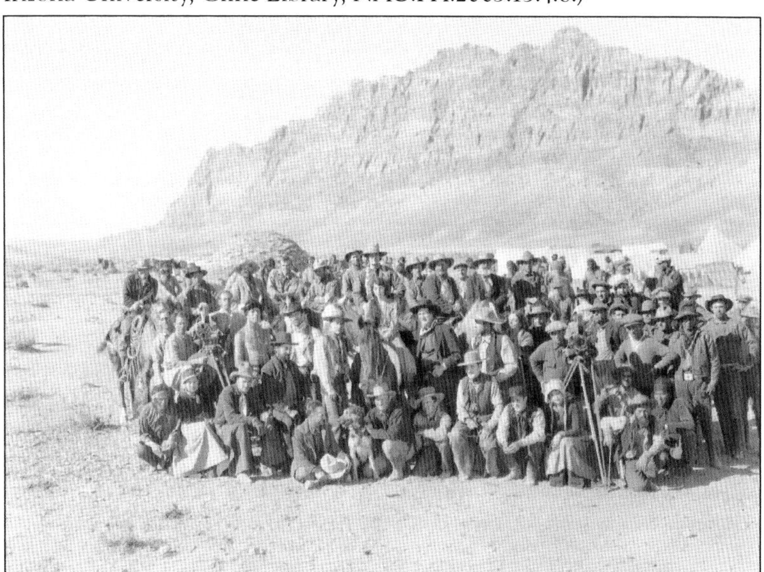

In 1928, the Famous Players-Lasky Corporation planned to film an adaptation of Zane Grey's *Avalanche* in the Cameron area. Its plans included using dynamite to blow up a mountain to create a landslide scene, and the mountain that they chose was Sunset Crater, a cinder cone created in an AD 1064 eruption. Local people in Flagstaff objected, and the production moved north to the Painted Desert, where the dynamite scene set off an explosion that sent boulders flying, killing one person and injuring the movie crew and onlookers. As a result of the protests and to protect the crater, the site was named a national monument in 1930. The photograph of Sunset Crater at right was taken by Fred Mang around the 1950s, and the image below, with a view looking north at the entrance to Sunset Crater National Monument on Highway 89, was captured in 1952 by Glen Haynes. (Right, courtesy of the National Park Service, No. SUCR422; below, courtesy of the National Park Service, No. SUCR645.)

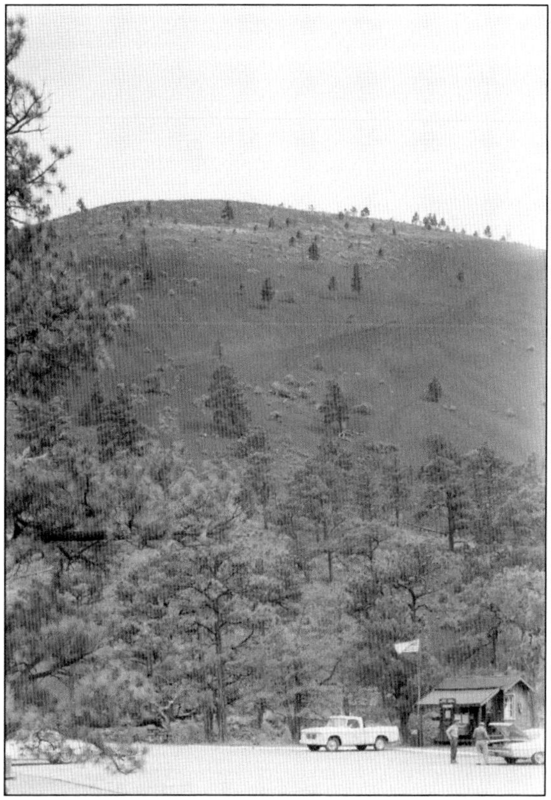

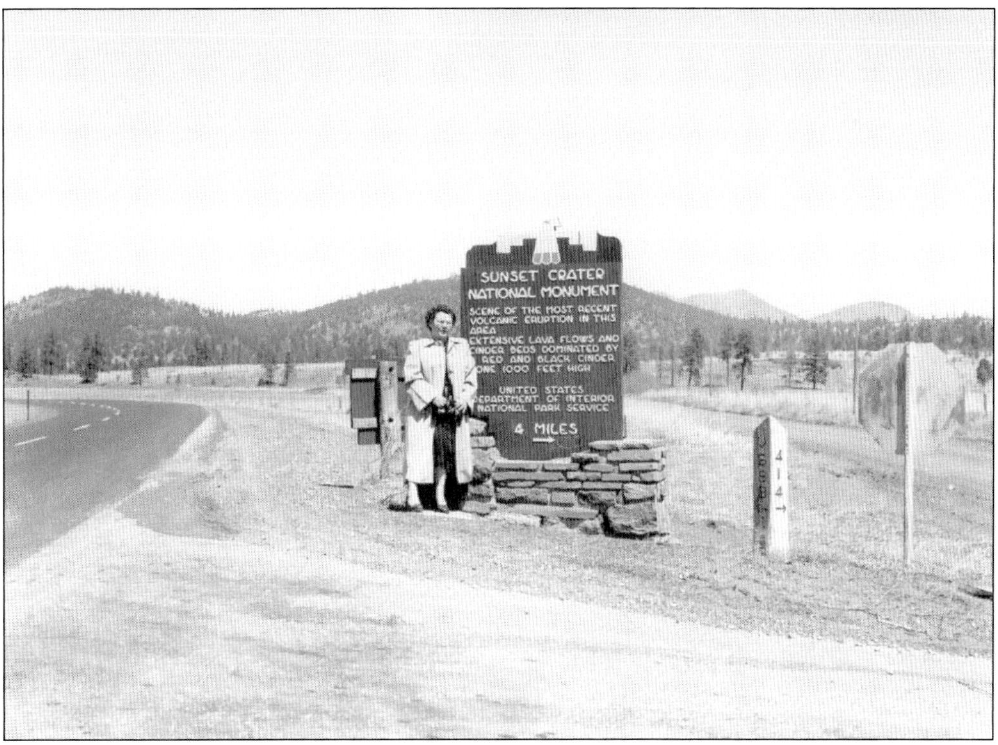

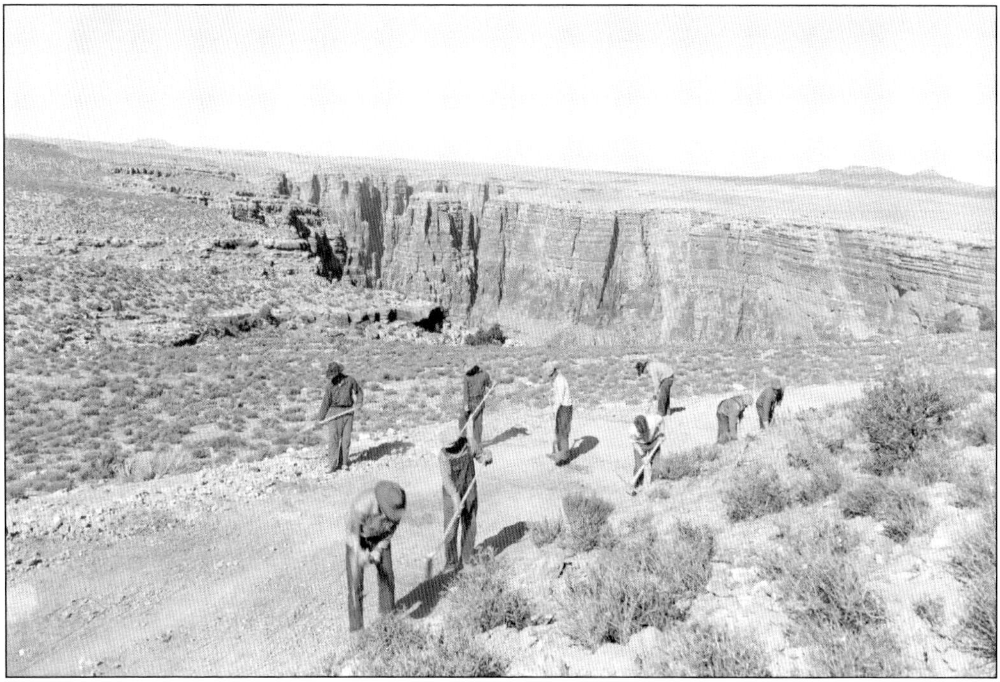

About 1924, the Fred Harvey Company began building the Navahopi Trail from the Grand Canyon to Cameron, and it was later designated as Highway 64. The graded road followed ancient foot trails used by Hopis and Navajos to reach sacred sites at the Grand Canyon. Fresno scrapers and a group of Navajo workers with picks and shovels, seen above, worked on the one-lane road that dropped 3,000 feet in 35 miles. Below, in this 1926 photograph, the two men at the right are Charlie Peshlakai (left) and Navajo John (right). The road was unpaved until 1936, when it was surfaced with an asphalt mix. (Above, courtesy of Grand Canyon Museum Collection, No. 02944; below, photograph by J.A. Metzger, courtesy of Grand Canyon Museum Collection, No. 17694.)

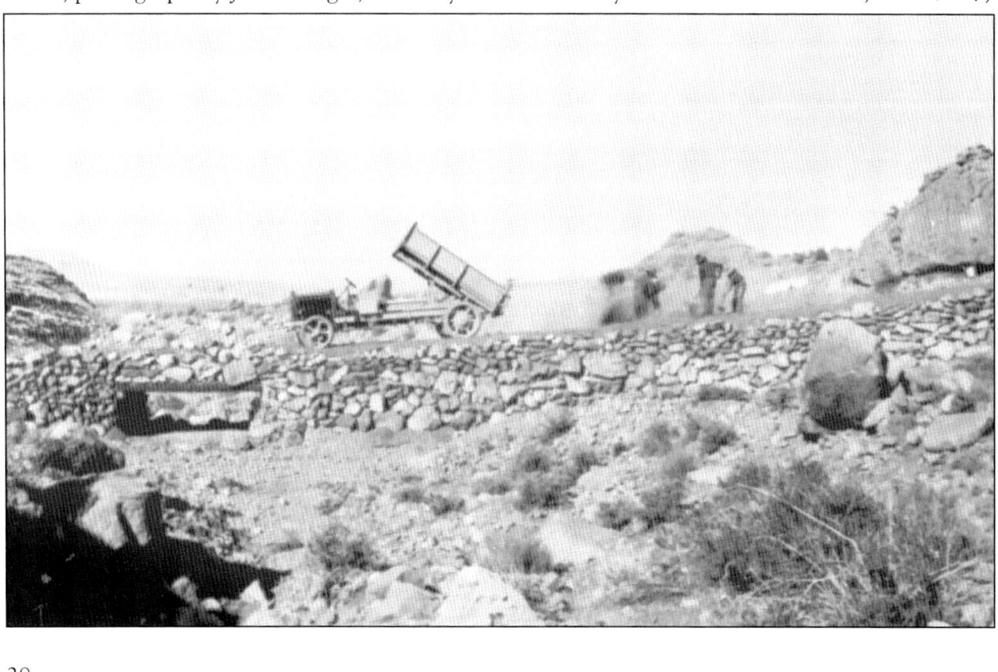

Water from Tappan Spring was used for the construction of the Navahopi Trail and also supplied Cameron Trading Post. In this 1926 photograph by J.A. Metzger, a line runs from a tripod at the truck to the wash below, and water was hauled up to the top from the spring. (Courtesy of Grand Canyon Museum Collection, No. 17695.)

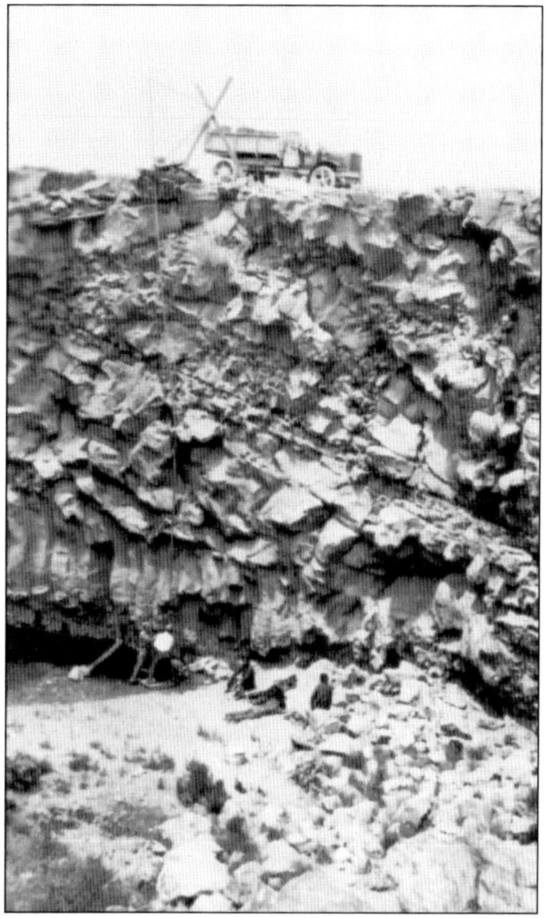

There were only a few places on the steep road that were wide enough to pull over to allow another car to pass from the opposite direction. In several places, there were sheer drop-offs down into the Little Colorado Gorge with only inches to spare at the unprotected edge of the road. One driver recalled that she just "took to the timber" when encountering another automobile. (Courtesy of Grand Canyon Museum Collection, No. 09447.)

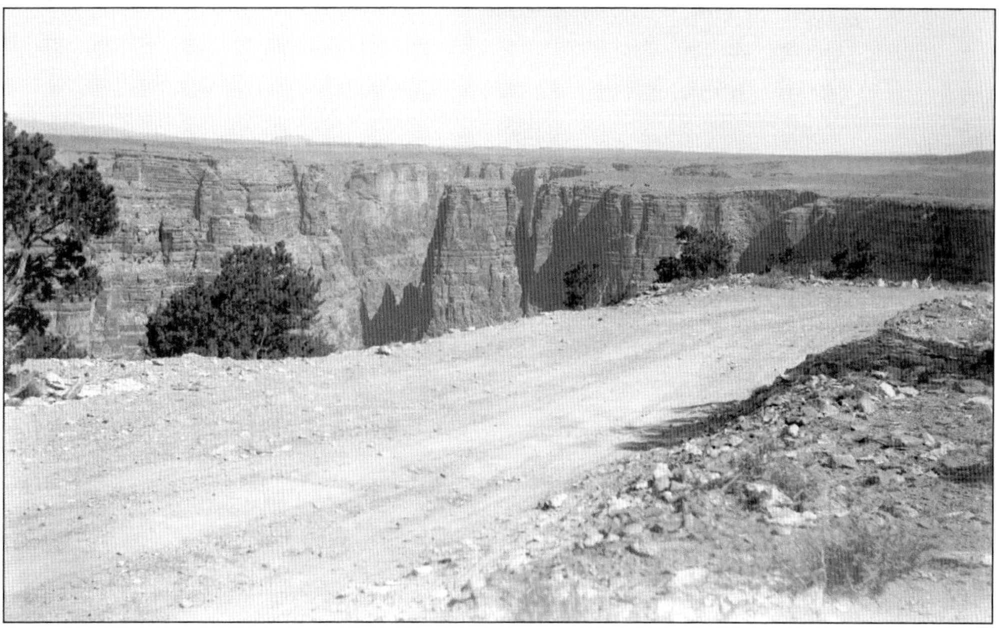

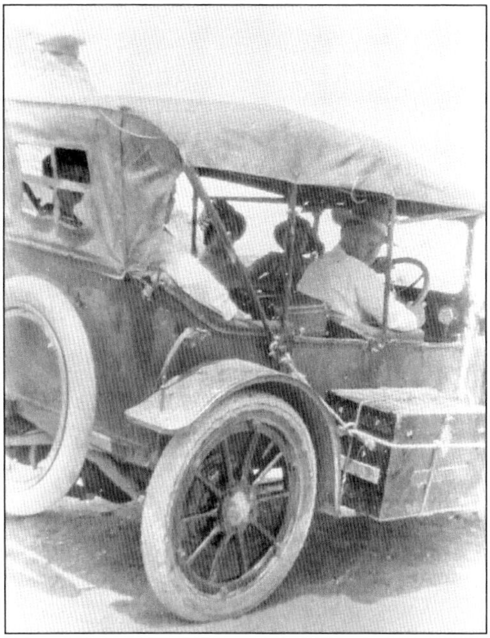

Construction of the Navahopi Trail brought an increase of visitors to Cameron. In the 1920s, Hubert Richardson built four new cabins and hired a cook to prepare meals for visitors. He also added a screened porch to the north side of the trading post that was used for dining. With trunks strapped to the automobile, Hubert likely is driving tourists to or from Flagstaff or the Grand Canyon. (Courtesy of Atkinson Trading Company.)

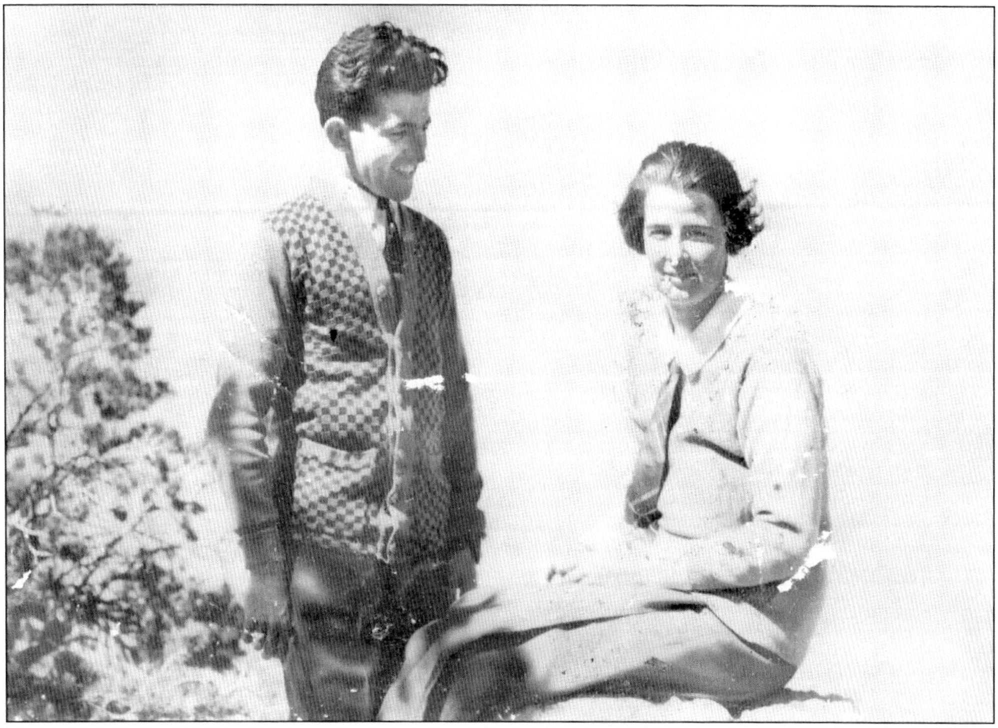

In 1926, when Elizabeth Hegemann and Mike Harrison visited Cameron, there was only the store and several cabins for workers and an occasional traveler. Everyone ate at a big table on the screened porch. When water was piped from Tappan Spring to Cameron, the Richardsons showed off their first bathroom. Before Cameron had running water, Elizabeth and Maybel traded gossip as they strolled and chatted on their way to the privy at the edge of the bluff above the river. (Courtesy of Harvey Leake.)

Elizabeth Hegemann recalled that there was little traffic on the main road across the bridge. When preacher Shine Smith, seen at right center with Tom Holiday, right and an unidentified man, performed a marriage in the middle of the bridge for Wes and Billy Case, not a single car had to be stopped. After the wedding, everyone enjoyed a supper on the porch, and the newlyweds retired to the trading post, where they spent their first night of married life on a stack of Navajo rugs. With only a 14-foot, one-lane roadway, the lightweight bridge would not hold heavy loads. Several years later, in 1937, the bridge nearly collapsed when herders crossed with a load of sheep. Drivers were required to honk their horns before driving across the bridge and flash their headlights at night. (Below, courtesy of Lisa Amaral.)

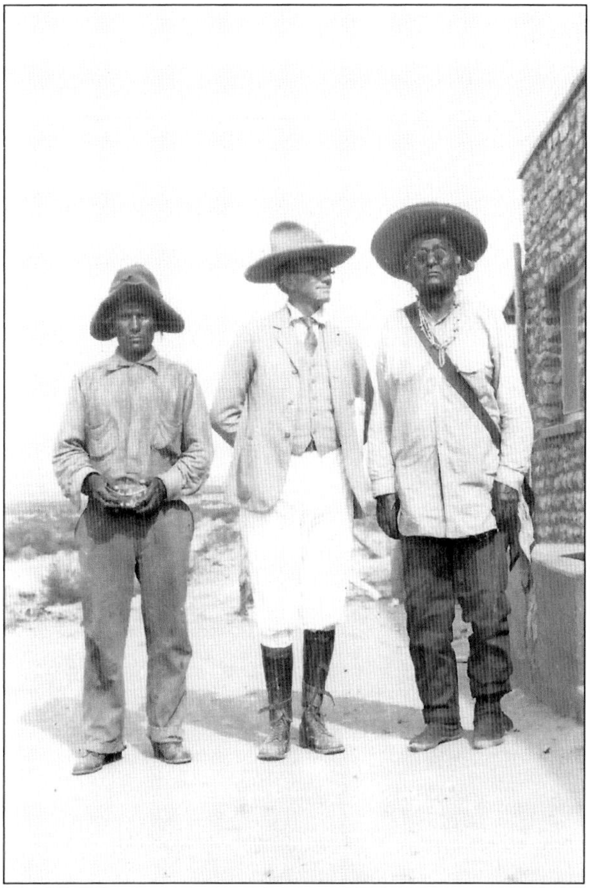

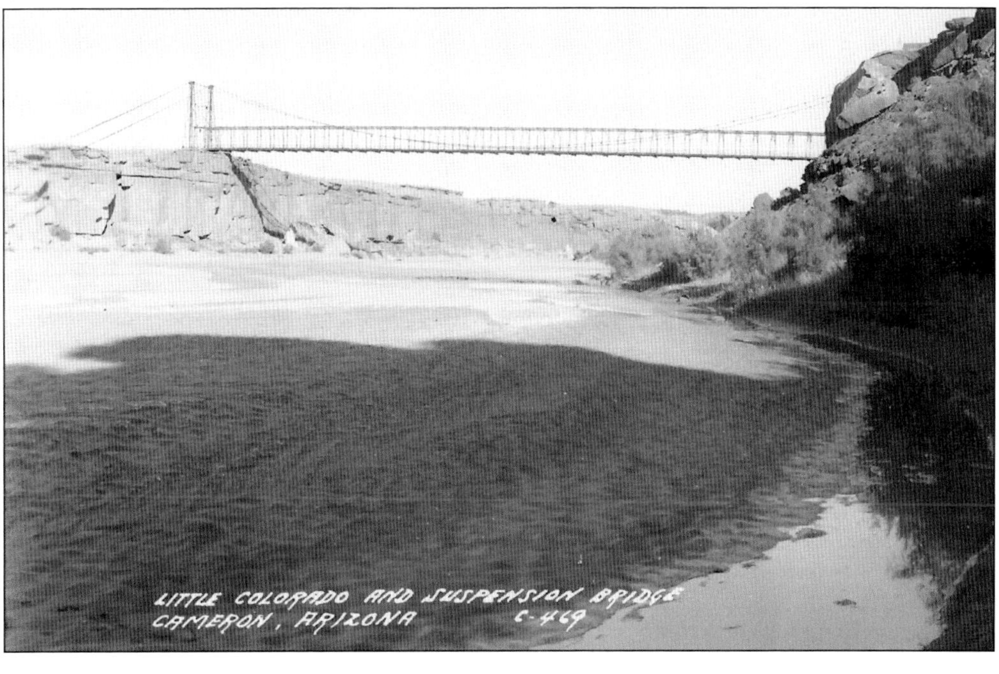

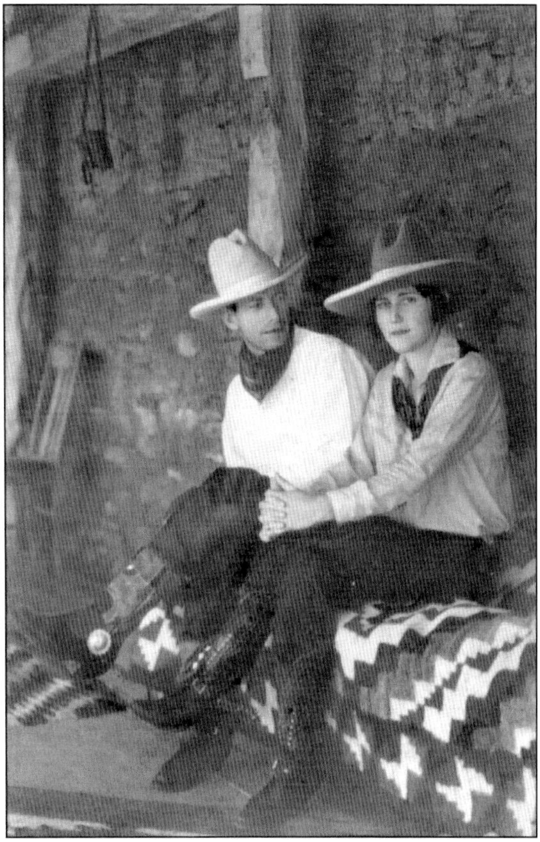

In the 1920s, Ida Mae and Stanton "Billy" Borum worked at Cameron, managing the store when Hubert and Maybel were in Winslow while their children attended school. In the 1930s, the Borums managed Leupp Trading Post as partners with Hubert Richardson. (Courtesy of Old Trails Museum/Winslow Historical Society.)

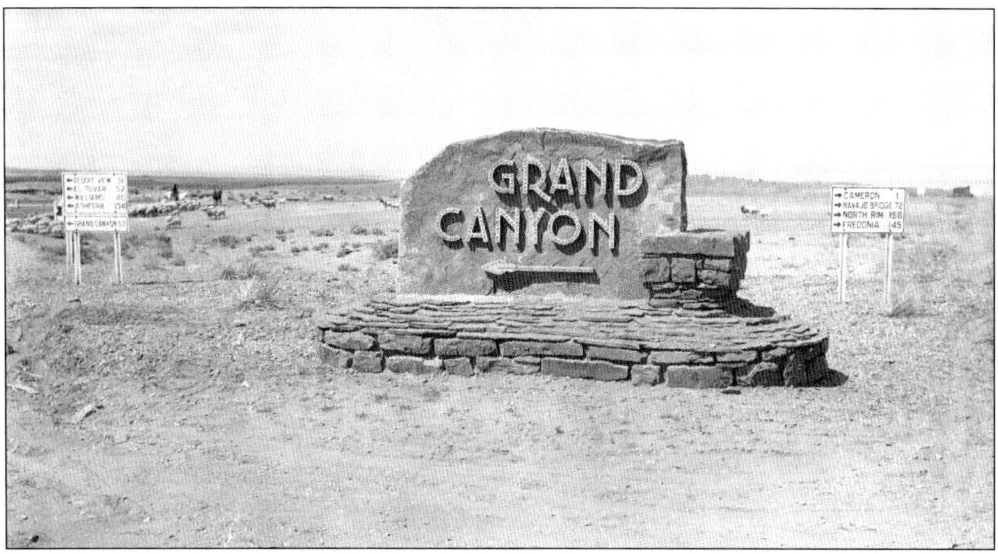

The journey to Cameron was rough in the early years. Sand blew across the road, and travelers recorded that stops were necessary to shovel sand and dirt to free the bogged-down tires. In the background, a Navajo woman on a white horse herds her flock of sheep across the dirt road at the turnoff leading to the Grand Canyon. (Courtesy of Grand Canyon Museum Collection, No. 07347.)

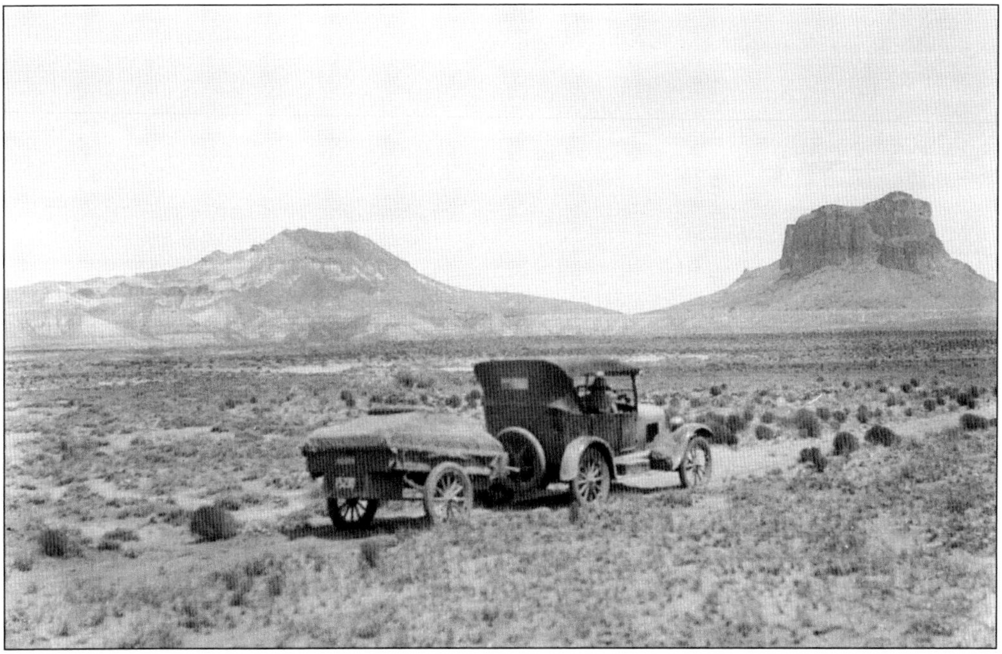

In 1927, Maud and Carey Melville from Worcester, Massachusetts, along with their three children, drove across the country. After stopping at Wupatki, they drove to Cameron, where they saw "red sand storms which looked like fire & smoke." At Cameron, the Melvilles were told that Fords (without vacuum-feed fuel delivery) could not make it to the Grand Canyon. Nevertheless, they decided to go ahead. At the road fork, there was a sign warning that Fords should not attempt the drive, and later, a man in a Buick stopped them and said "You'll never make it." Maud wrote that the view of the Little Colorado Canyon was grand, but eventually, the Ford stopped. They had to unload the trailer and "push hard for ¼ mile up" to where they found a camping place. That night, they put up their tent among the "stones, cedars & cactus." (Both, courtesy of Robert Arnold.)

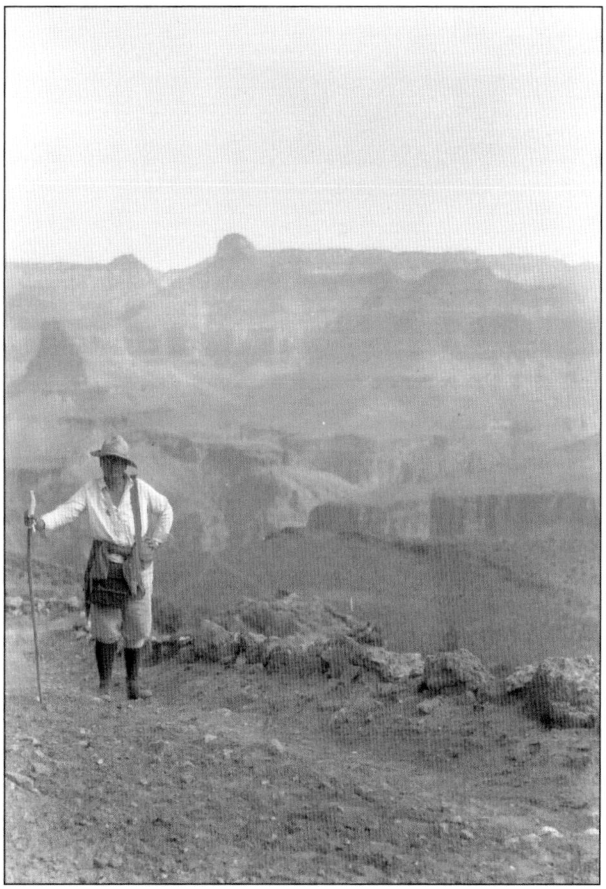

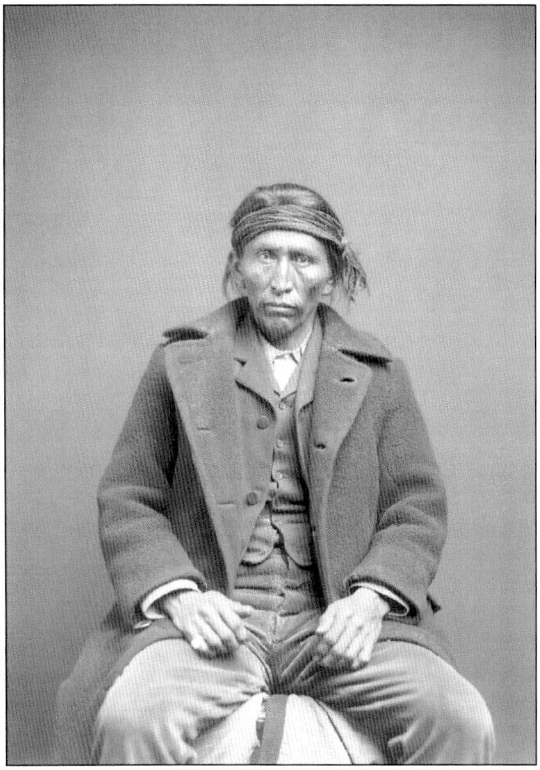

Peshlakai Etsidi, Silver Smith, of Naakai Dine'e ("First Clan"), lived in the Wupatki area west of the Little Colorado River and south of Cameron. As a boy in 1866, Peshlakai and his family participated in the Long Walk to Fort Sumner, New Mexico. When the government released them, the families returned to Wupatki, only to have conflicts with Anglo cattlemen. Ultimately, Etsidi's lands were incorporated into Wupatki National Monument. Etsidi always claimed to have been the first Navajo, along with his friend "Red Whiskers," to make silver jewelry. As a boy, he watched smiths at Fort Sumner as they made bridles using iron. Etsidi was photographed by Thomas William Smillie in 1904. Below, the circular ruins show traces of early Navajo homes scattered across the Painted Desert, in the area where Peshlakai Etsidi lived. (Left, courtesy of National Anthropological Archives, Smithsonian, No. 396700; below, courtesy of Scott Thybony.)

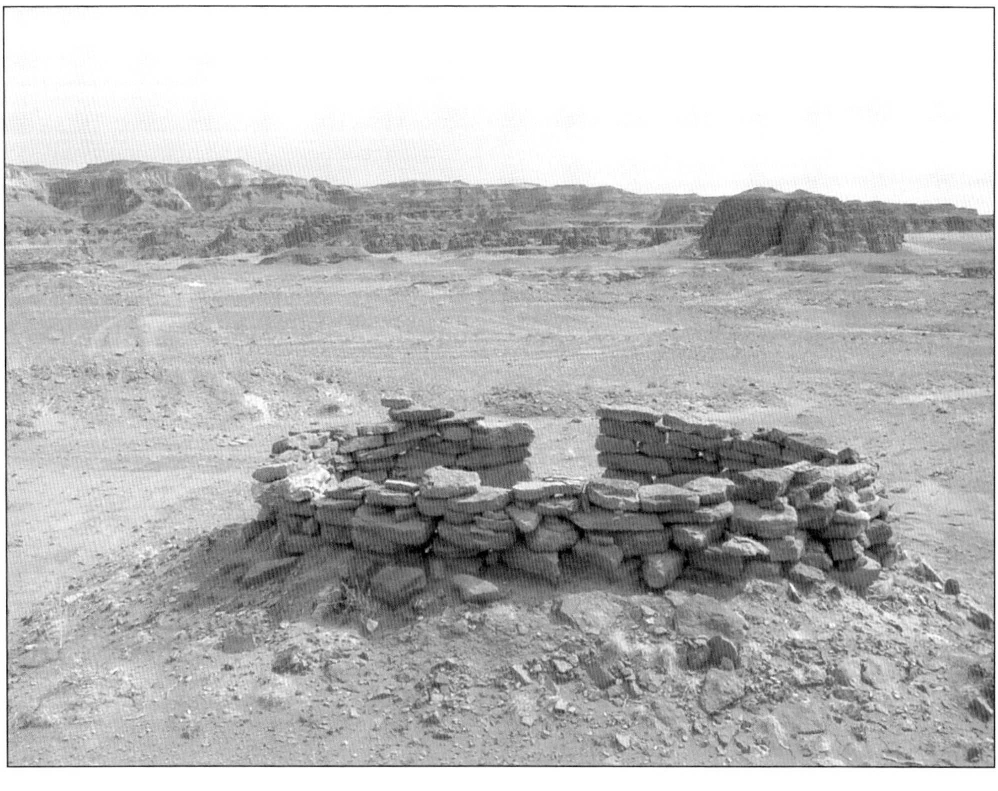

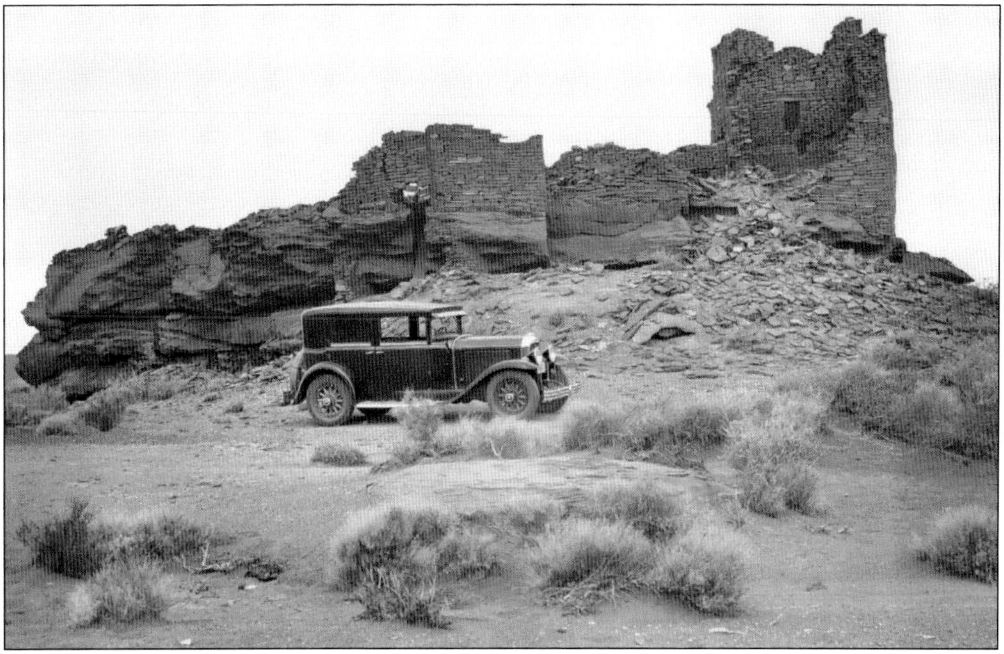

There are more than 800 ruins within Wupatki National Monument, just south of Cameron, and several are large Anasazi and Sinagua pueblos built on mesa tops and canyon rims. Wukoki, above, was photographed in 1930 by M.J.E. Colter. Many Navajo families have historically lived in the Wupatki area, but when the boundaries of Wupatki National Monument were drawn, those families were required to leave, with many relocating to the Cameron area. Peshlakai Etsidi traveled to Washington, DC, to meet with Pres. Theodore Roosevelt to argue the boundaries in 1904, but to no avail. His granddaughter Stella Peshlakai Smith is the last of the Peshlakai clan living on Wupatki land. Generations of Peshlakais have lived on this land, and when Stella dies, the rest of the family must leave. (Above, courtesy of the National Park Service, WUPA 15968; below, photograph by W.C. Bullard, courtesy of the National Park Service, WUPA 15800.)

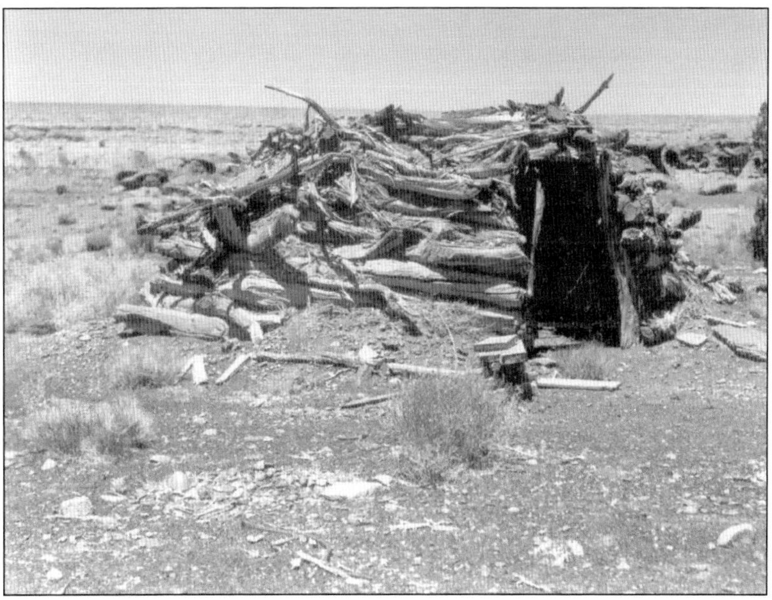

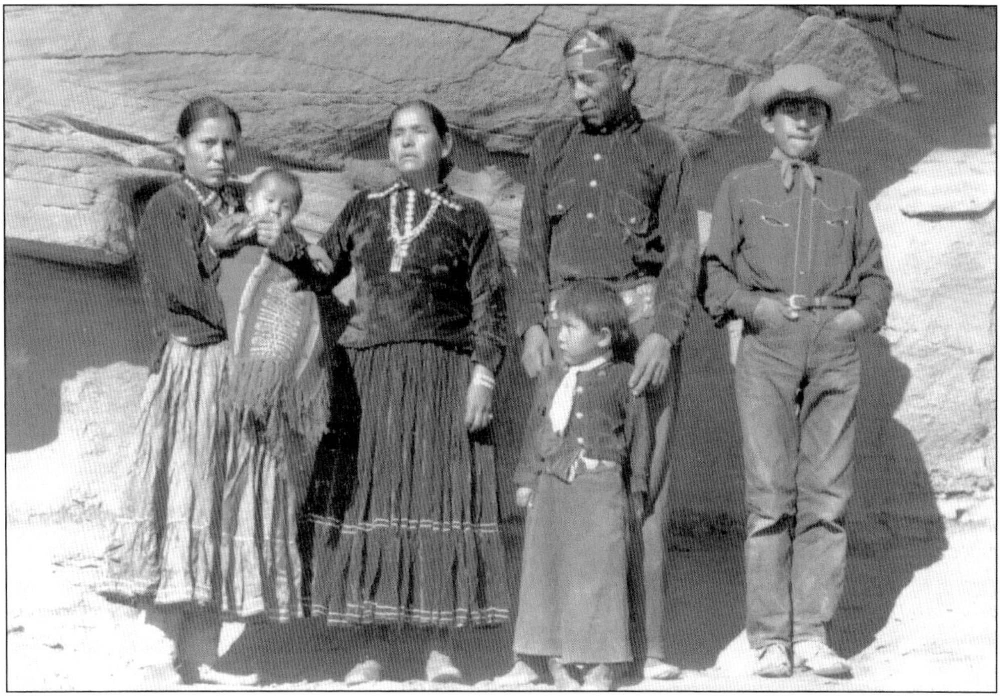

Clyde Peshlakai, son of Peshlakai Etsidi and Vera Standish, was born near Black Point on the Little Colorado River in 1882. He was married to at least four women, including sisters Sallie and Katherine. Clyde was allowed to live at Wupatki National Monument after the monument boundaries were drawn, serving as an honorary custodian. He is pictured above with his family about 1941; from left to right are Katherine (holding their daughter Eleanor), Sallie, Clyde, Clyde's son Charley Clyde, and an unidentified man. Clyde often gave tours of Wupatki ruins, and once, he painted a large oblong rock green and told visitors it was a prehistoric watermelon. At his death in 1979, Clyde was buried in his hogan at Wupatki. (Above, courtesy of the National Park Service, WUPA 15599; below, courtesy of the National Park Service, WUPA 15803.)

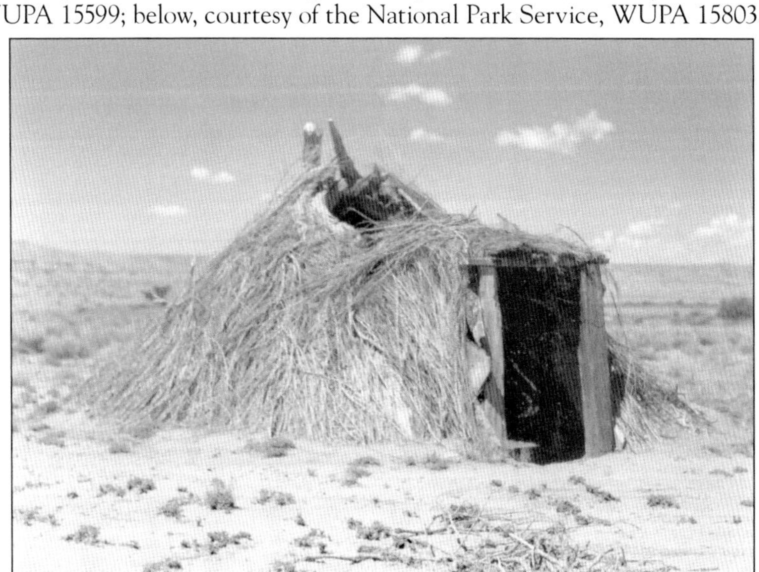

Clyde Peshlakai married Sallie in 1937. They did not have any children together, although they both had children from previous marriages. About two years later, Clyde took Sallie's half-sister Katherine out of school to live with him, even though she was only 13 or 14 years old at that time. He did not officially marry Katherine until 1946, after Sallie divorced him (and married Emmet Lee from the Tuba City area). Clyde and Katherine had eight children together. In the 1939 photograph at right, Katherine (left) and Sallie shear sheep. Below, Sallie spins the cleaned and carded wool into lengths of yarn, in preparation for weaving a rug. (Both, courtesy of National Park Service, above, WUPA 15558, below, WUPA 15563.)

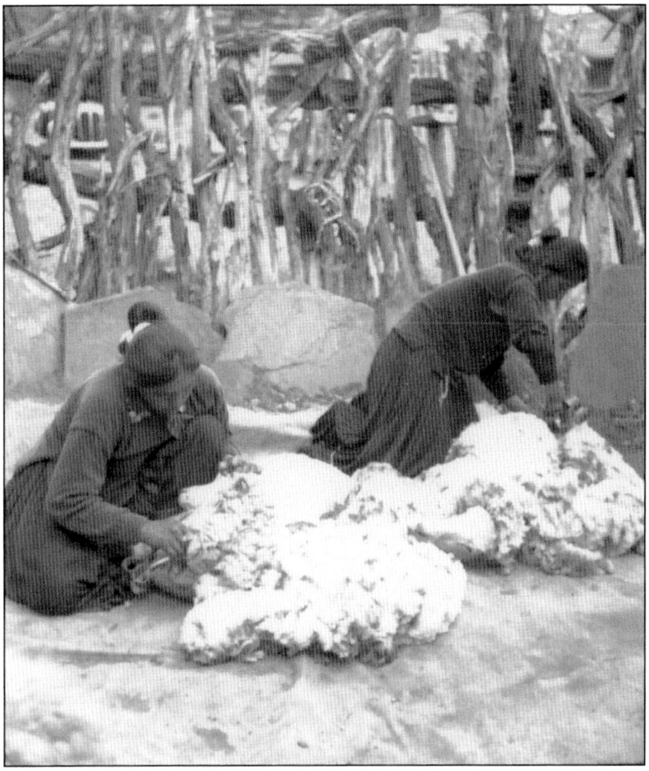

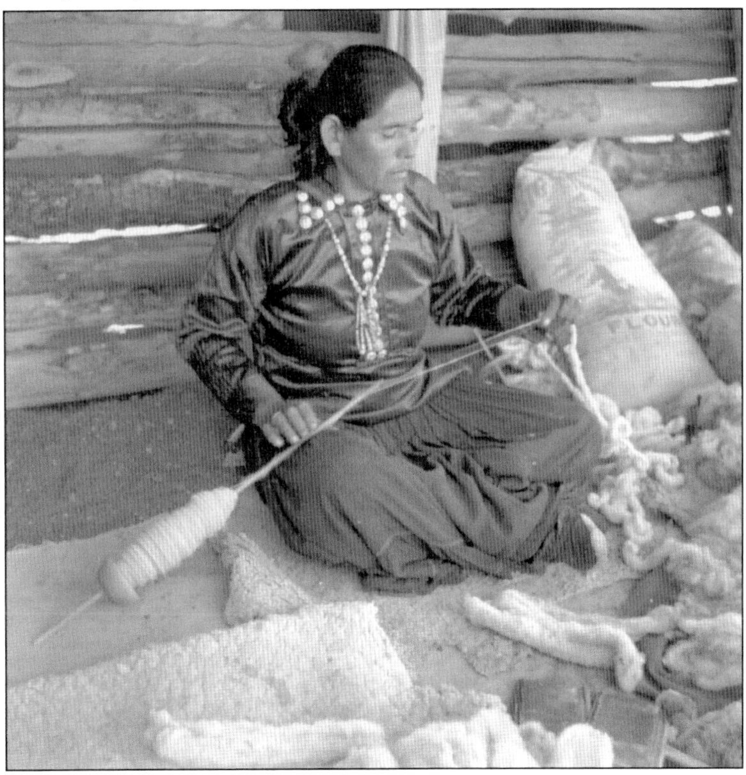

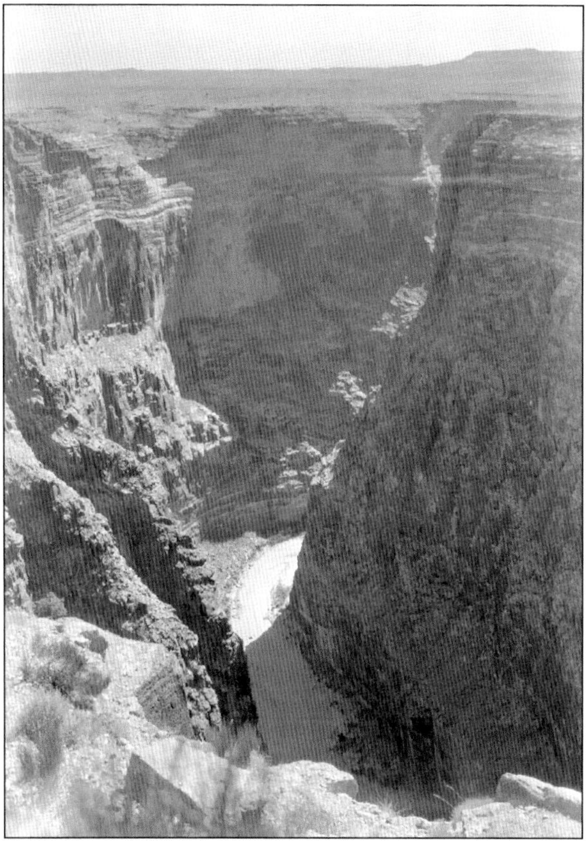

During the Long Walk in 1864, when Navajos were forced to walk to New Mexico, a pregnant woman of the Bitter Water Clan, knowing she could not survive the journey, was hidden in a cave in the Little Colorado River Gorge. After the baby was born, she was rescued by her relatives who were returning from the Long Walk. They lowered a braided yucca rope. The site in the gorge is known as Pull Up the Baby Canyon. (Courtesy of Grand Canyon Museum Collection, No. 00409.)

A Navajo girl stands in front of her wood-sided hogan. A blanket with the corners tied to the top of the frame serves as a door.

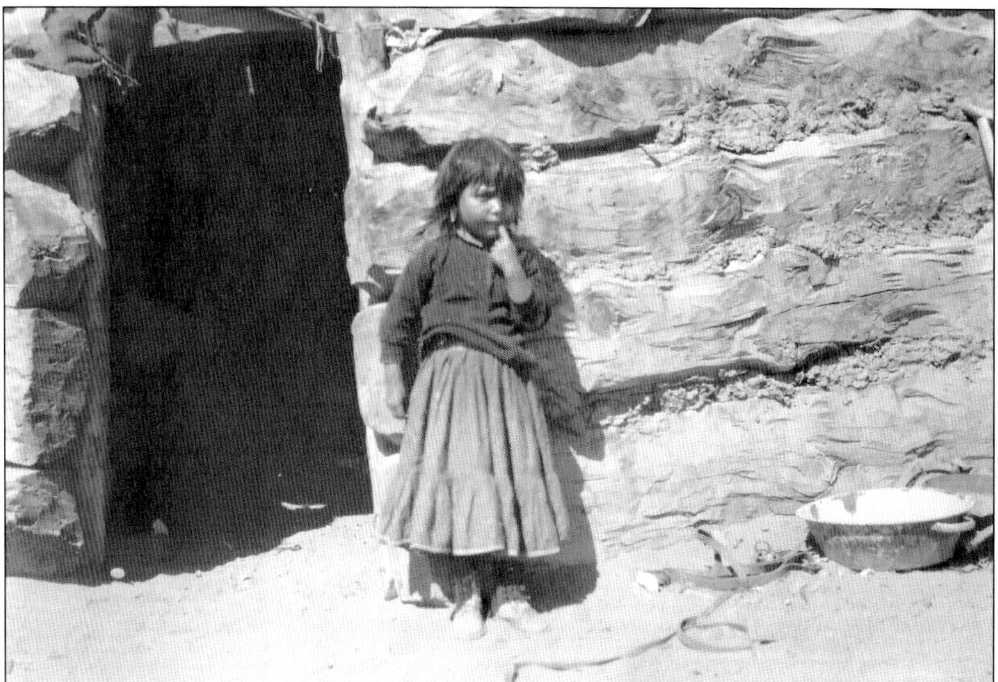

Two

An Oasis in the Desert

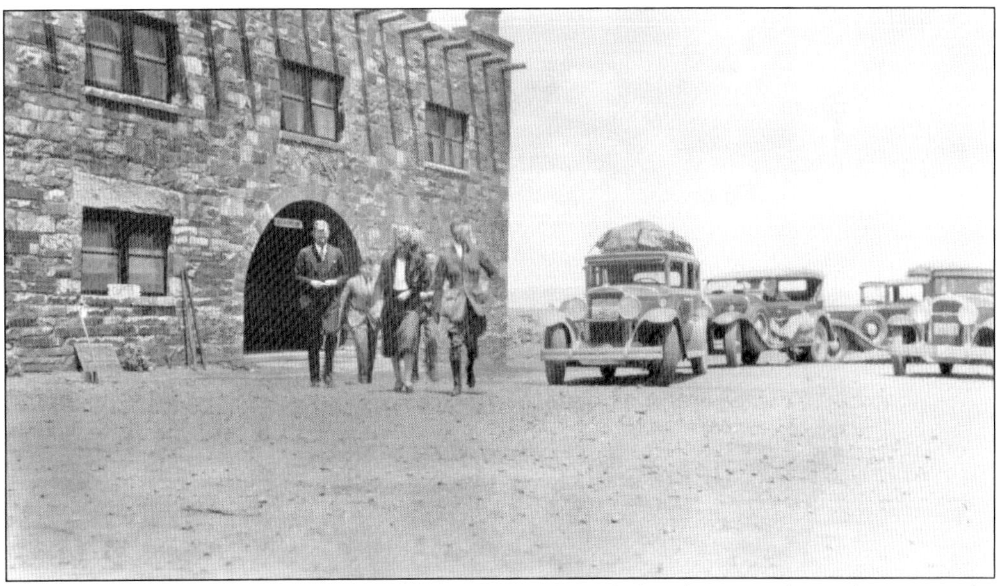

In the spring of 1928, Hubert Richardson built a pueblo-style hotel next to the trading post. The building, constructed of natural red stone, was known as the Klo-a-chee-kin Hotel, the Little Red Rock House. The hotel had a ground-floor kitchen, dining room, lobby, and a small apartment at the back for the caretaker. There were six rooms upstairs for guests. (Courtesy of Atkinson Trading Company.)

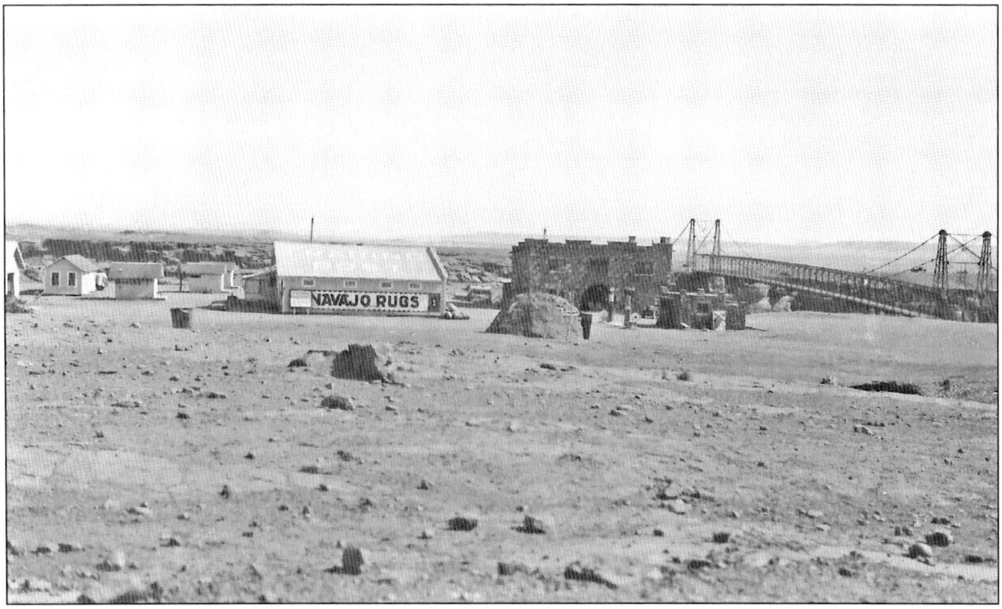

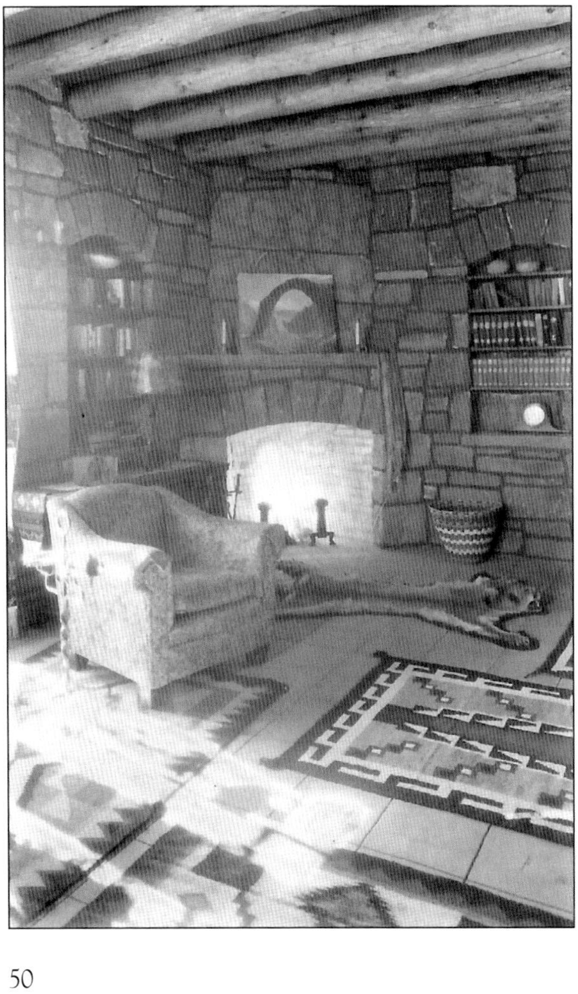

After construction of the new hotel at Cameron, the word spread and more tourists visited the trading post. The lobby of the Klo-a-chee-kin Hotel, adjacent to Cameron Trading Post, was considered to be surprisingly luxurious, given its remote location. Decorated with Navajo rugs, baskets, and Pueblo pottery, the hotel was a comfortable spot in northern Arizona. Several stone blocks in the interior walls of the lobby were imbedded with the dinosaur tracks found in nearby Dinosaur Canyon. The *Arizona Daily Sun* called Cameron "a veritable oasis in the desert at the edge of the Navajo Reservation." There were also one or two guest hogans for visiting Navajos, and the number of tourist cabins behind the store grew each year.

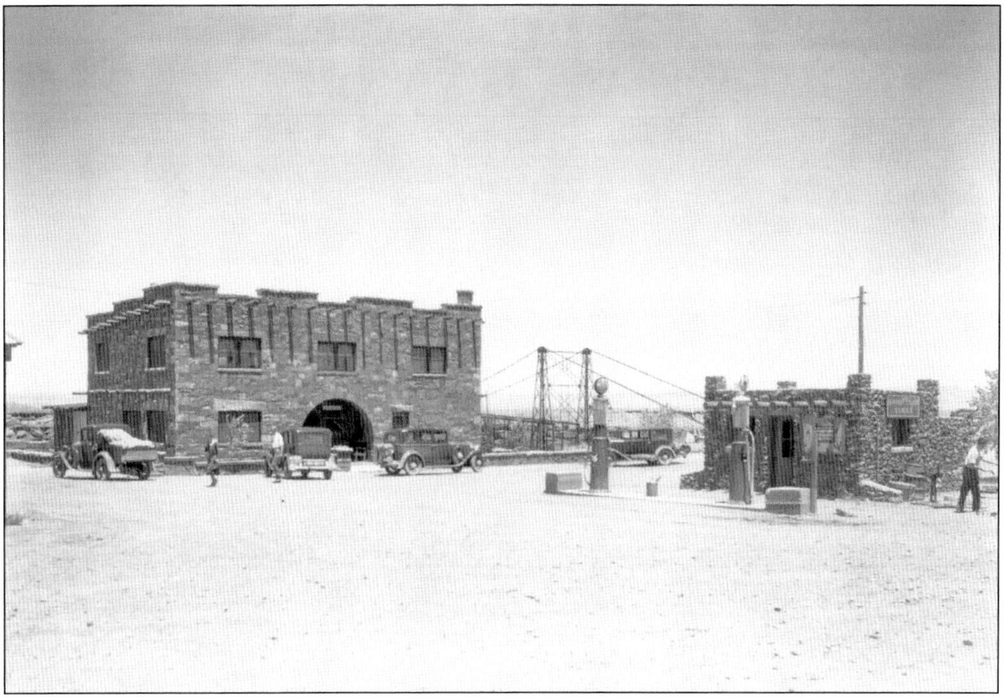

More and more tourists were driving their automobiles to Cameron and beyond. Cameron offered Texaco gasoline and Goodyear tires for travelers. North of the bridge over the Little Colorado River and west to the Grand Canyon, the roads were all unpaved; sand, rocks, and washouts were real hazards. Gasoline and automobile tires would have been valuable for travelers, as there were no services for many miles beyond the trading post. The unidentified girl below stands at one of the gasoline tanks. (Above, courtesy of Grand Canyon Museum Collection, No. 03976; below, courtesy of Atkinson Trading Company.)

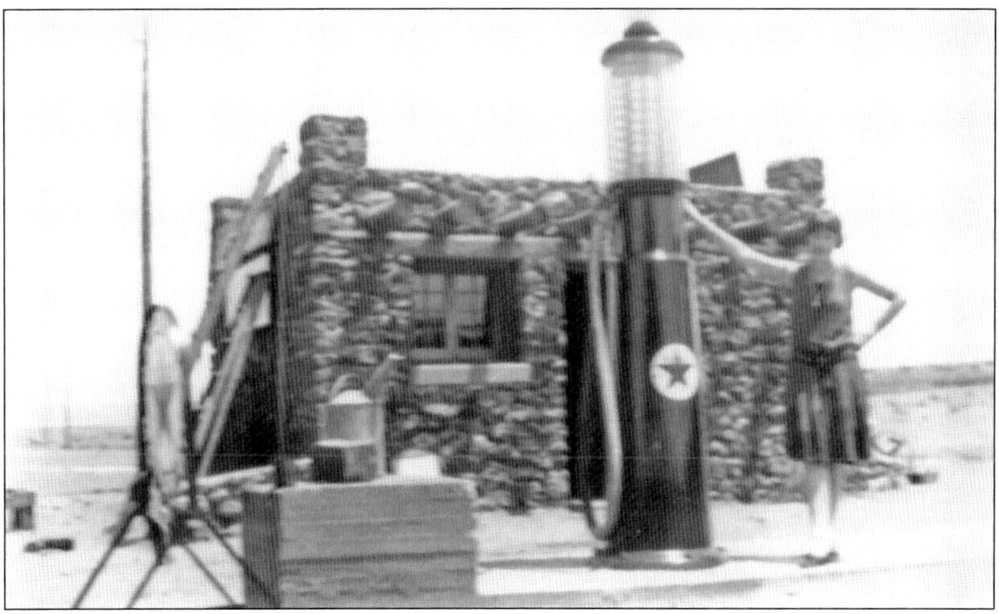

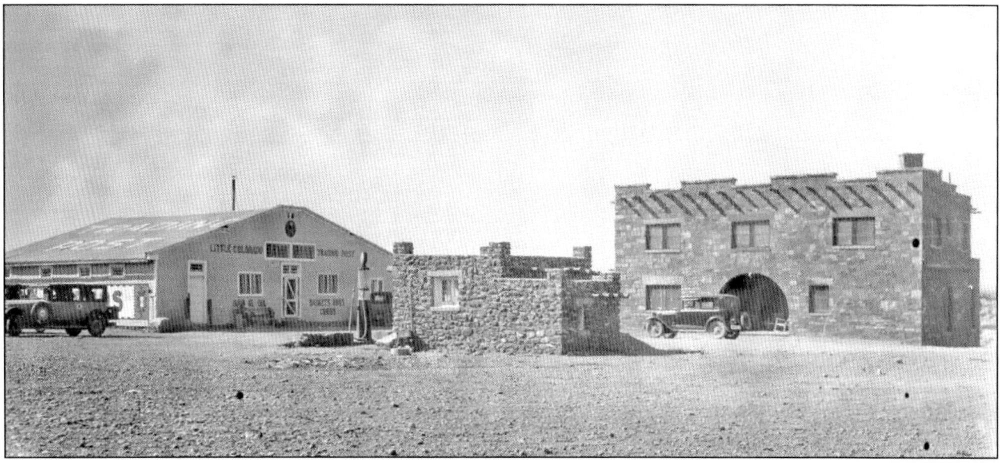

The Fred Harvey Company offered Indian Detours for railroad travelers visiting the West; travelers were called "detourists." The one-to-three-day tours were advertised as visits to "Indian Country" and the Grand Canyon, at a cost of $3 to $10, and $14 in the 1930s. Cameron Trading Post was always a stop on the Painted Desert, Grand Canyon, and northern Arizona trips. Above, a Harvey car can be seen in front of the trading post. These luxury automobiles were large Cadillacs, Franklins, and Packards. Their powerful engines were necessary to climb the steep road from Cameron to the Grand Canyon. As Elizabeth Hegemann recalled, the Harvey tour cars barreled up and down the narrow road, sometimes running other drivers off the road to avoid a collision or a drop into the sheer canyon. (Above, courtesy of Lisa Amaral; below, courtesy of Grand Canyon Museum Collection, No. 14052.)

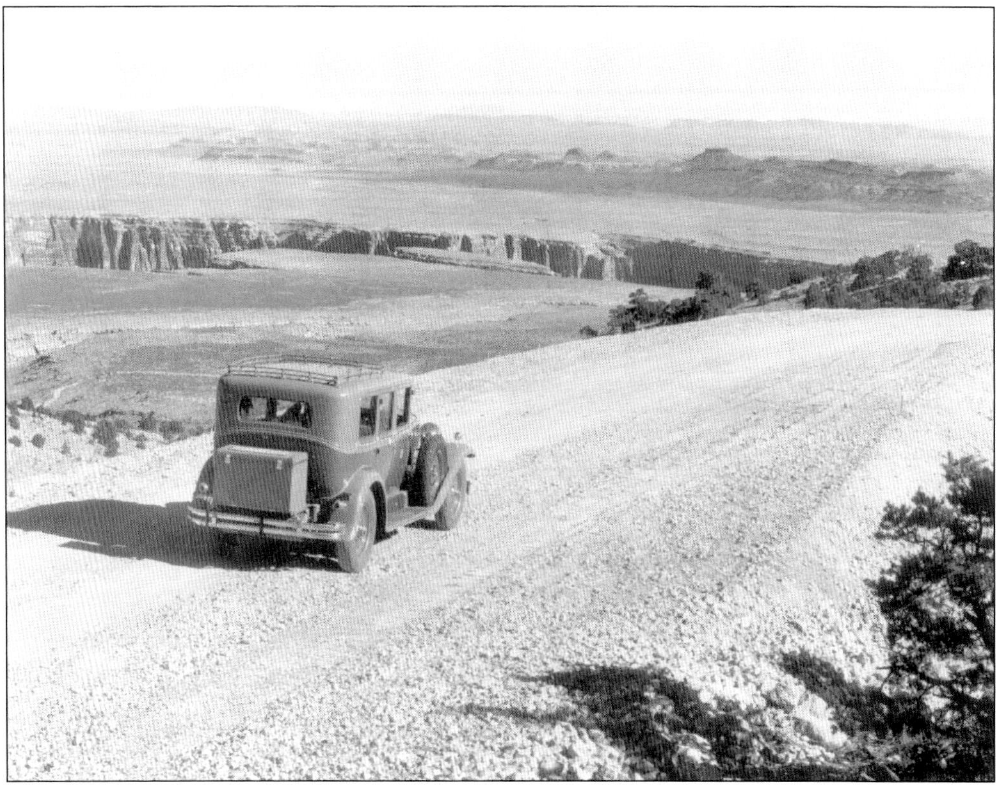

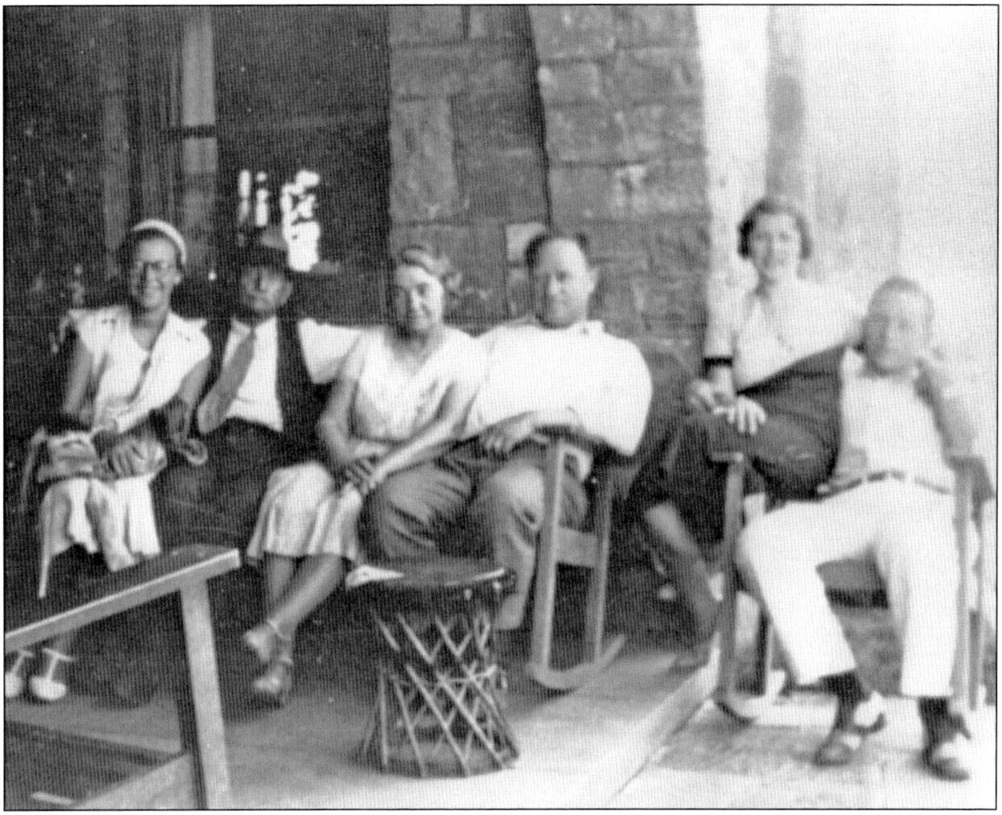

Above, the Richardson family poses for a photograph, lounging in rockers on the patio of the recently built stone hotel across from the trading post. From left to right are daughter Jeanette (in her mid-teens), Hubert's father, John W. Richardson, Maybel, Hubert, a woman identified as "Aunt Jane," and Richardson's eldest son, John "Jack" Richardson. Jack worked at Cameron until his death in an automobile accident in 1955. Jeanette attended Julliard and later married and moved away. The youngest son, Keith, who went by "Buddy," worked at Kaibito, Bellmont, and later, Cameron. Maybel planted a lush garden behind the hotel. Called "Maybel's Oasis," it was a shady and cool spot in the harsh landscape of the Painted Desert. (Above, courtesy of Lisa Amaral.)

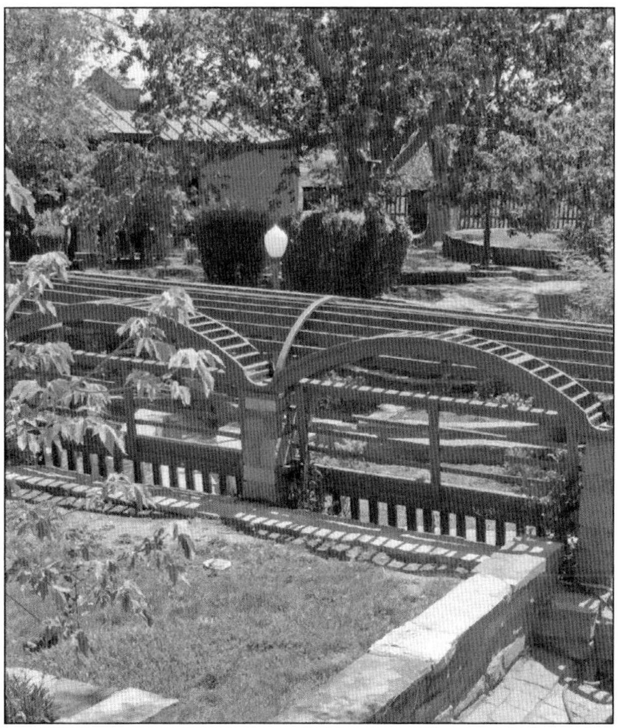

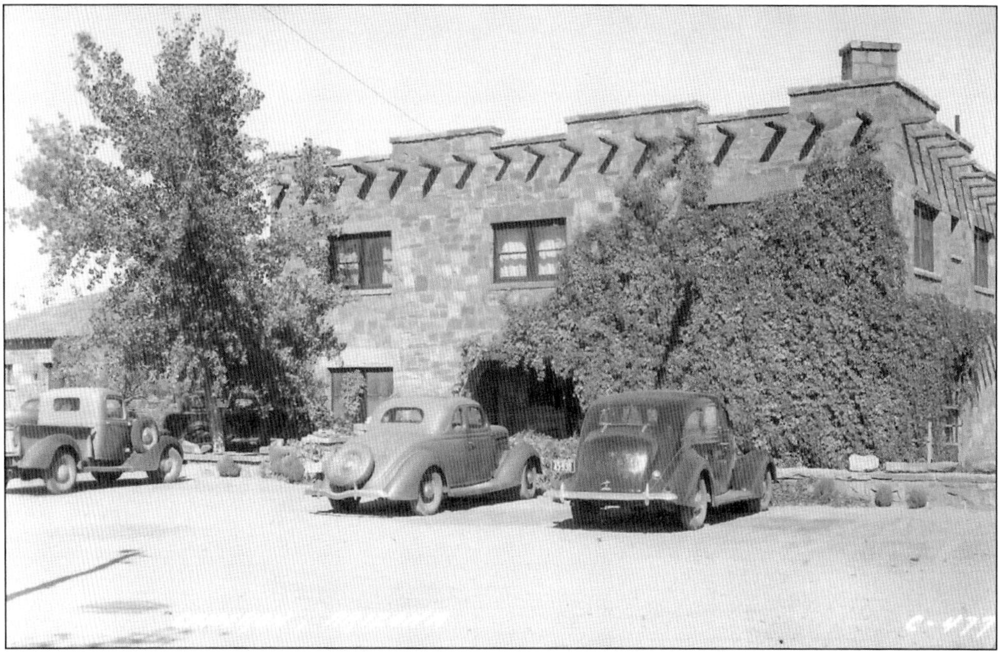

Maybel Richardson was the person responsible for the plantings at Cameron. She loved flowers and shrubbery, as can be seen in the photograph above with trees and vines growing up the side of the hotel. Below, Maybel and Hubert rest on a bench in her garden behind the hotel. (Both, courtesy of Lisa Amaral.)

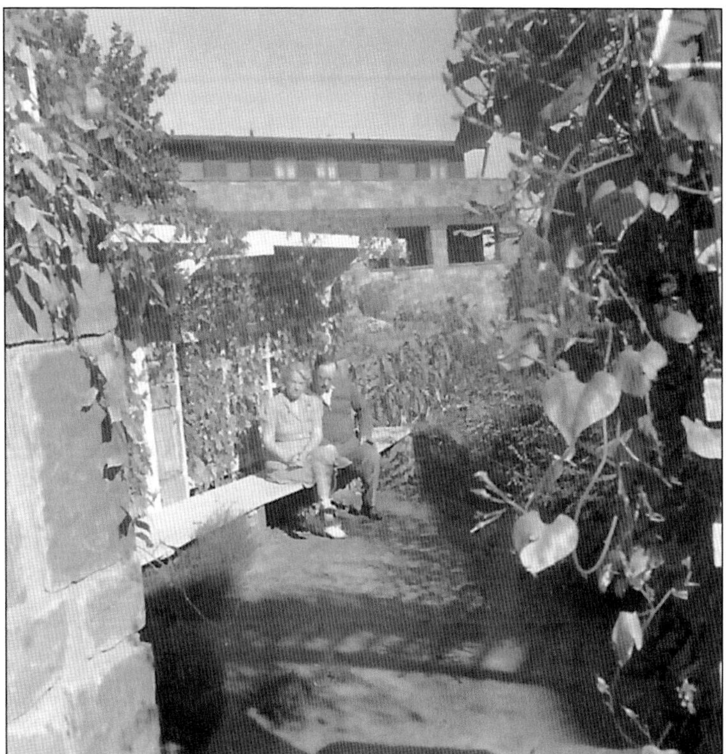

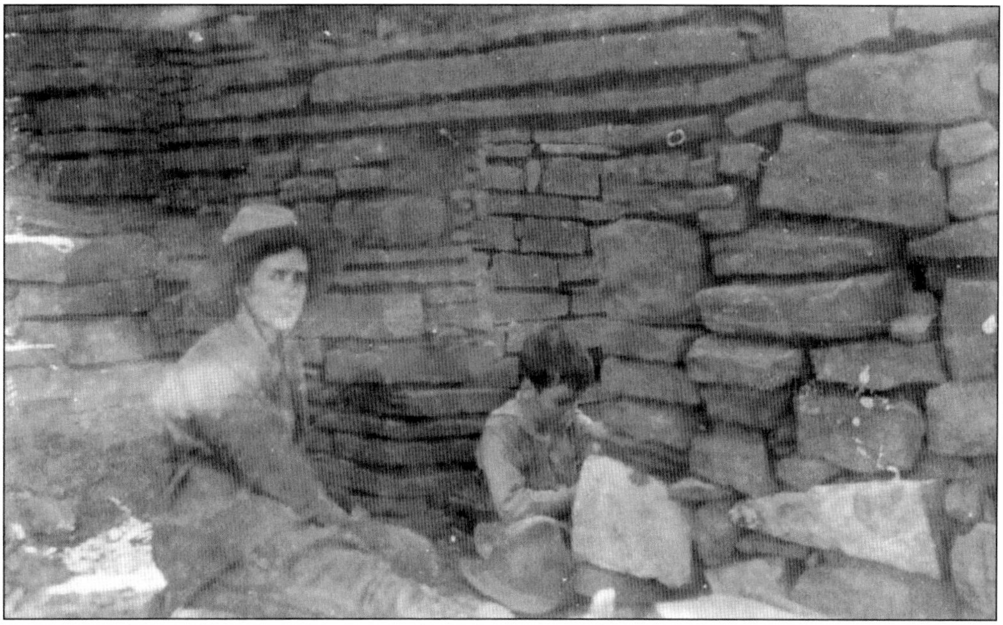

Mary-Russell Ferrell Colton (1889–1971) studied art in Philadelphia before moving to Arizona with her husband, Harold, in the early 1920s. In 1928, they cofounded the Museum of Northern Arizona in Flagstaff. The Coltons both had an interest in the country and the people of the area and spent time exploring their new state. On those trips, Mary painted landscapes, the Painted Desert, and the country near Cameron Trading Post. The Little Colorado River and the river's dramatic gorge were often subjects. Mary, pictured above with her son, Ferrell, painted *The Lonesome Hole, Valley of the Little Colorado* in 1929. (Above, courtesy of the National Park Service, WUPA 24473; below, courtesy of Mark Sublette Medicine Man Gallery.)

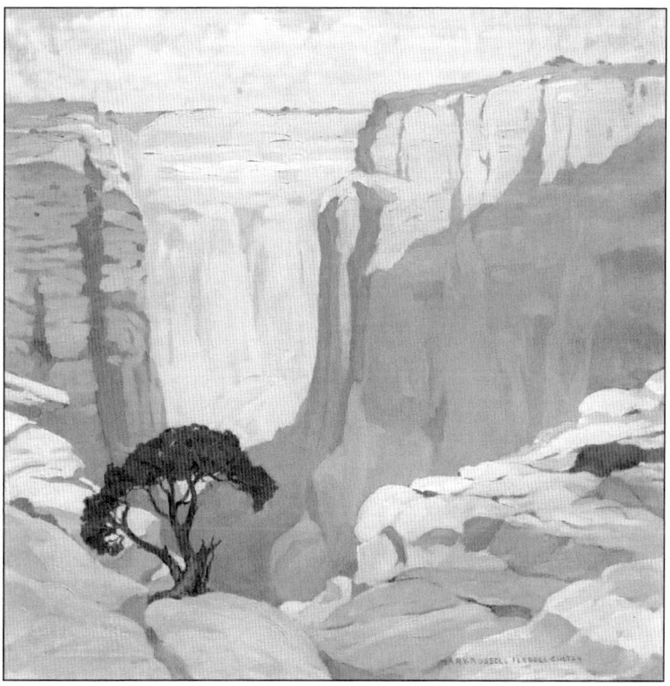

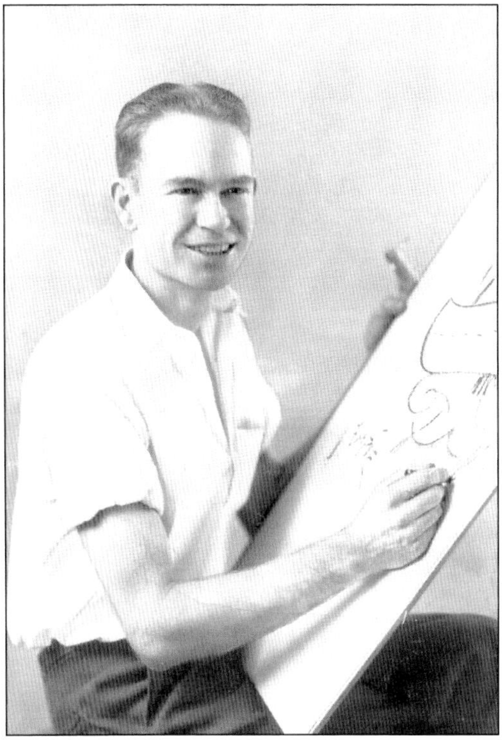

Born in 1909 in a dirt-floored adobe house in eastern Arizona, Hart Haller "Hal" Empie was a self-taught artist. A pharmacist by training, Hal operated a pharmacy in the small ranching community of Duncan, Arizona, on the Gila River. He set up his easel in the store and painted in between filling prescriptions. When time permitted, Empie traveled around Arizona to paint desert landscapes, with Cameron being a favorite stopping place. His *Little Colorado* painting was done in 1951. (Left, courtesy of Ann Empie Groves; below, courtesy of Joanne DeVine.)

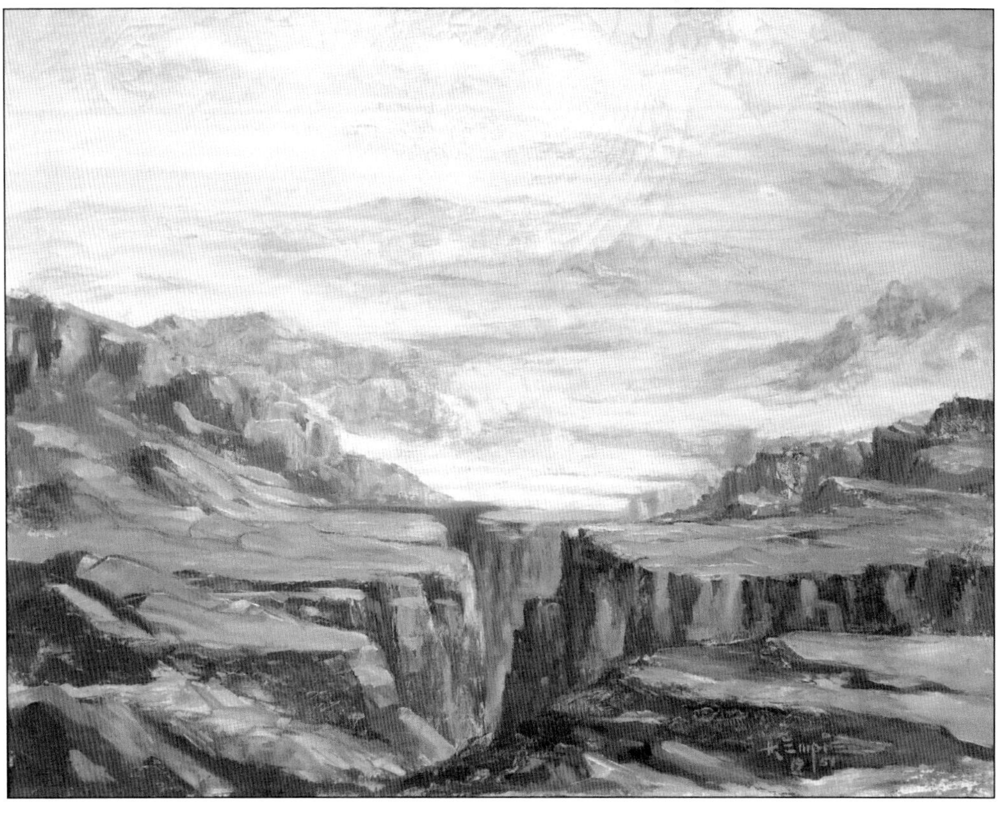

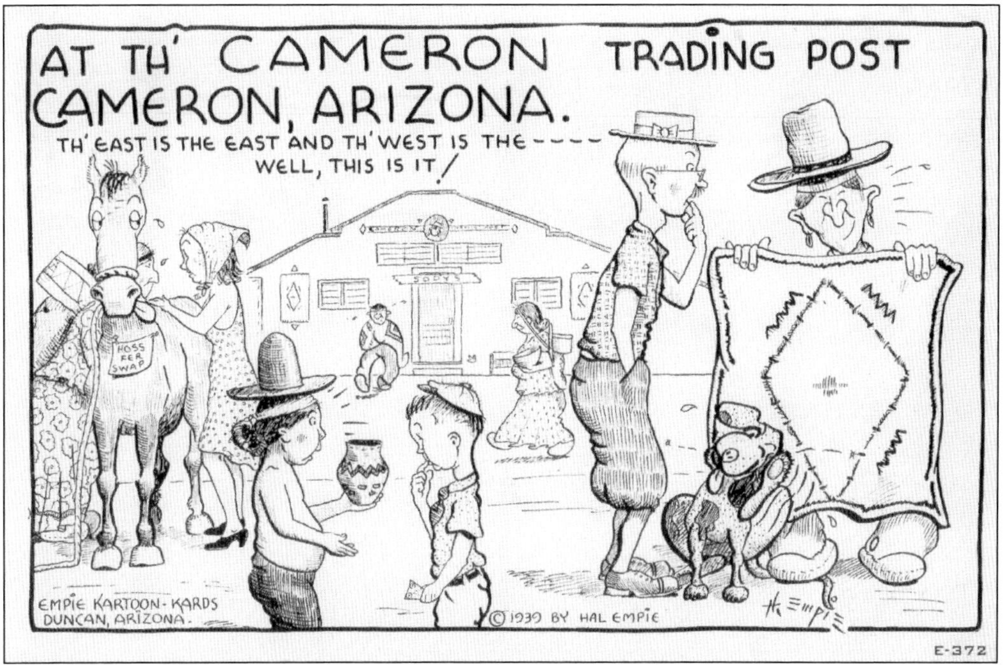

In addition to his oil paintings, Hal's "Empie Kartoon Kards" were among the earliest copyrighted western cartoons. They were frequently featured in *Arizona Highways* magazine, and his cartoon postcards were marketed in 38 states. When he died at age 93 in 2002, Empie was the oldest continuous resident artist in Arizona. (Both, courtesy of Ann Empie Groves.)

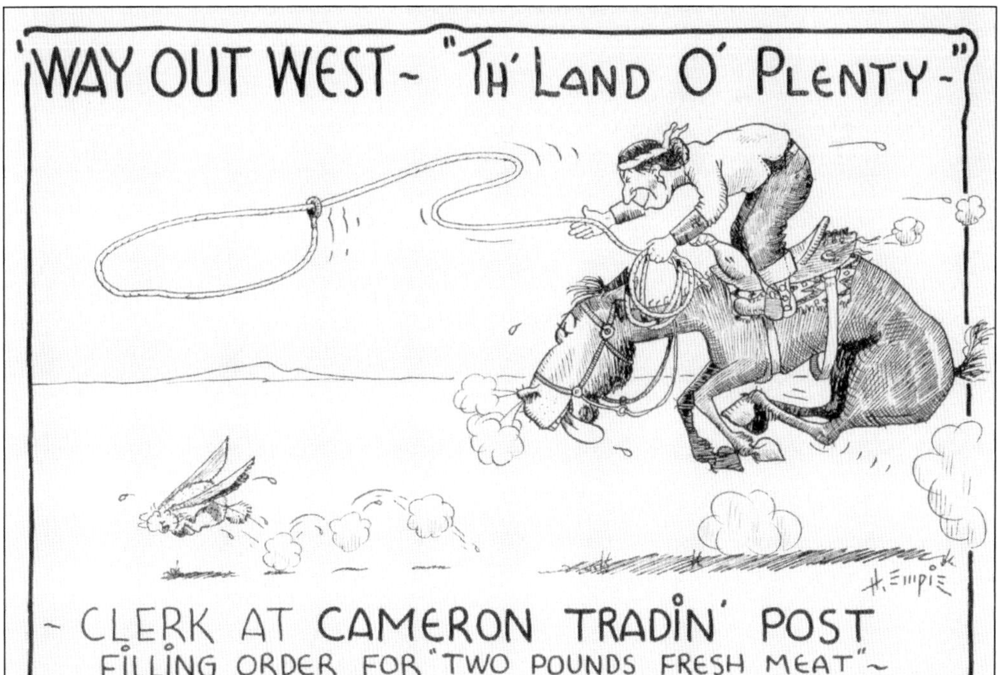

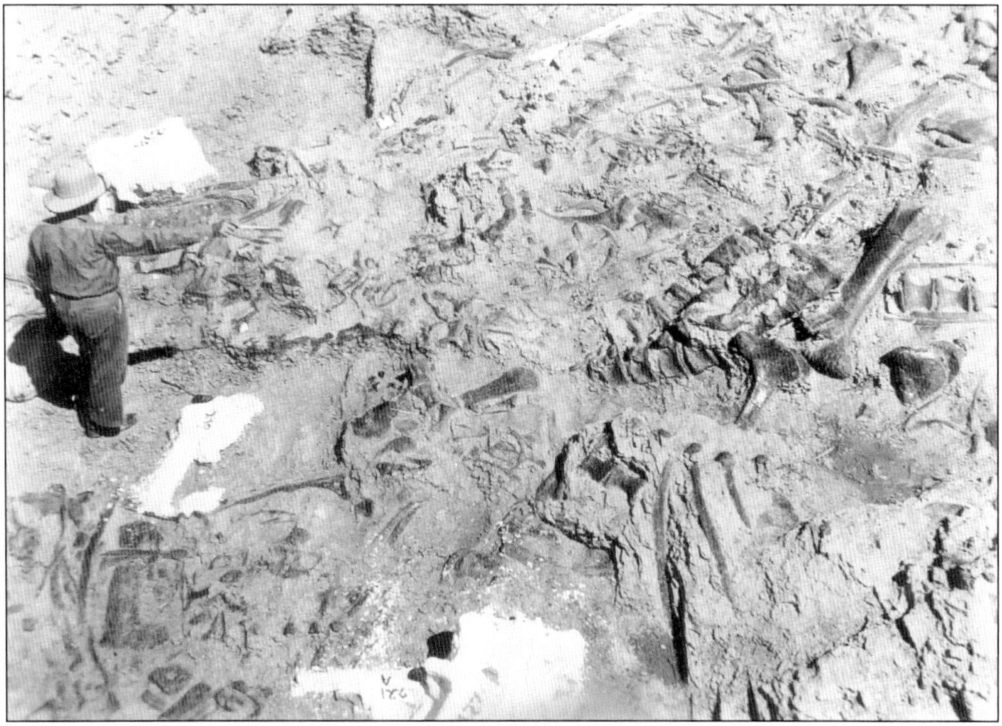

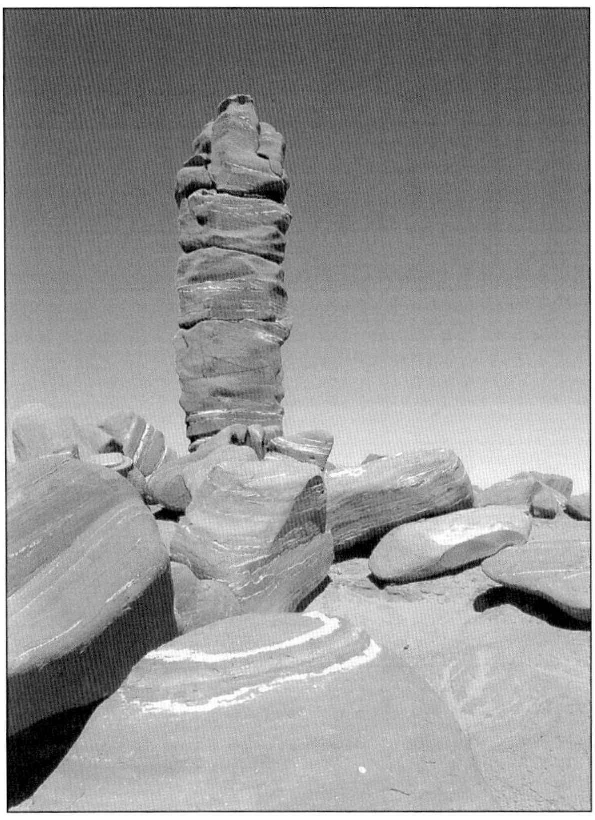

Barnum Brown, shown above examining bones of sauropods, was a paleontologist from the American Museum of Natural History, best known for his discovery of a *Tyrannosaurus rex* skeleton. He was known as "Mr. Bones" and hosted a popular radio show where he related tales of his worldwide explorations. Brown first visited the Cameron area in 1902, collecting fossil pinecones for the Smithsonian Institution. He also discovered fossil tree trunks standing upright north of Tanner's Crossing. Brown later became acquainted with Hubert Richardson and returned to Cameron several times after a local Navajo man, Goldtooth Semallie, told him of dinosaur tracks and a fossil bed in Dinosaur Canyon east of Cameron. The spire in Dinosaur Canyon, pictured at left, is named for Barnum Brown. (Above, courtesy of US Geological Survey; left, courtesy of Scott Thybony.)

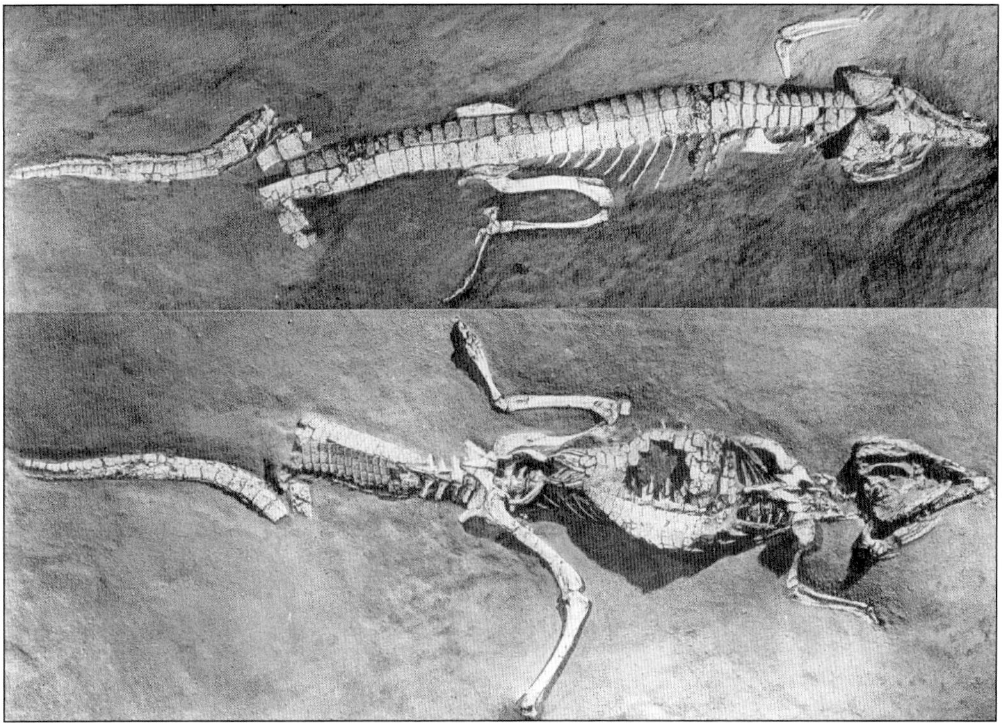

Barnum Brown returned to Cameron in 1931. Richardson took Brown to Dinosaur Canyon in his Packard, with others in the expedition following behind. With a storm nearing, they fled the canyon that morning, but near Tanner's Crossing, Brown uncovered a huge phytosaur skull, 54 inches long, as well as the complete skeleton of an ancestral crocodile from the Upper Triassic, seen above. As the rain fell, Hubert announced that they had better leave the area. Arriving back at Cameron, Maybel let the group know that she had been worried. Brown replied, "Haven't I always told you never to look for a fossil-hunter until you can see him?" Brown named his discovery *Protosuchus richardsoni* in Hubert's honor. His inscription in Dinosaur Canyon, pictured below, reads: "B. Brown Am Museum Nat Hist New York." (Above, courtesy of US Geological Survey; below, courtesy of Scott Thybony.)

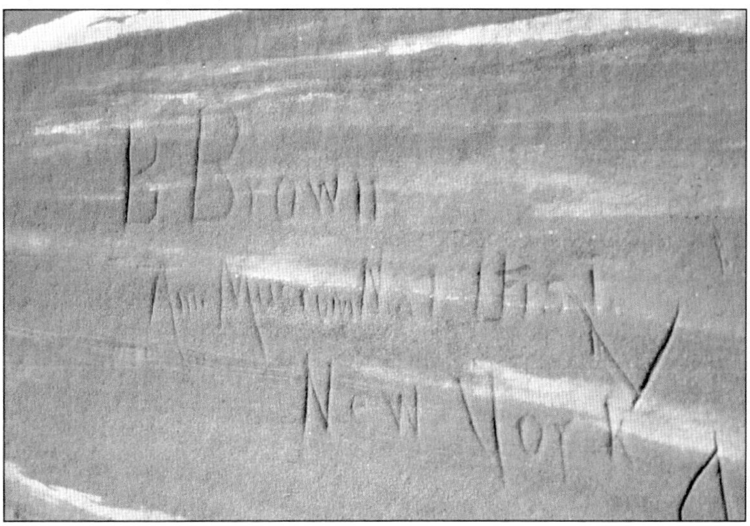

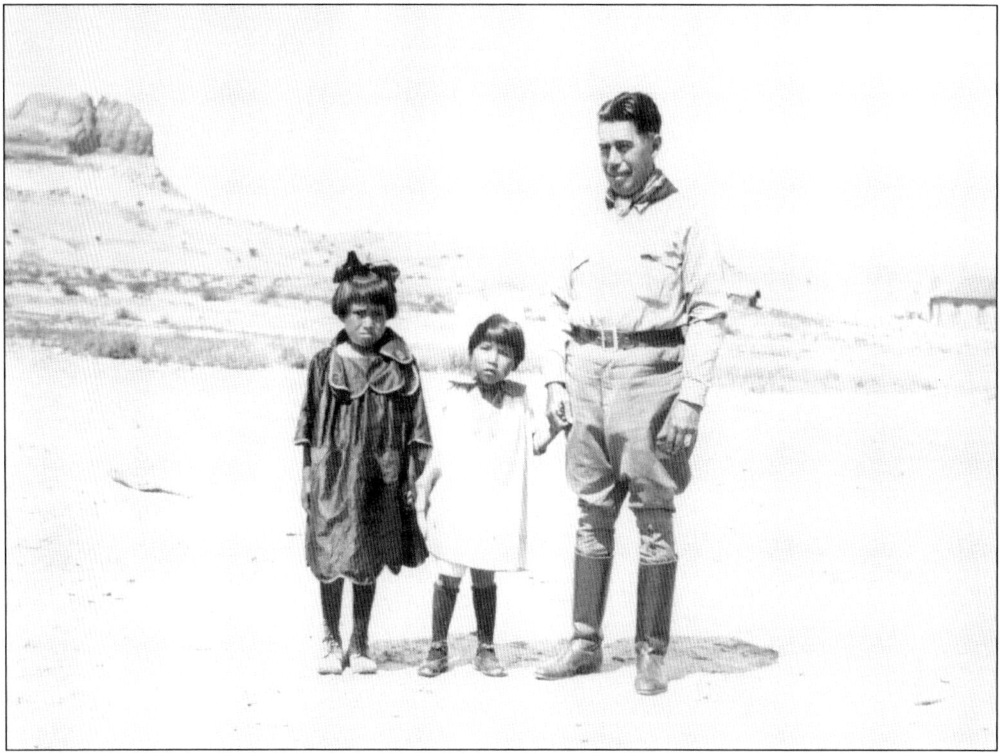

Cameron Trading Post was often a home base for California cartoonist and landscape painter James "Jimmy" Swinnerton (1875–1974). About 1906, when living in New York City, Swinnerton contracted tuberculosis and was told he had two weeks to live. He boarded a train for the West and spent the rest of his years in California and Arizona. According to Hubert Richardson's granddaughter, the artist was a close friend of the Richardsons and even gave them a painting of Monument Valley. Other paintings of the Cameron area featured the Little Colorado River. In addition to his paintings, Swinnerton was known for his cartoon strips, including *Canyon Kiddies*, which appeared in *Good Housekeeping* magazine from 1922 to 1941. Above, Swinnerton poses with John and Louisa Wetherill's adopted daughters Betty (left) and Fannie at Kayenta. Swinnerton's painting below is titled *Wetherill's Front Door*. (Above, courtesy of Harvey Leake; below, courtesy of Mark Sublette Medicine Man Gallery.)

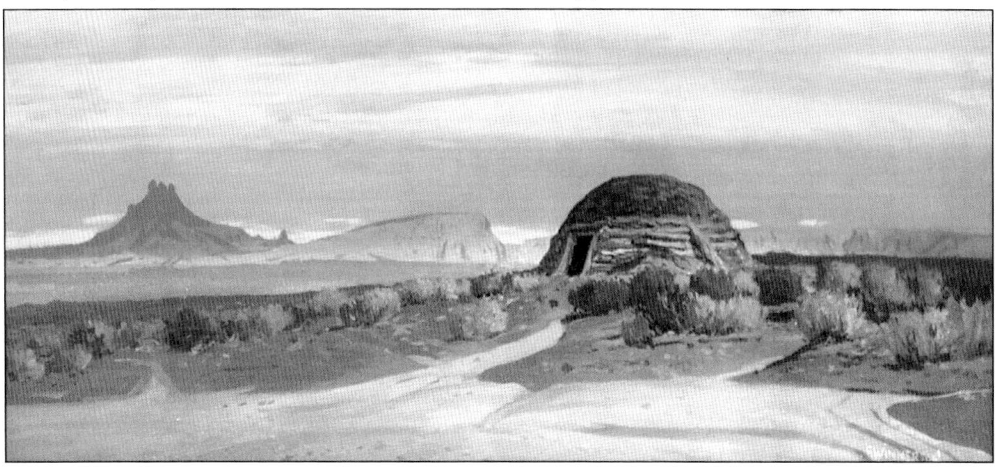

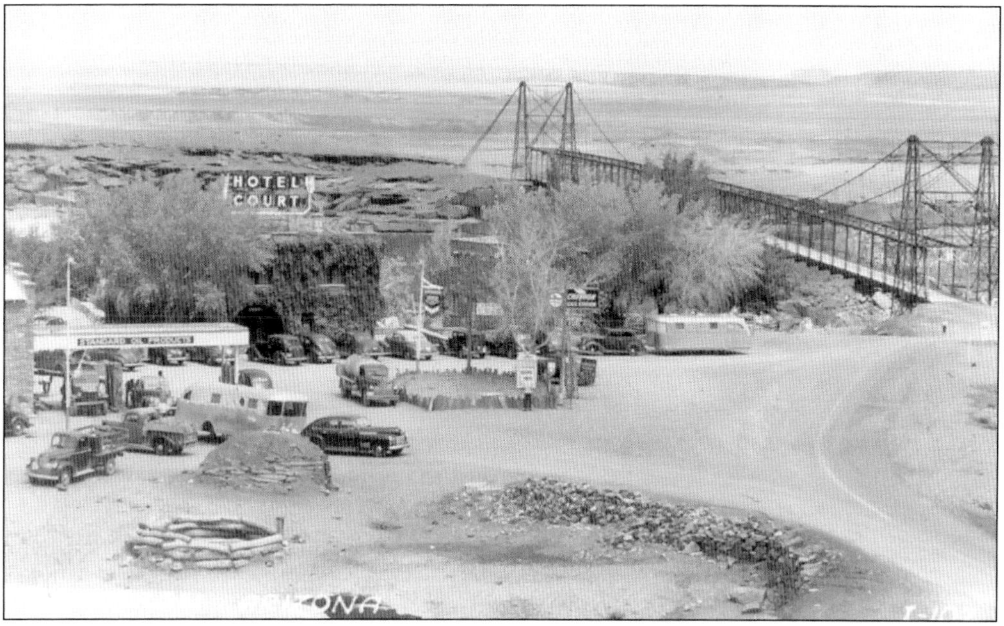

The Hopi building, a separate motel addition, was built north of the store in the 1930s. There were four kitchenettes on the west side, two upstairs and two downstairs, with eight single rooms on the east side. This building was remodeled in 1994. There were also two guest hogans for Navajo visitors to Cameron, but by the 1930s, there was so much tourism that Hubert Richardson tore them down because tourists had to drive around the hogans to reach the gas pumps and he realized that the Navajos had already stopped using them. Hubert remarked that "the Indians started traveling in cars and pickups about 1930." The image below shows the back of the trading post with tourist cabins lining the rim above the river. (Above, courtesy of Tom Collins; below, courtesy of Lisa Amaral.)

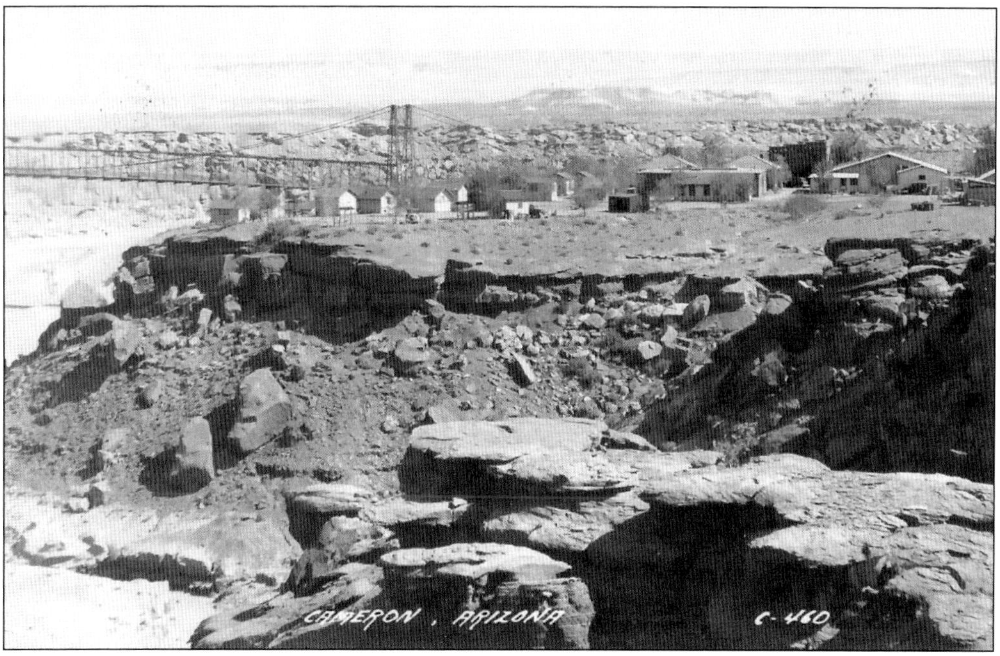

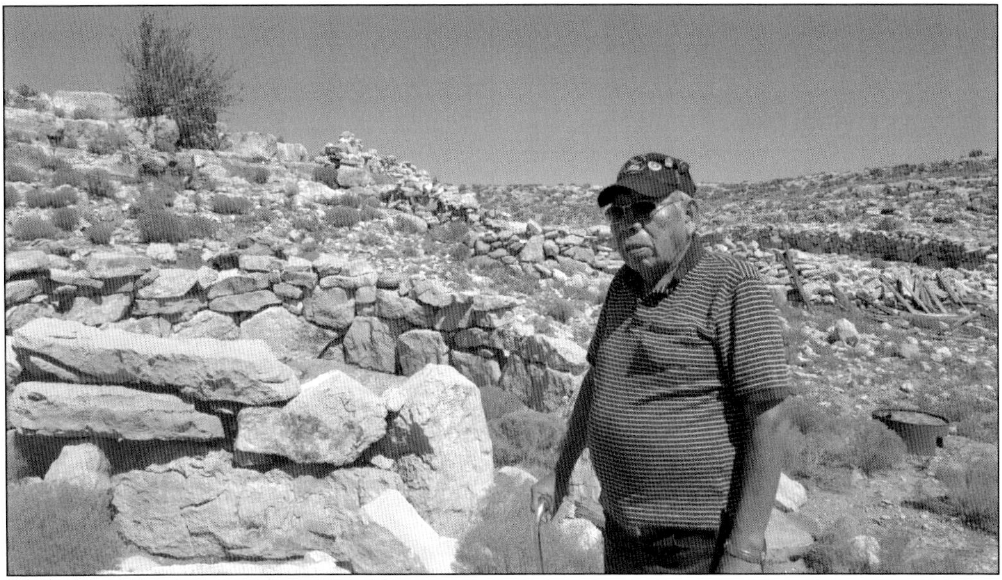

Paul Talker was born west of Cameron off Highway 64 toward Gray Mountain, seen below, a few years before the road to the Grand Canyon was paved. He stands at the stone foundation of the hogan where he was born in 1932. The larger, circular rock foundation behind him was the corral where sheep were penned at night. Paul recalled that as a boy, when he was out herding sheep, he always went to the road if he saw an automobile approaching, perhaps seeing only one or two cars a month. Tourists usually stopped and wanted to take his picture, and he was often given candy in return. Behind the hogan, the land falls down to the Little Colorado River Gorge near Pull Up the Baby Canyon.

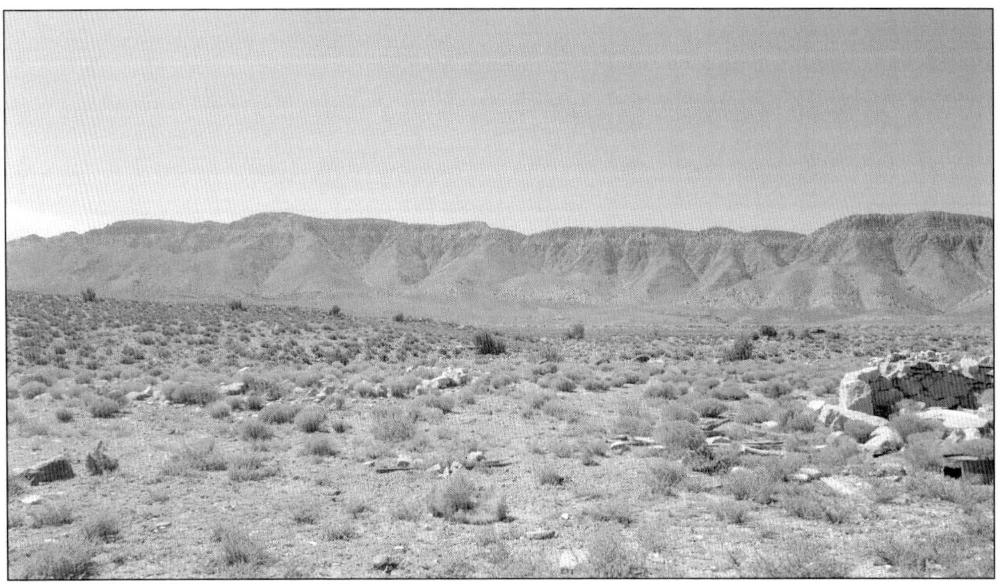

Paul Talker's father, Silas Talker, or Ha'dilch'alii Sani, was a medicine man. He is pictured on the right at Cameron Trading Post in 1957. Paul recalls that his parents traveled 10 miles to Cameron for supplies, and they also made the trip if rains were scarce and water could not be collected in natural rock pools near their hogan. Then, they went to Tappan Spring or to the trading post to get water. Paul's mother, Mary Yazzie, is pictured below in her hogan preparing food. (Right, courtesy of Harvey Leake; below, courtesy of Paul Talker.)

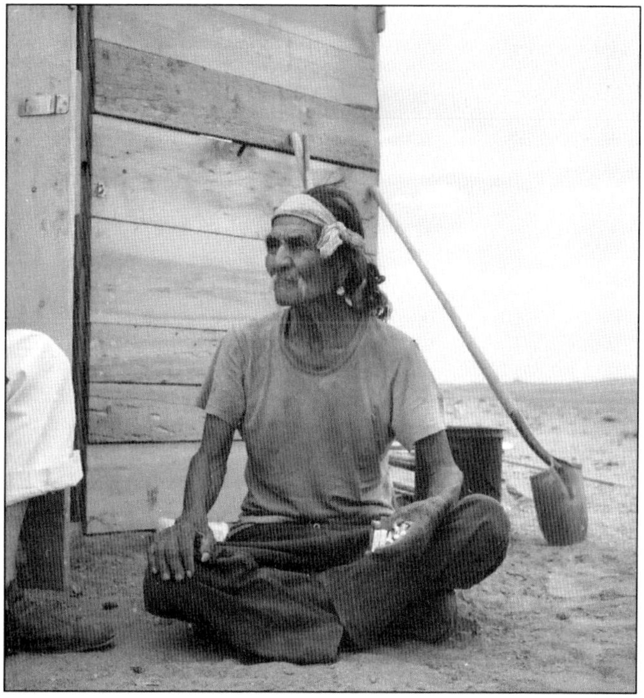

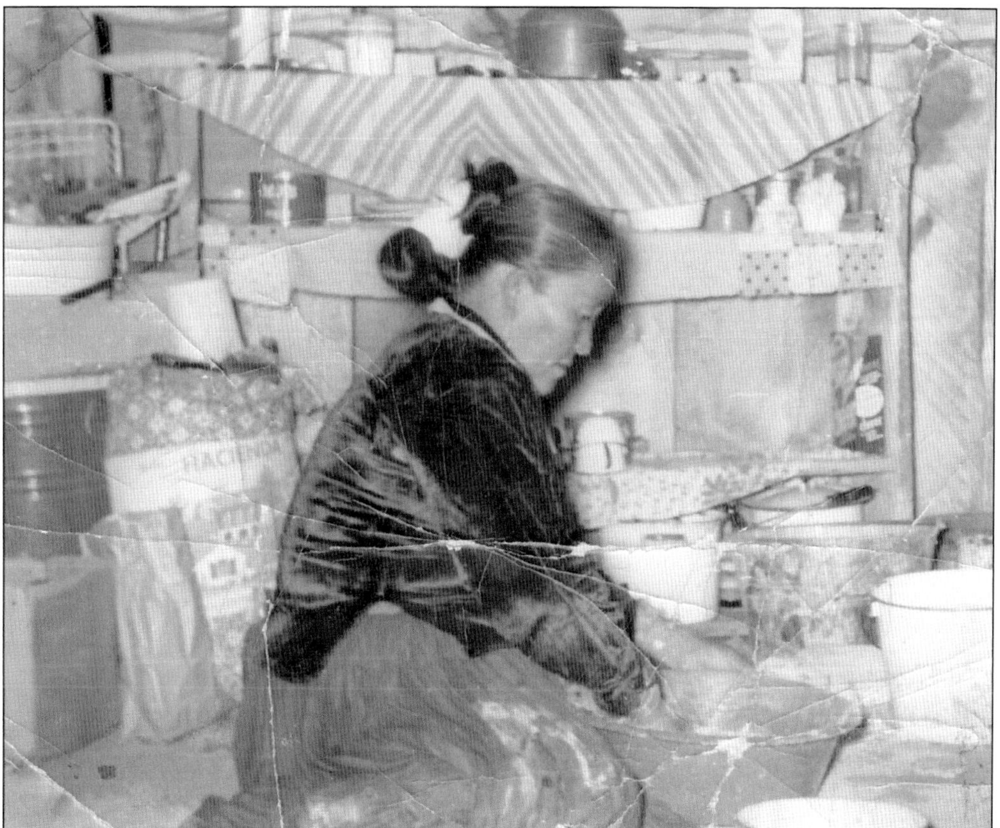

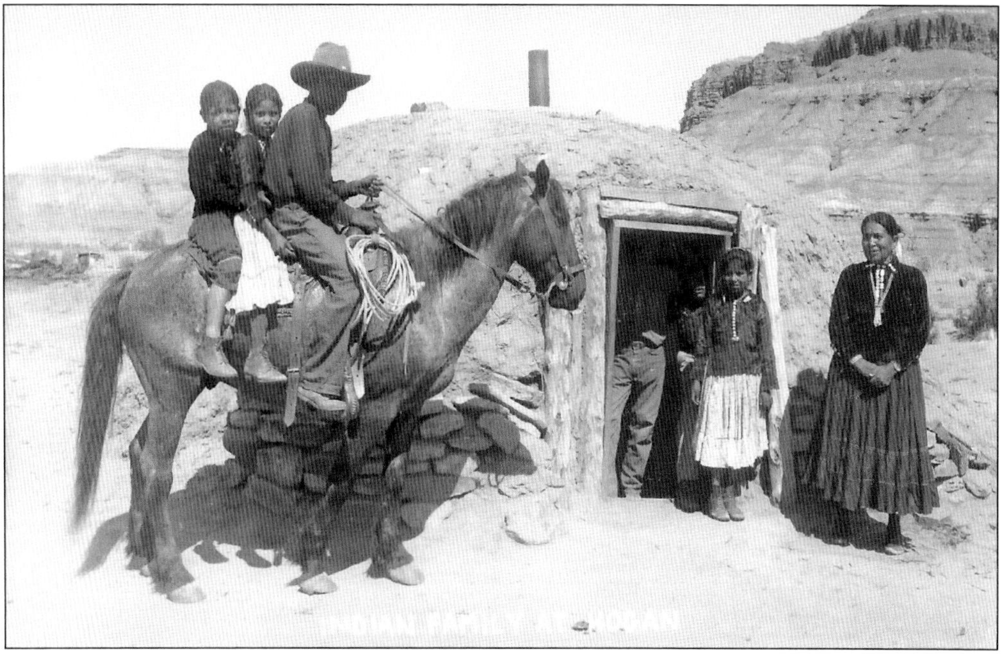

In his later years, Paul Talker and his family lived north of Cameron in the Tuba City area near the old Kerley Trading Post. Pictured at the family hogan, from left to right, are Maxwell Yazzie's daughter Mary May, unidentified, and Paul's brother Stacey Talker (who contracted tuberculosis and died in 1945), Paul's uncle Maxwell Yazzie (who built the hogan), unidentified, Paul's cousin Laura, and Paul's grandmother Doris Yazzie. (Courtesy of Paul Talker.)

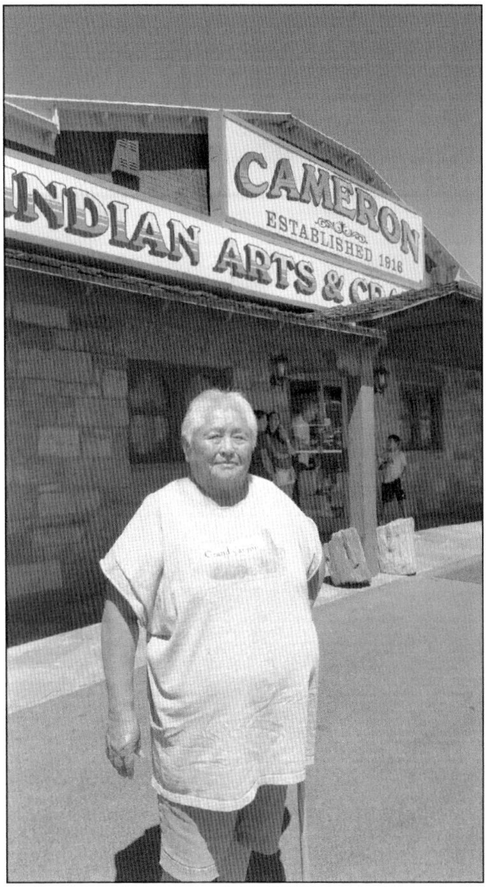

Mae Talker's mother and grandmother were weavers. Her grandmother once wove a huge rug that stretched from floor to ceiling. At the age of two, Mae moved from Kaibito to Cameron with her mother. She remembers going to the trading post with her mother when she was trading her weavings. Mae also remembers seeing the ledger books in which transactions, sales, and credits were recorded.

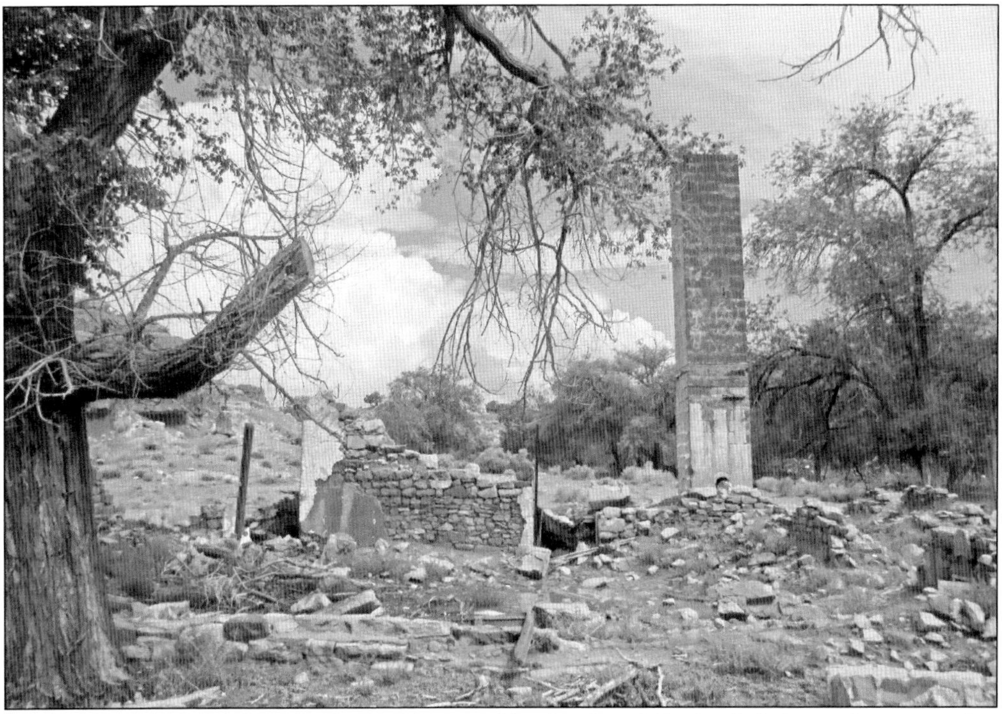

Around the time of the Depression, Hubert and his brother C.D. divided the trading posts that they jointly owned. Banks were closing, and the economy was collapsing. C.D. took Kaibito, now in ruins, as seen here, and Shonto, telling Hubert that at Cameron he would never make a living selling to tourists. Hubert took Cameron, Leupp, and Winslow.

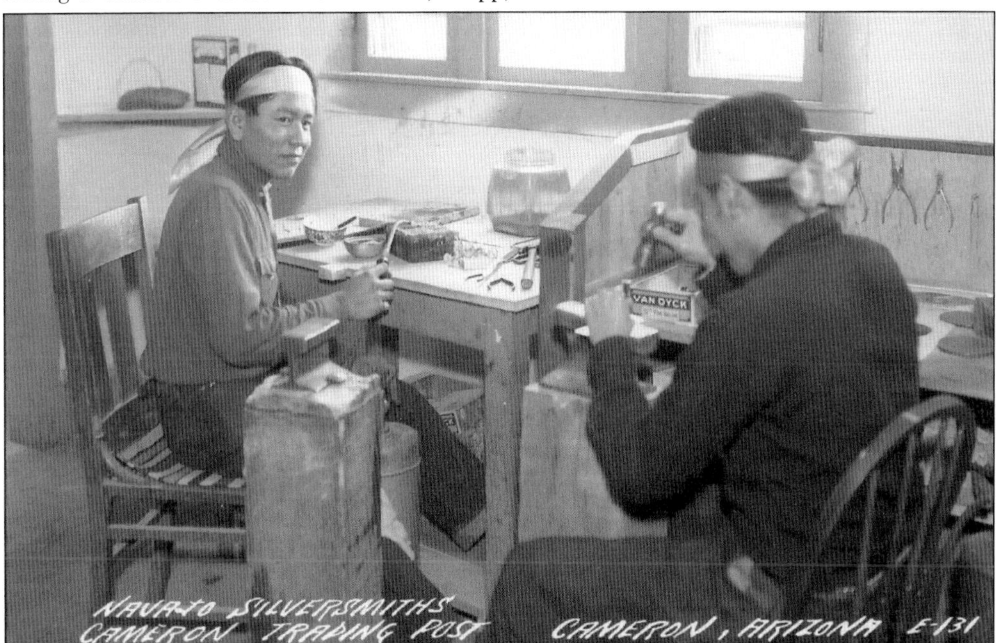

Riley Jones (left) was originally from Gray Mountain. He worked at Cameron for Hubert as a silversmith and served in World War II. The man at the right is unidentified. (Courtesy of Lisa Amaral.)

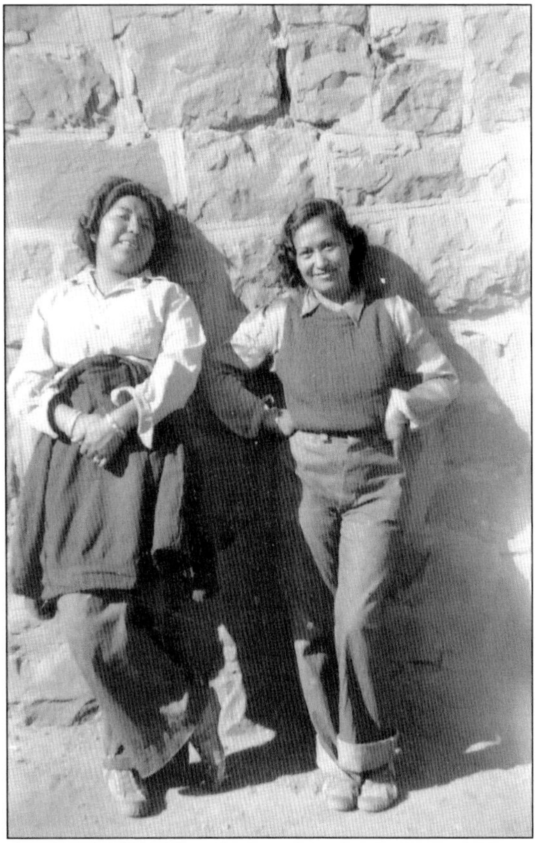

Pictured at left, Fannie (left) and Betty were the adopted Navajo daughters of Kayenta traders John and Louisa Wetherill. Betty's middle name was Zane, for Zane Grey, a frequent visitor to northern Arizona and Cameron and Kayenta Trading Posts. Betty married Buck Rodgers, a freighter from Texas, and the couple built a trading post two miles south of Cameron at the junction of Highways 89 and 64. There was opposition to their trading post because Buck was Anglo, but the couple was allowed to get a trader's license because of Betty's Navajo heritage. Hubert Richardson also objected to the post because of the competition with Cameron Trading Post. Below, Fannie Wetherill and her daughter Gretchen lounge in front of the trading post, about 1939. In this view looking south, the empty road leads to Flagstaff. (Both, courtesy of Wilma Rodgers Seeley.)

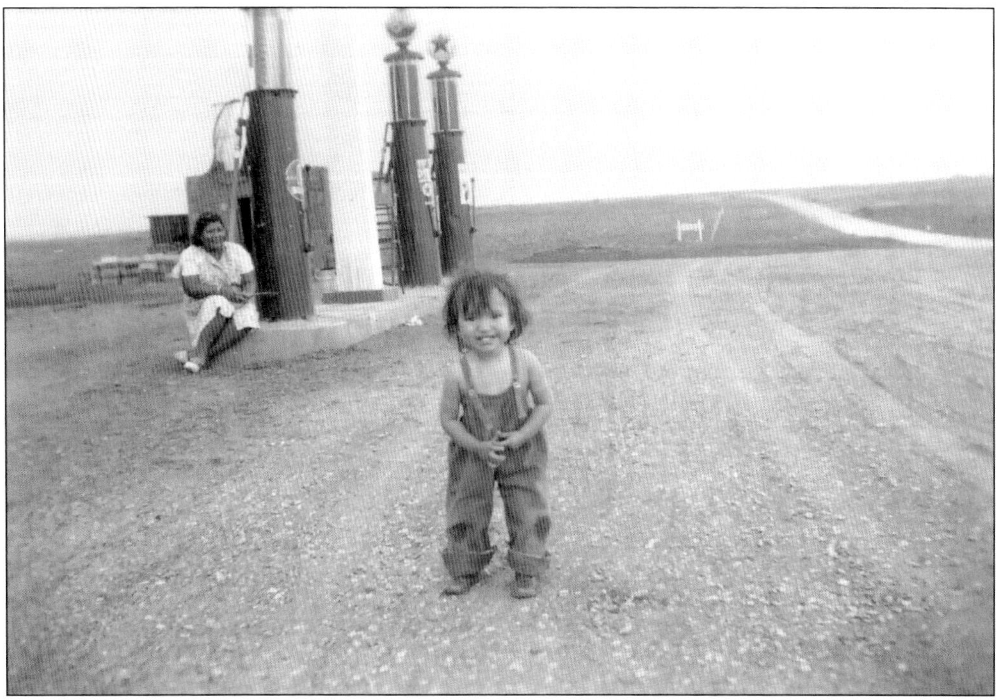

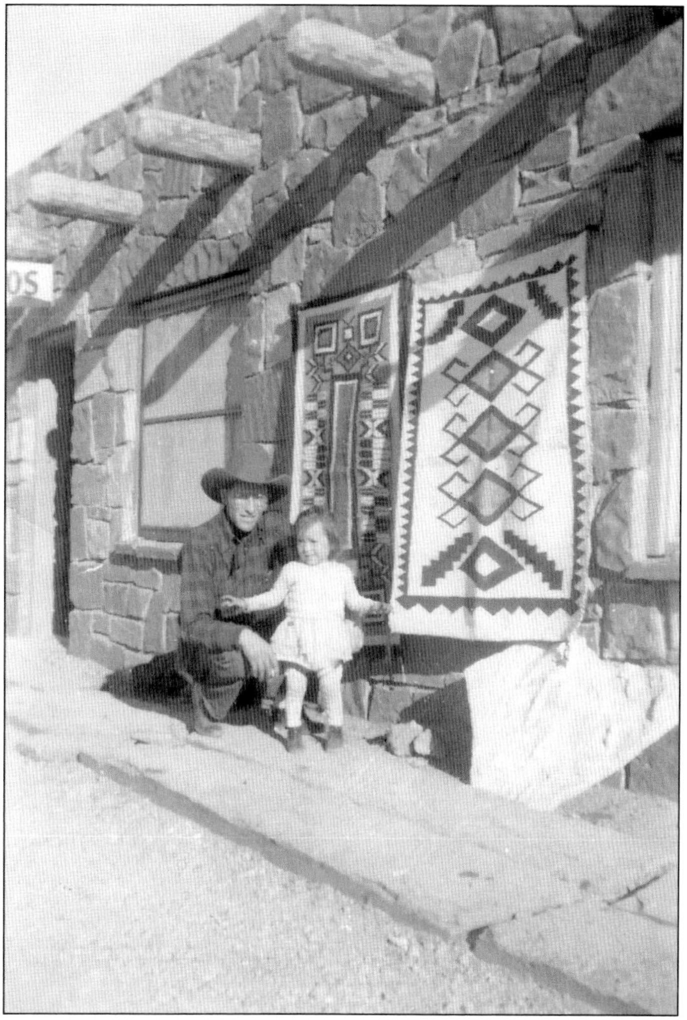

Little Betty Rodgers—named for her mother, Betty—was born in 1939, just a few months after her parents built their trading post. Buck, a freighter, met his wife, Betty, at Kayenta Trading Post north of Cameron. Their son Joe recalled that Betty spoke Navajo and Buck spoke "enough." The Rodgers had five children who walked two miles each way to school at Cameron. The Rodgers soon put in a hand-pumped Texaco gasoline dispenser, a restaurant, and motel. Betty cooked, and all of the children worked at the store. Buck continued with his freighting business, mostly hauling livestock. Below, Wilma and Stanley Rodgers pose in front of the guest hogan at the trading post. Buck Rodgers Trading Post burned down in 1975. Today, there is a gas station and convenience store at the site. (Both, courtesy of Wilma Rodgers Seeley.)

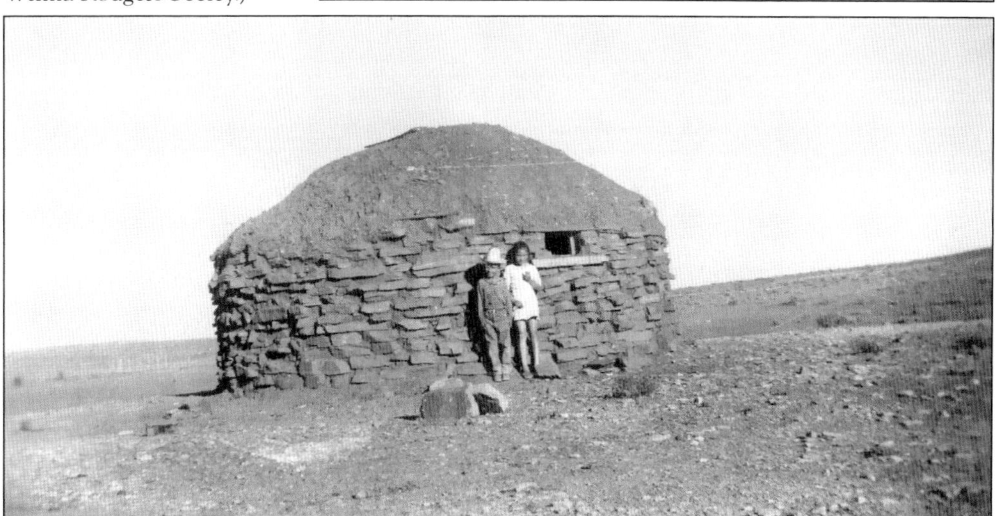

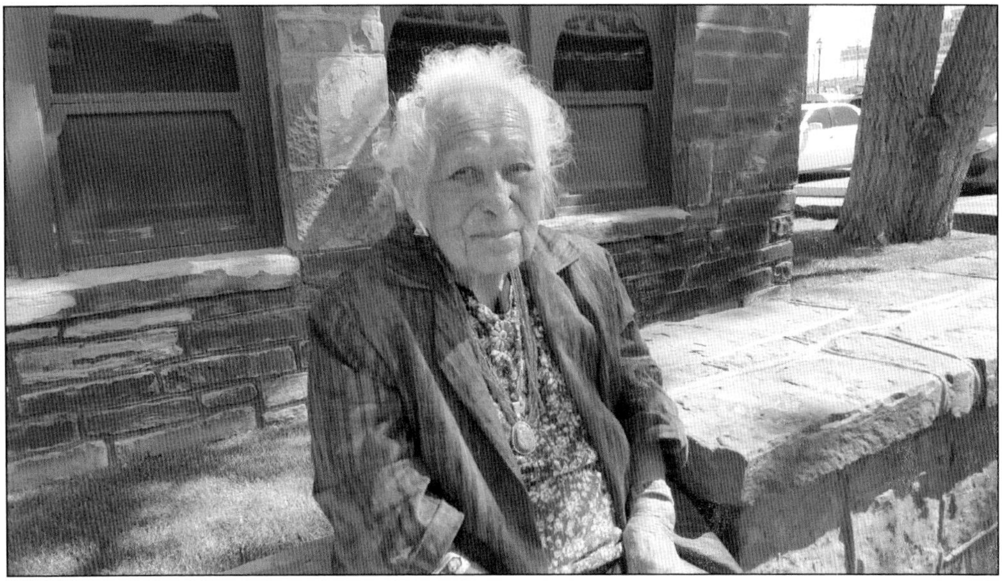

Sally Preston was born in 1921 and lived at Gray Mountain, seen below, west of Cameron. Her family had a summer camp on the mountain and moved to the base of Gray Mountain in winter. She remembers coming to Cameron Trading Post as a girl. Her father, Tom Largewhiskers, hauled supplies in a wagon for Hubert Richardson. During World War II, Sally's husband, Jimmie Preston, served in the South Pacific, so she moved her family back to Gray Mountain. Her children herded their flock of sheep throughout the year, and Sally supported the family by trading her weavings at Cameron. She saved all of the allotment checks sent to her during the war, and afterward, she had enough money to build a small house behind Buck Rodgers Trading Post, where she later worked as a dishwasher. (Below, courtesy of Tom Collins.)

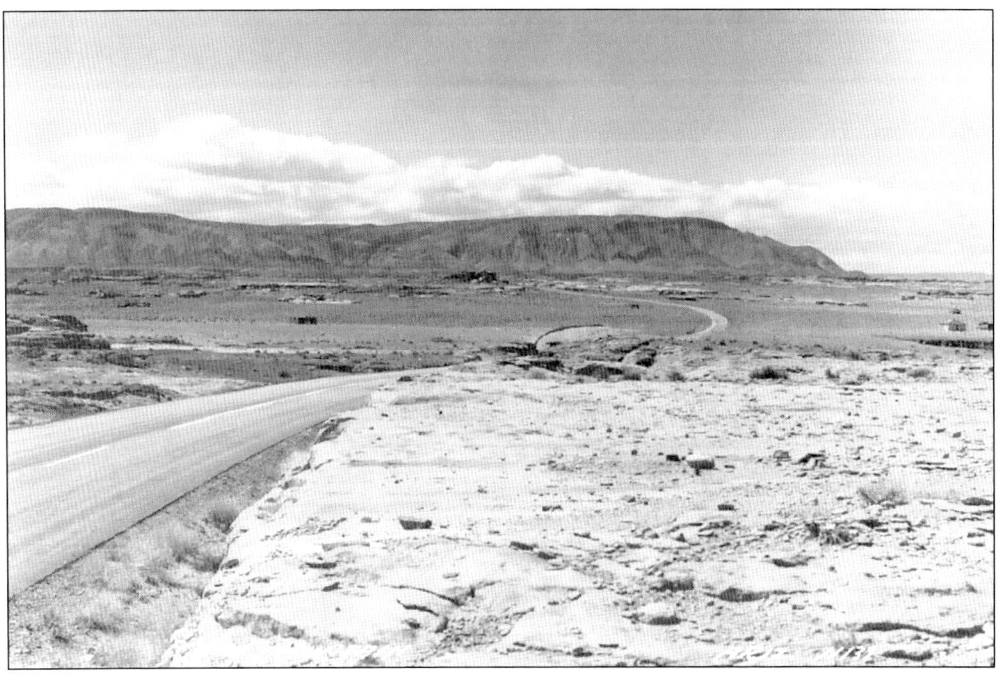

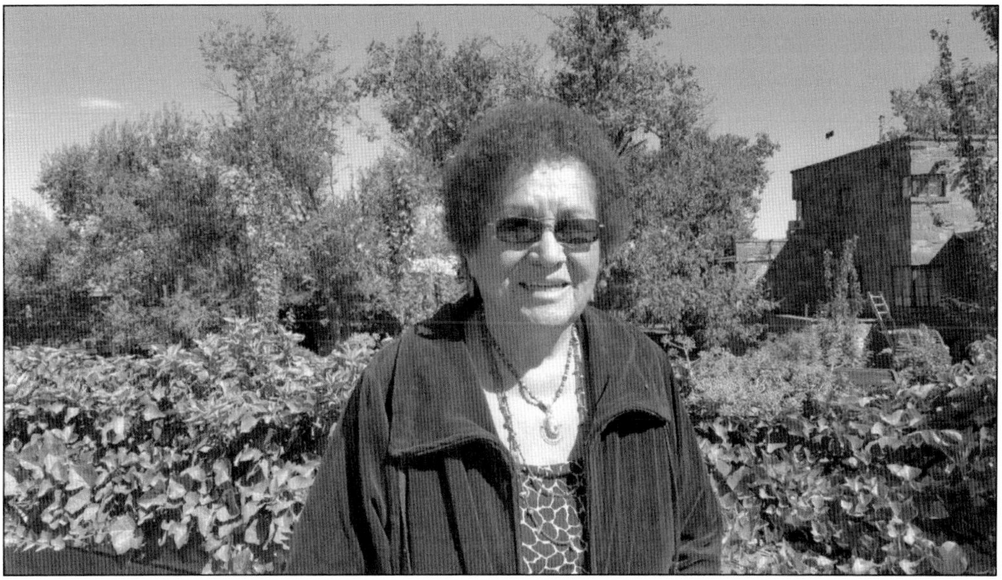

Luana Boyd, Sally Preston's daughter, recalled herding sheep in the snow when the family lived near Gray Mountain. She remembers going to Cameron with her father and buying sardines, crackers, and strawberry sodas. Later, in the late 1950s, living near Buck Rodgers Trading Post when the second bridge was built across the Little Colorado River, Luana and Louie and Elmer Jenkins sold Kool-Aid to motorists waiting in line during bridge construction. Luana's grandfather was Samuel Preston, the Tuba City trader who built the first trading post at Cameron during the 1911 bridge construction. (Below, courtesy of Lisa Amaral.)

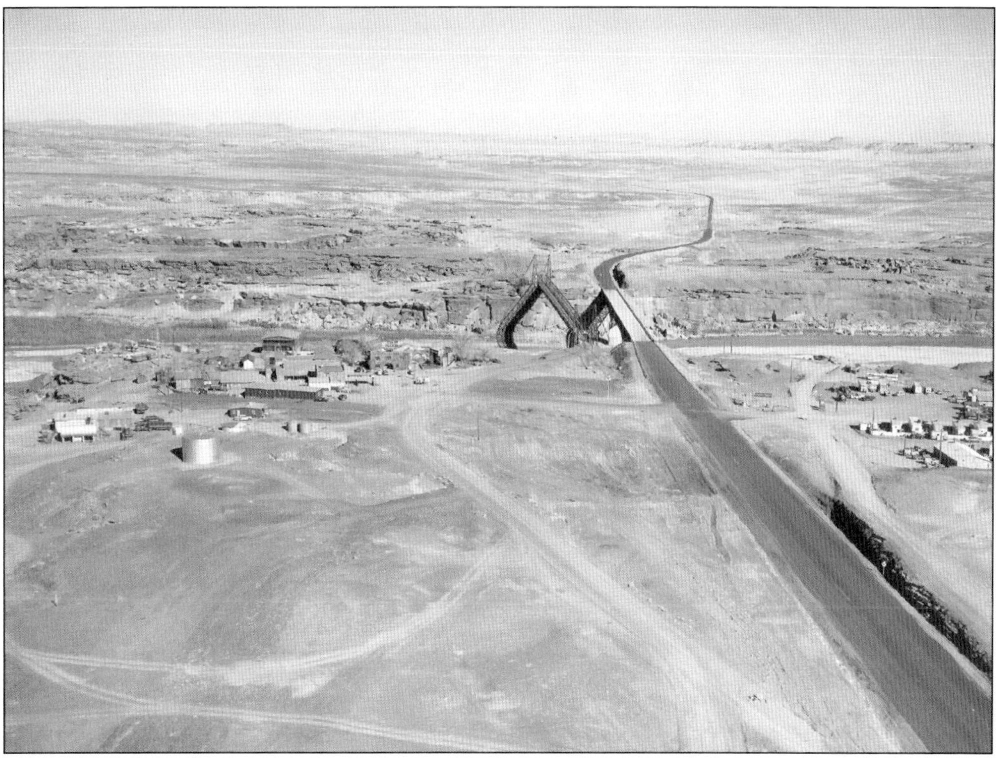

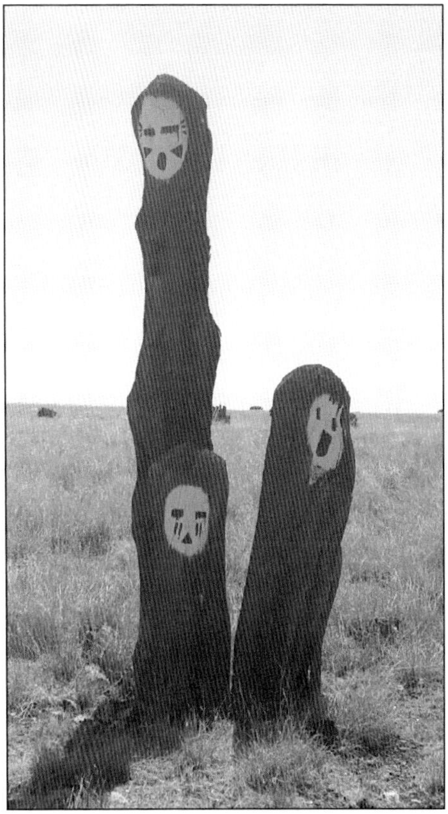

About 1938, when Buck and Betty Rodgers built their trading post, Hubert Richardson became more aggressive about advertising Cameron Trading Post. He commissioned Frank Goldtooth Sr. to erect a sign on the highway north of Flagstaff as well as another one at the intersection of the Grand Canyon Highway. The original signs had two sets of three logs with painted faces and "Cameron Trading Post" between the posts.

A group of local Cameron people gathered for a photograph about 1941. From left to right are (first row) Norman Huskon, Betty Ann Huskon, Bertha Blackhair, Jean Cody, Jenett Huskon, and Dzaani (partially obscured); (second row) Max Tone, Evans Huskon, Charlie Huskon, Ashkii Tso, Harrison Sloan, and Moody Semallie. (Courtesy of Frashers Fotos.)

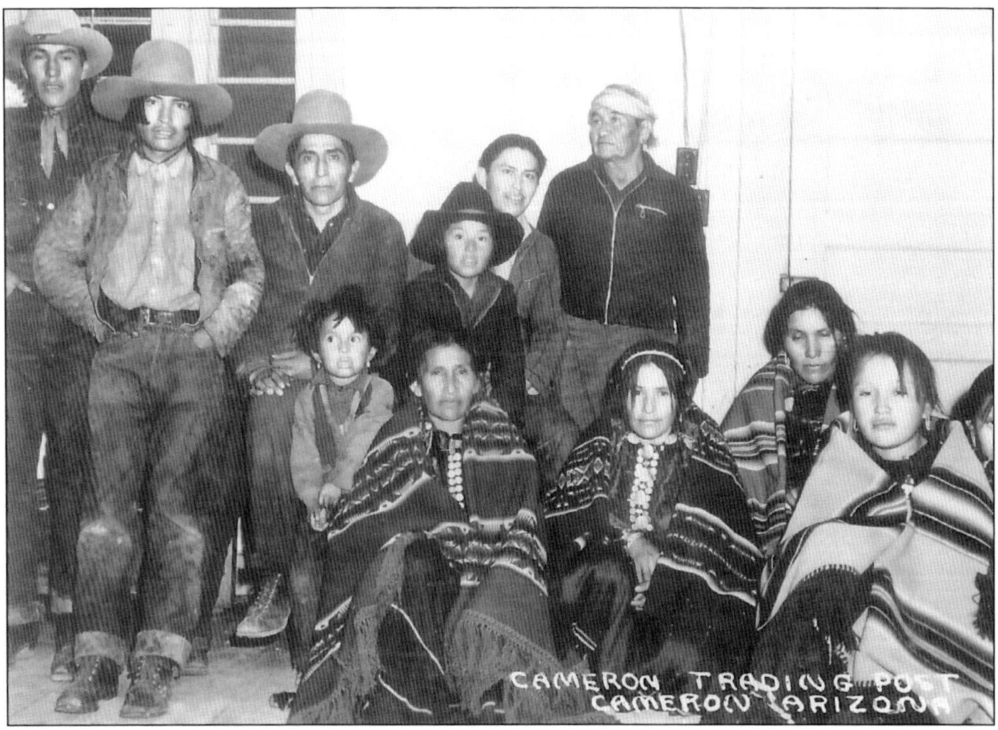

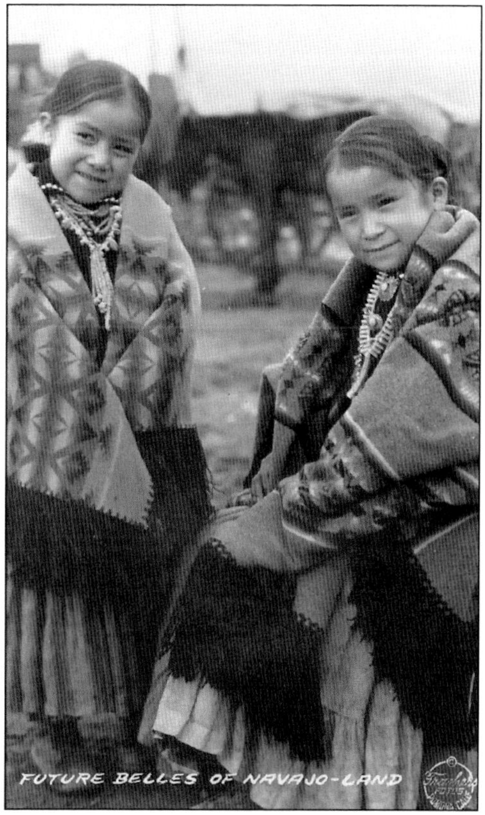

Lilly Cowboy (left) and Rose B. Tracy are seen in this charming image from the late 1930s. The girls wear their finest skirts and turquoise jewelry and are wrapped in Pendleton shawls. Lilly was a rug weaver and lived in Cameron all of her life. Rose was a silversmith for Cameron, but she also was a weaver, made moccasins, and raised sheep and cattle. (Courtesy of Frashers Fotos.)

Sally Littlesmith, also known as Astidi yazhi bee Asdzáá, translated as "little silversmith's wife," belonged to the Towering House Clan. She was a weaver and traded her rugs at Cameron. Her hogan was located about two miles north of Cameron, and her family still lives in the area today. (Courtesy of Lisa Amaral.)

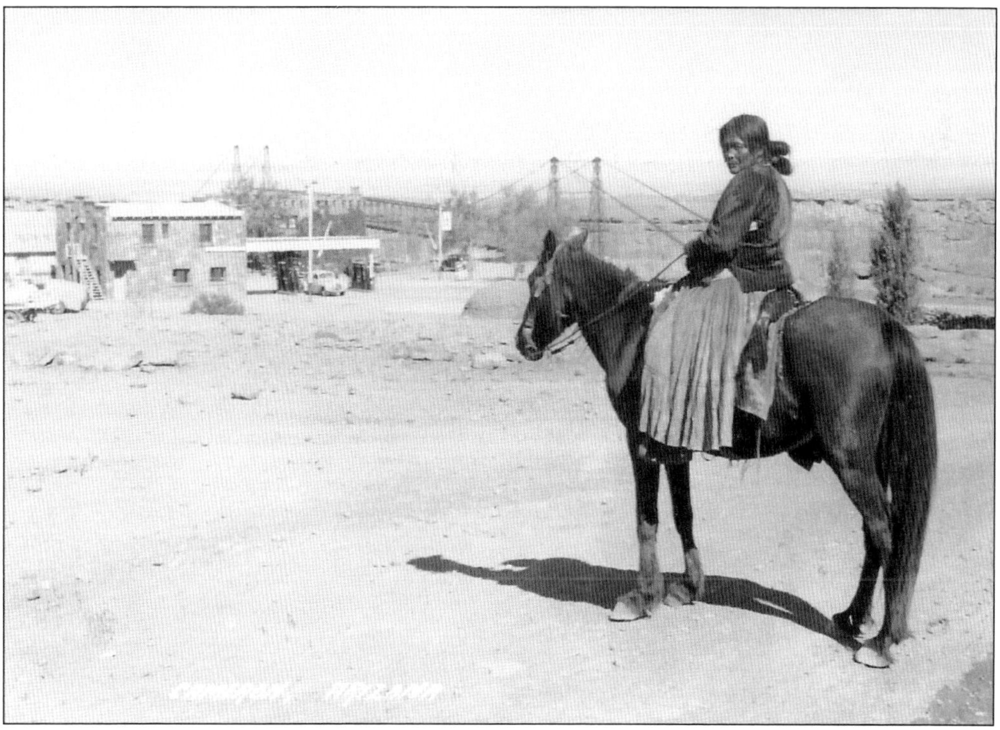

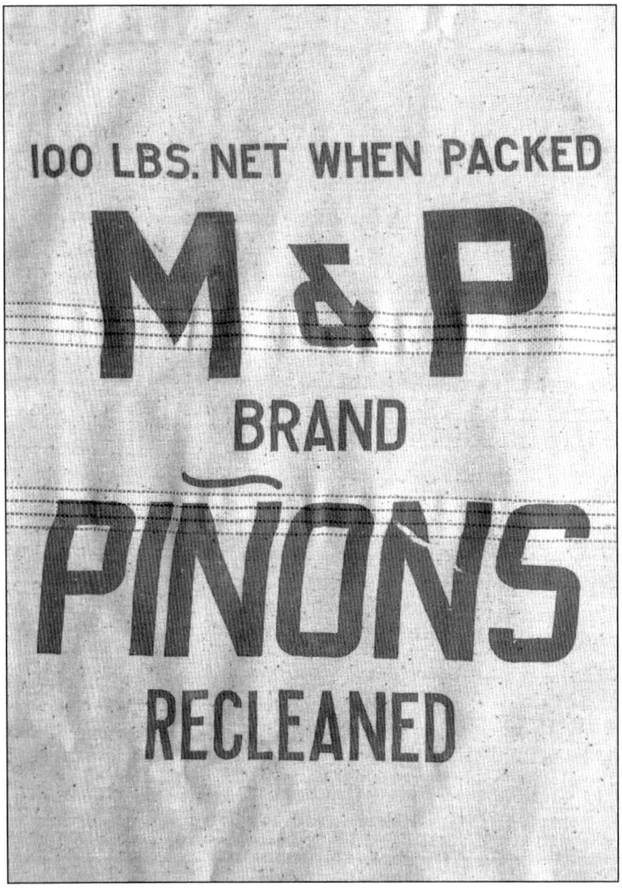

Christmas, or "Kissmuss," as the Navajos call it, was a time to gather at Cameron Trading Post. In 1938, Maybel Richardson cooked a special Christmas Eve dinner for the family and, by early afternoon, Navajos from Gray Mountain came by horseback and wagon to trade piñon nuts. Hubert gave out beef, flour, coffee, sugar, and lard, and the women began cooking a Christmas feast. Around the trading post, campfires glowed throughout the night, and Navajo men could be heard singing through the cold desert air. More families came to trade the following morning, and Maybel's sister-in-law Katherine Wilson wrote that even though it was the end of the season, $500 worth of piñons were traded on that holiday. More than 175 people came to Cameron, and on the afternoon of Christmas Day, Hubert passed out candy, oranges, apples, and Cracker Jack. (Below, courtesy of Lois McMindes.)

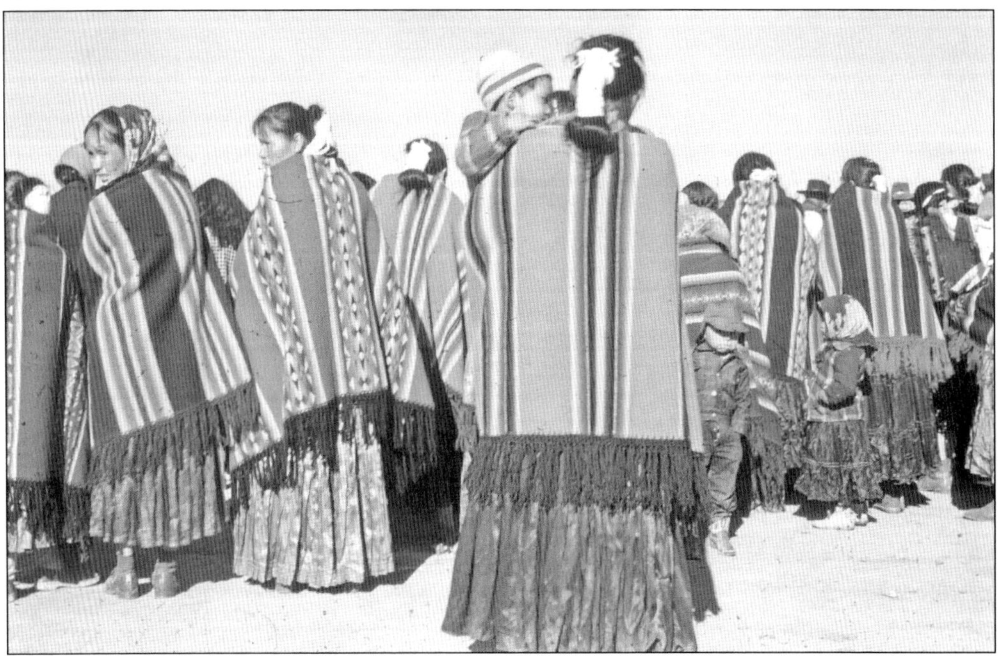

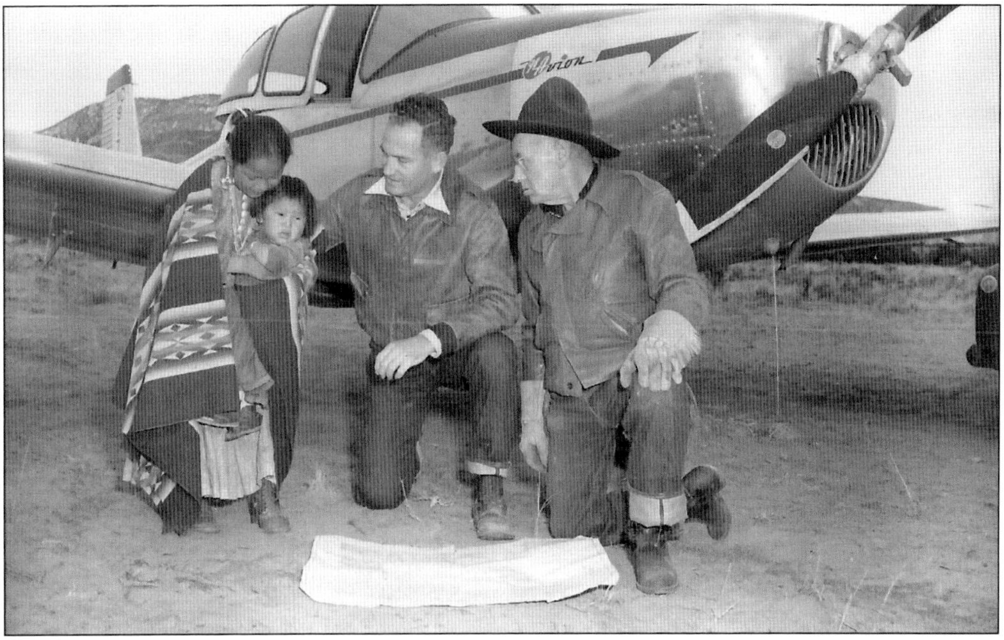

Besides operating Cameron Trading Post, Hubert Richardson owned other stores and properties. In 1942, he sold his half interest in Rainbow Lodge and Trading Post to Peggy Goldwater, who bought the store for her husband, Barry, the future Arizona senator and US presidential candidate in 1964. Above, Bill Wilson (right), Maybel Richardson's brother, is pictured with Goldwater and two unidentified Navajos. Wilson retained his half interest at Rainbow and operated the store and guided tourists on mule-pack trips 14 miles to Rainbow Bridge. Goldwater never operated the trading post, but he loved the country and often flew his airplane to Rainbow Trading Post, stopping at Cameron, where there was a dirt landing strip. Goldwater was a friend of the Richardsons, and Hubert's granddaughter Lisa recalled a flight with Goldwater's female pilot, who flew Lisa and her mother, Hazel Richardson, to Palm Springs. (Both, courtesy of Lisa Amaral.)

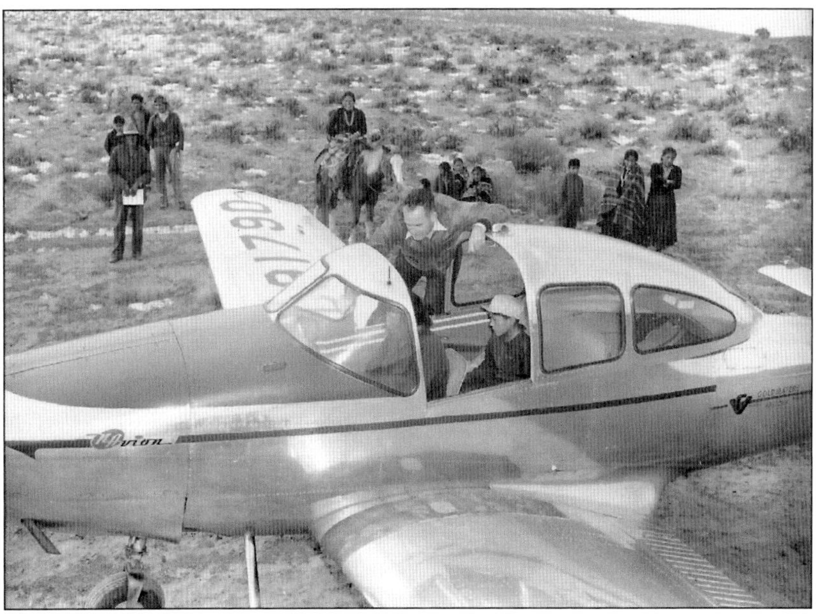

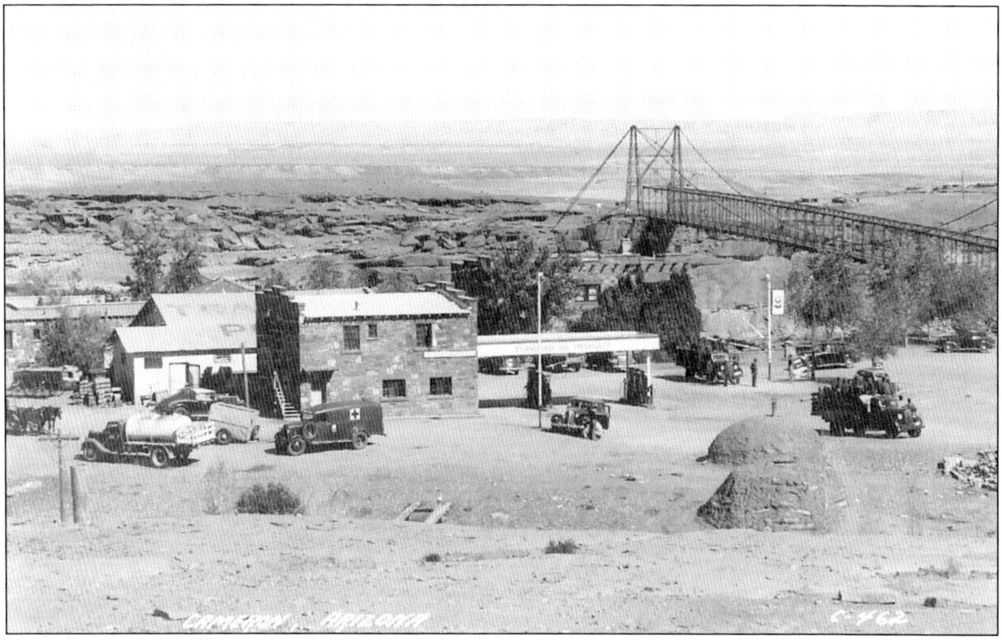

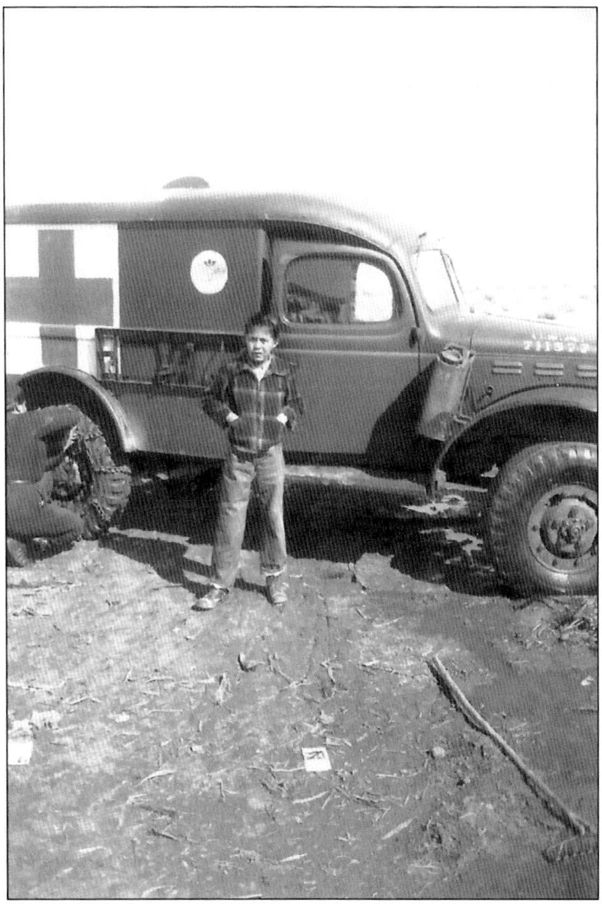

During World War II, the military opened an ordnance depot at Bellmont west of Flagstaff. Hopi and Navajo workers were employed at the site, which eventually grew into a village. Hubert Richardson was asked to open a store with a traditional trading post flavor, carrying items that were preferred by the workers. The store was placed halfway between the Navajo hogans and the Hopi village. Richardson kept a flock of sheep to supply mutton, and stocked cowboy hats, soda pop, velveteen, and Pendleton shawls. Hubert's brother-in-law Billy Young and Buddy Richardson managed the store. It is believed that the above photograph of Cameron is a wartime image. There is a Red Cross ambulance to the left and two open trucks filled with men in uniform. At left, Johnny Begay stands in front of an ambulance. (Above, courtesy of Tom Collins.)

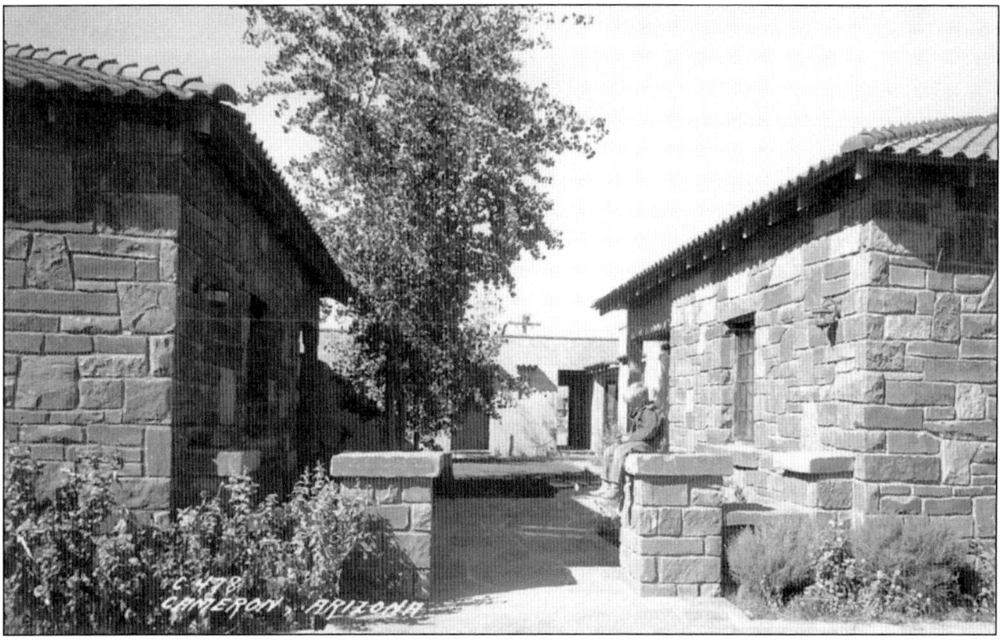

Hubert Richardson added a second motel building in the 1940s. Zuni Court was built of the same red rock as the 1928 hotel, but it was constructed in a U-shape. Located behind the hotel and to the side of the store, the structure had eight rooms, with a courtyard down the center. The photograph below of Zuni Court was taken from the roof of the hotel, with the tourist cabins in the distance, set along the bank of the Little Colorado River. Today, Zuni Court has been incorporated into the expanded trading post and the courtyard was roofed with glass. Joe Atkinson commented that the skylight turned the space into an oven, so it was painted black and later covered. (Both, courtesy of Tom Collins.)

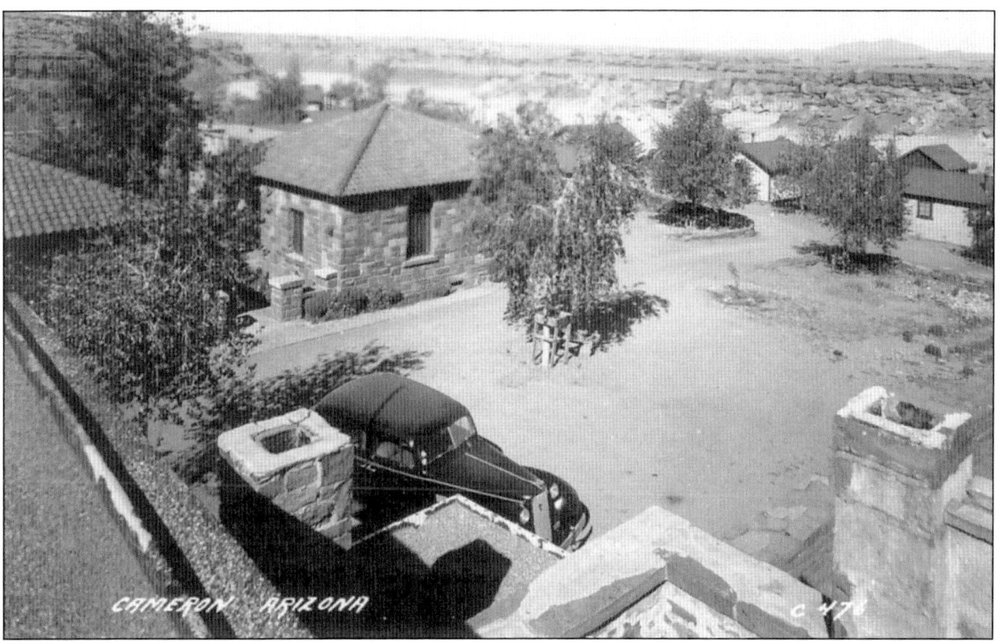

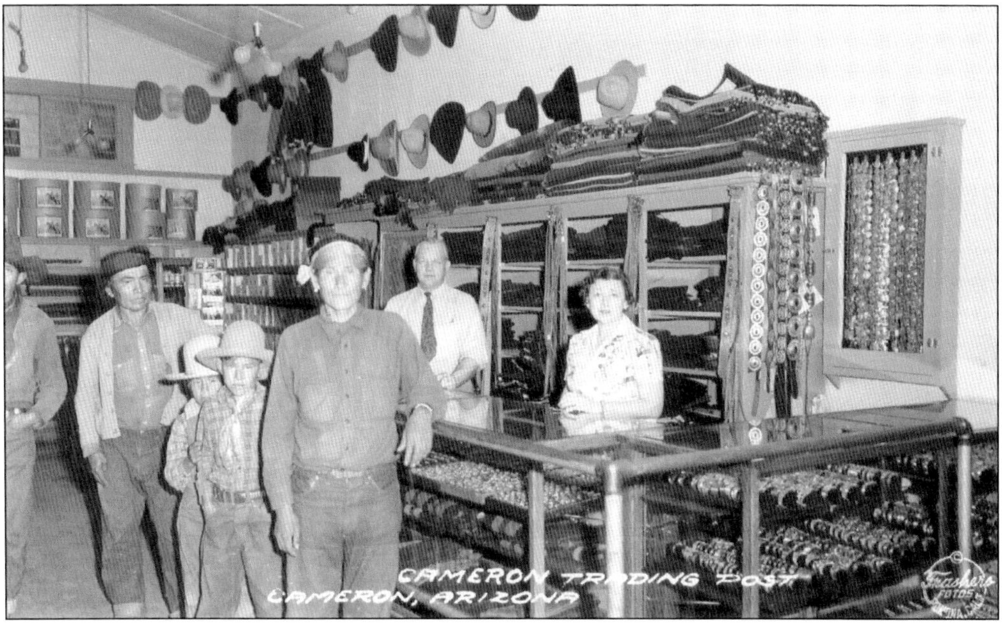

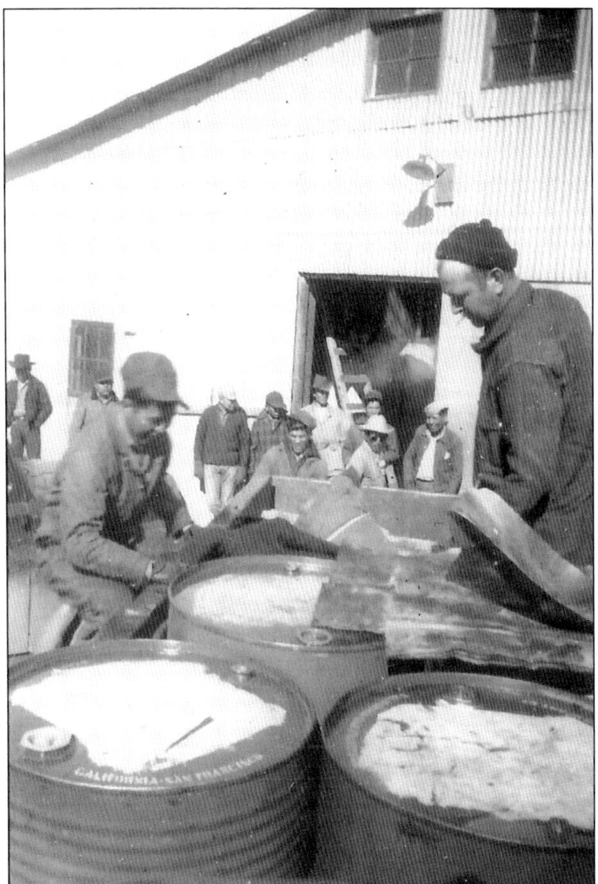

This interior photograph shows the variety of goods sold at the trading post. The glass cases hold turquoise and silver jewelry, concho belts hang at the right, folded clothing and Pendleton blankets are displayed on the shelves, and hats line the walls above the shelves. Visitors to the store are, from left to right, Moody Semallie, Roger Semallie, John Semallie, and their father Pete Semallie; the two store clerks are unidentified. (Courtesy of Frashers Fotos.)

When deep snows fall on the Painted Desert, Navajo families living in the backcountry can be trapped with little food and few supplies; deep snow and freezing temperatures are deadly to people and livestock. In one memorable storm in 1949, six feet of snow fell. Planes dropped food and bales of hay at isolated hogans, some with "SOS" stamped out in the snow. Families were stranded, and rescue groups were sent out from Tuba City. (Courtesy of Editha Watson.)

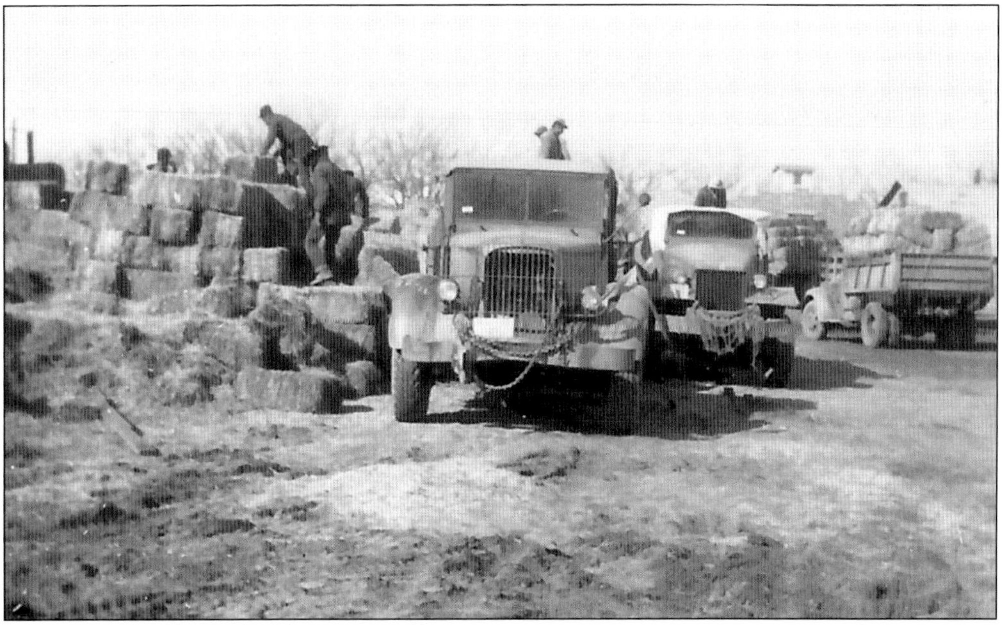

Hubert Richardson loaded his heavy delivery truck with food and hay and sent his son Jack to Gray Mountain to aid stranded families. Richardson said he believed that many other people were stranded in higher elevations north and east of Tuba City. James Stewart, superintendent of the Navajo Indian Reservation, was reported to say that he believed that all livestock in the northwestern part of the reservation had perished in the 1949 blizzard. (Both, courtesy of Editha Watson.)

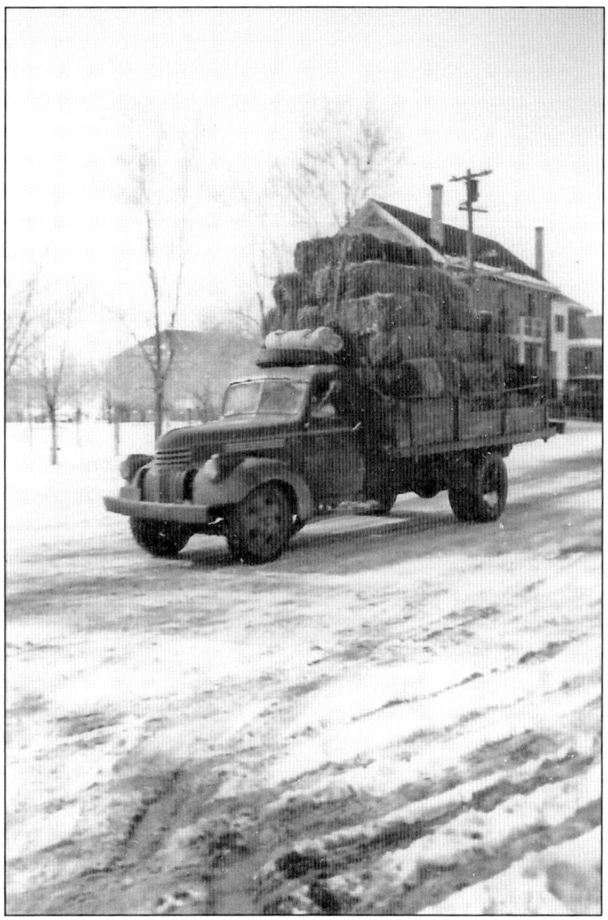

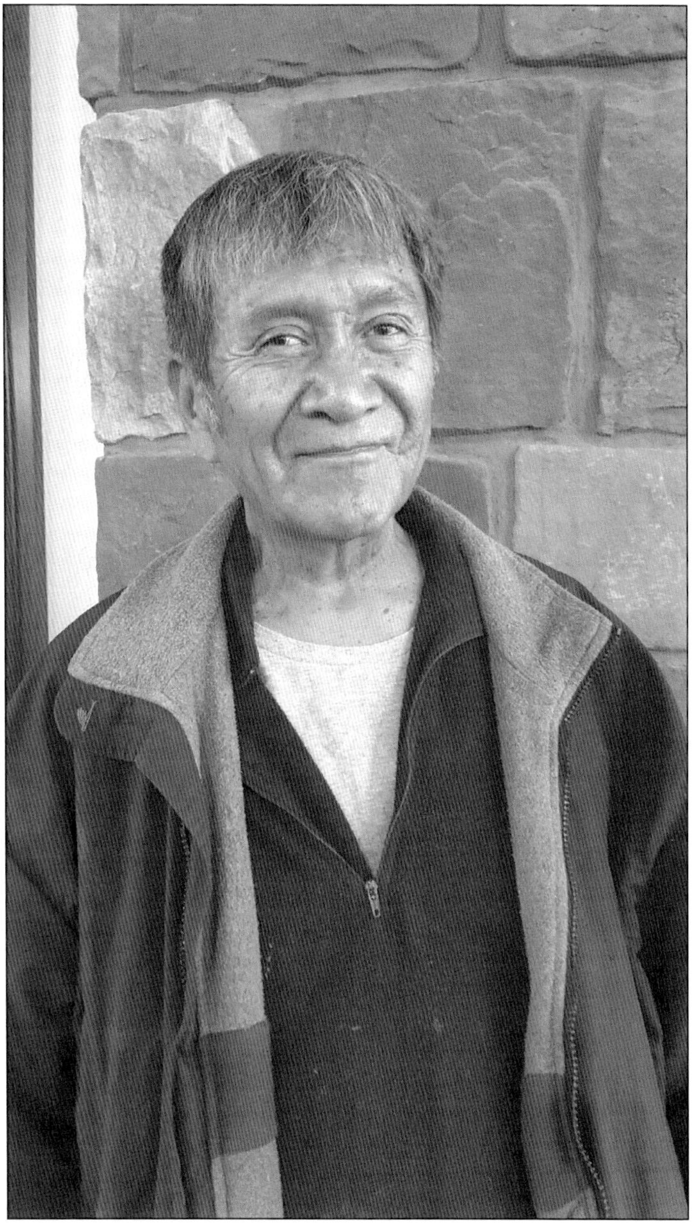

Two blizzards hit northern Arizona in December 1967, dropping up to seven feet of snow. It was the time of the Vietnam War, and in early December, Virgil Bigsinger was out herding sheep on Gray Mountain when the first storm began. His cousin came to tell him that he had been drafted and was to report to Flagstaff. Catching a ride to town, Virgil, who claimed at the time he "still got my sheep clothes on," was sent to Fort Bliss, Texas. As Christmas approached, the recruits were allowed to take leave, so Virgil hitched a ride back to Flagstaff. So much snow had fallen in Flagstaff, volunteers were recruited to shovel snow off collapsing rooftops. Virgil shoveled for seven days and then got a ride to Gray Mountain Trading Post. From there, he made it through the snow to his mother's home. Virgil walked into her hogan and learned that she did not even know that he had been away. With no telephone, no communication, and blocked roads, she assumed that he was still up on the mountain, snowed in with the sheep.

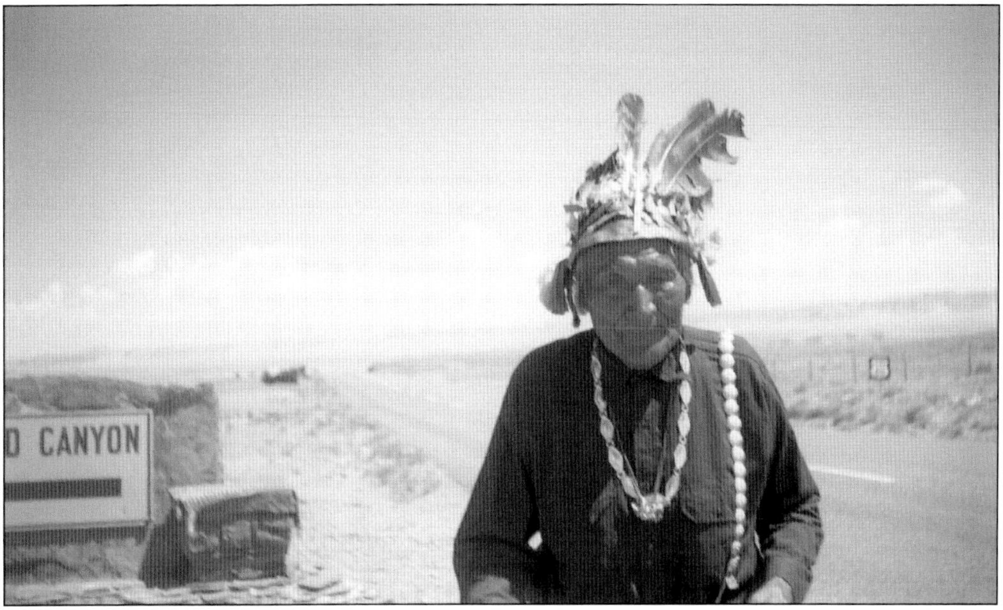

Hosteen Noodái, often called "Old Chief" (his English name was Sellers), lived in the Cameron area. Most days, he would put on his curio-purchased warbonnet and sit at the intersection of Highway 89 and the road to the Grand Canyon. Tourists who stopped to see him paid $1 to take his photograph. Local people say that Dead Indian Bridge, a few miles west on Highway 64, was named for Noodái. One day, when waiting for a tourist to pass, he crawled under the bridge and fell asleep. The next tourists who stopped thought that he was dead and contacted authorities. From then on, the bridge was known as Dead Indian Bridge. It was completed in 1935 at a cost of $44,000. Noodái died peacefully in his hogan in the 1950s. (Below, courtesy of Grand Canyon Museum Collection, No. 02917C.)

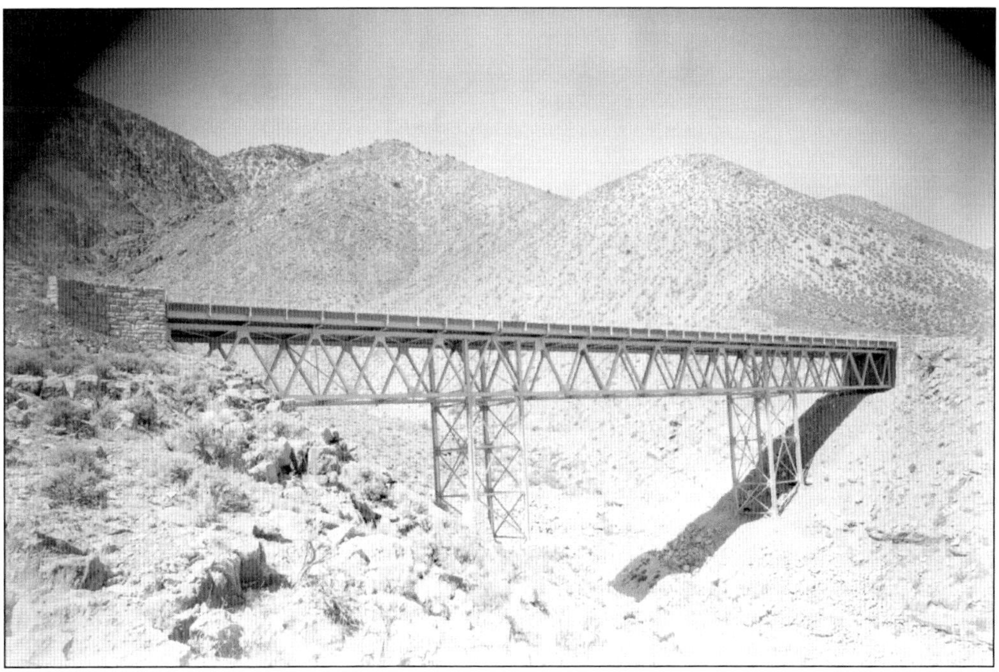

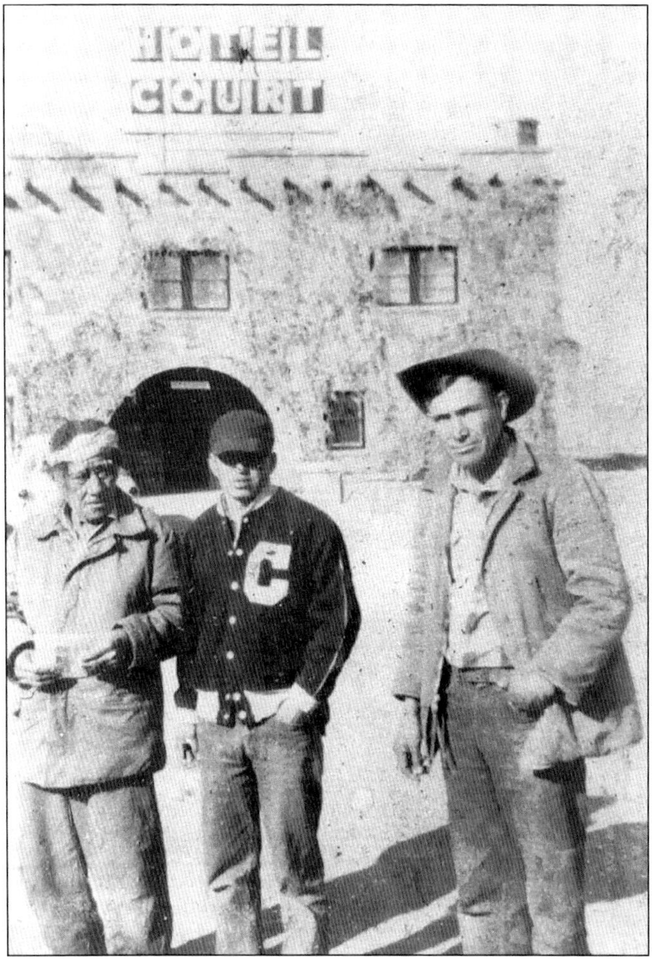

During World War II, Jimmie Preston (right) was a Navajo code talker in the South Pacific. His father-in-law, Tom Largewhiskers (left), was a medicine man and said to be 114 years old at the time of his death about 1968. Largewhiskers's son Richard Keetso is in the center. The men are standing in front of the original hotel. (Courtesy of Jennifer Beard.)

This 1940s image shows the old road that curved in front of Cameron Trading Post. Later, the road was straightened and went directly to the bridge. A loading dock has been built on the side of the store. (Photograph by Charles E. Leake, courtesy of Harvey Leake.)

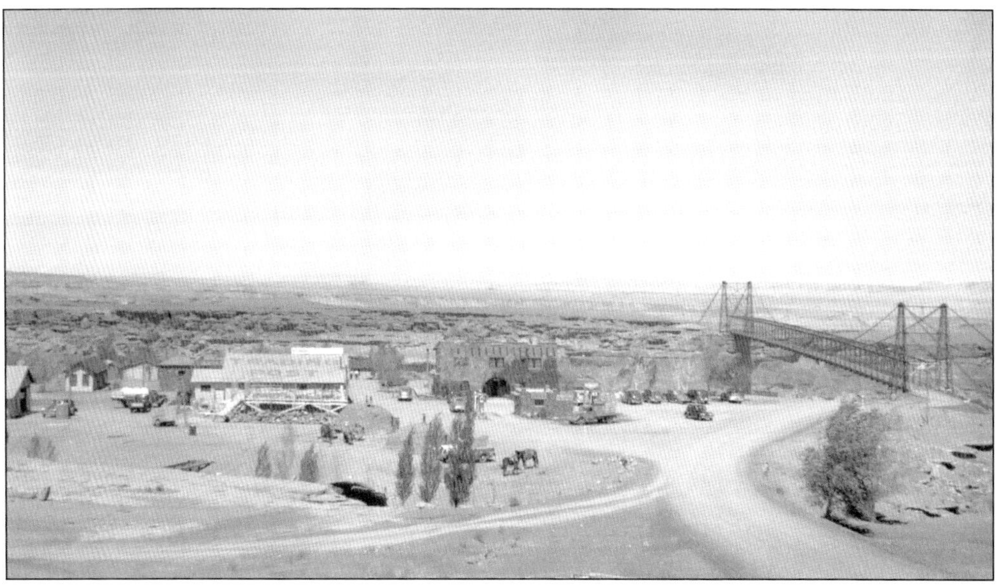

Three

A Century of Trading and Tourists

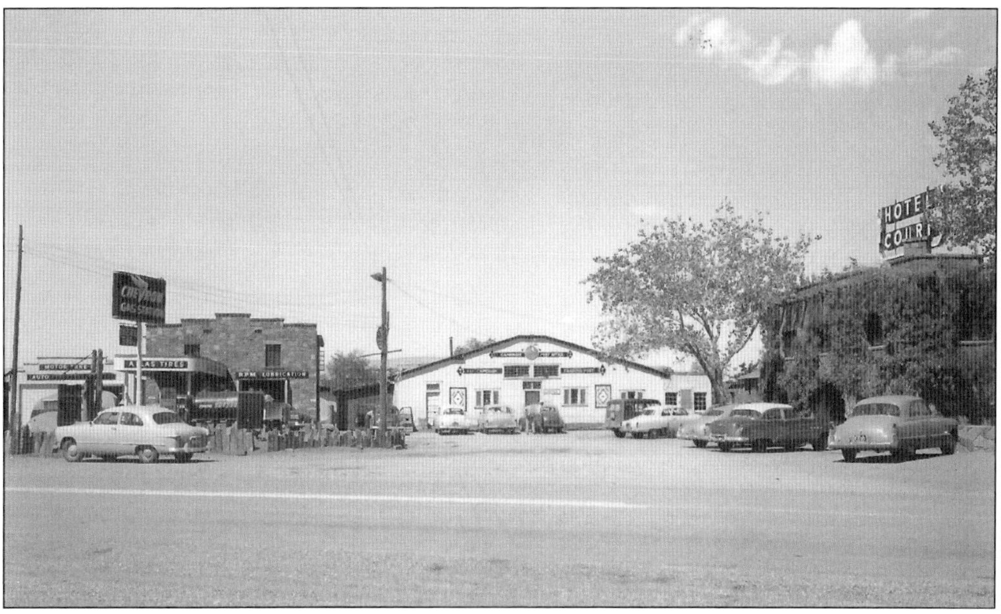

Tourism increased at Cameron after the war and into the 1950s. Visitors noted on their postcards that they could purchase gasoline, groceries, and souvenirs at the store. One traveler wrote that they had just gotten to Cameron in time, because "the place is all filled now." The stone building at the left housed the service station, and upstairs was housing for store employees. (Courtesy of Tom Collins.)

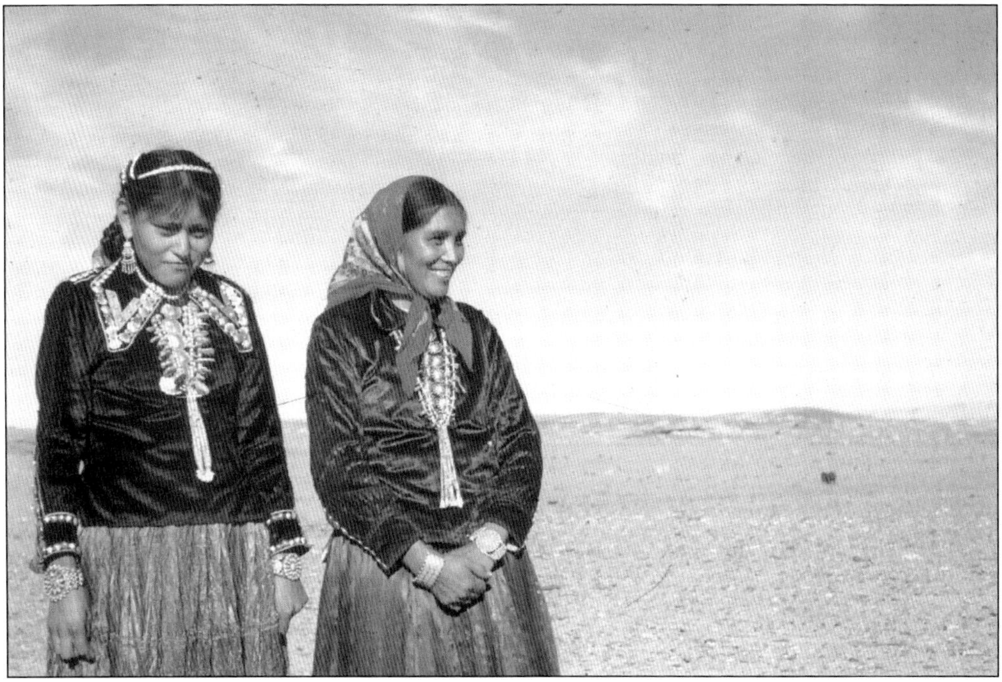

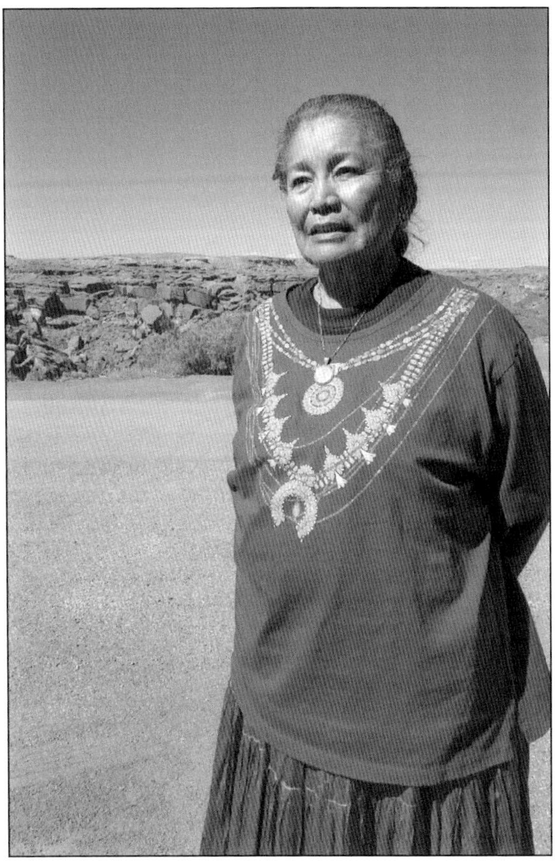

Pictured above, Sisters Nora Robbins (left) and Nancy Horse lived near Cameron and were photographed at a 1954 Christmas party at Buck Rodgers Trading Post. Both sisters were weavers and always had a flock of sheep. Nancy married Juan Horse and had six children, including May Stevens, seen at left. The family lived on the north side of the Little Colorado River and usually crossed the river on horseback. They could hear the water coming when floods swept down the river, and Stevens remembers a time when the river was a mile wide. The color of the water indicated which drainage the floodwaters were coming from. While attending the Tuba Boarding School as a girl, May was told that she must think and talk in English, so today, it is a "sweet bitterness" for her to teach the Navajo language at local schools. (Above, courtesy of Lois McMindes.)

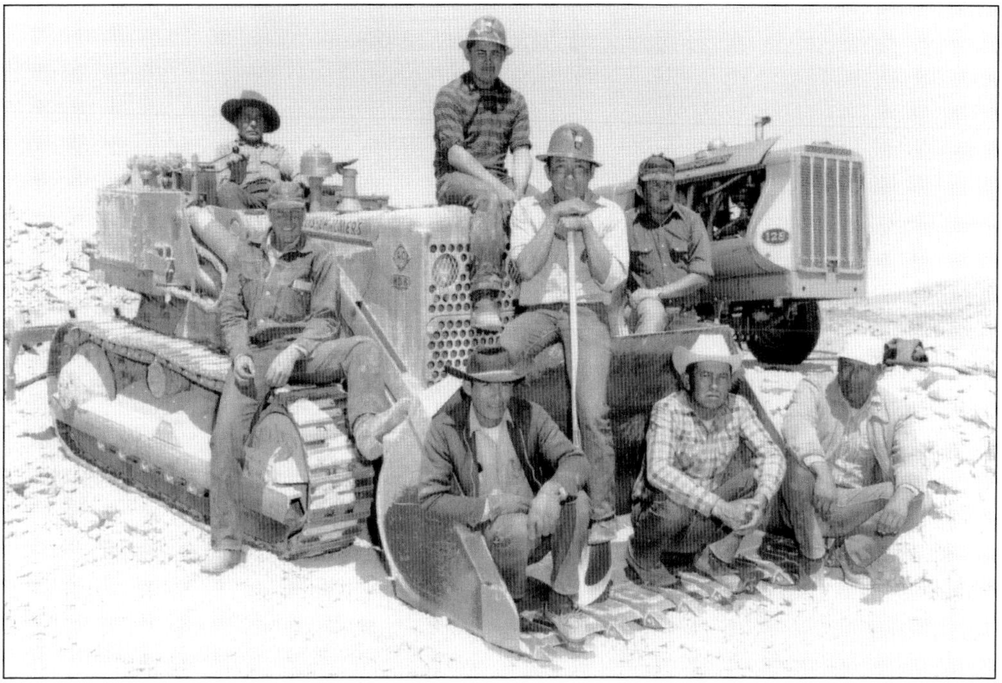

Rich deposits of uranium, known as "yellow dirt," lay under the Navajo Reservation. In the 1950s, during the Cold War, the US government needed the radioactive mineral to produce atomic bombs. Several Navajo prospectors staked claims near Cameron. After the uranium boom, lakes appeared in the old uranium pits. No one knew of their deadly contaminants until later when sheep died and children were born with birth defects. One Cameron resident recalls prospecting for uranium with her grandfather, others remember swimming in the abandoned pits. Efforts are being made to clean up the approximately 520 mines, but estimates on this long-term project predict that it will cost hundreds of millions and up to billions of dollars. In these 1956 photographs, miners from Cameron are shown working at one of the nearby uranium mines. (Above, courtesy of Northern Arizona University, Cline Library, NAU.PH.85.3.94.18; below, courtesy of Northern Arizona University, Cline Library, NAU.PH.85.3.93.151.)

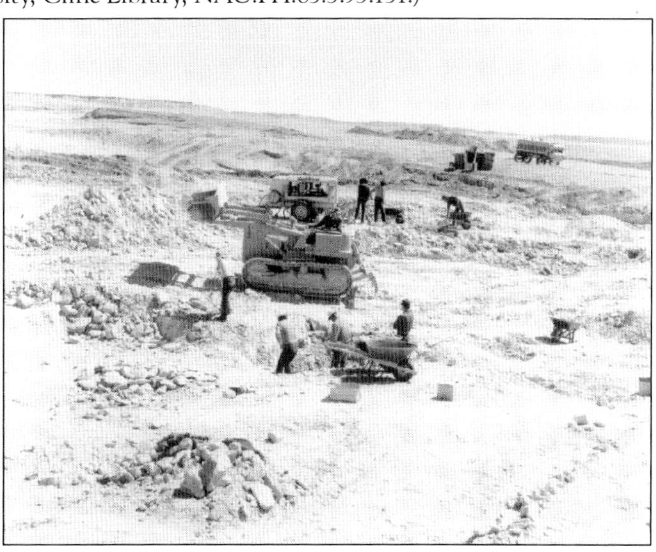

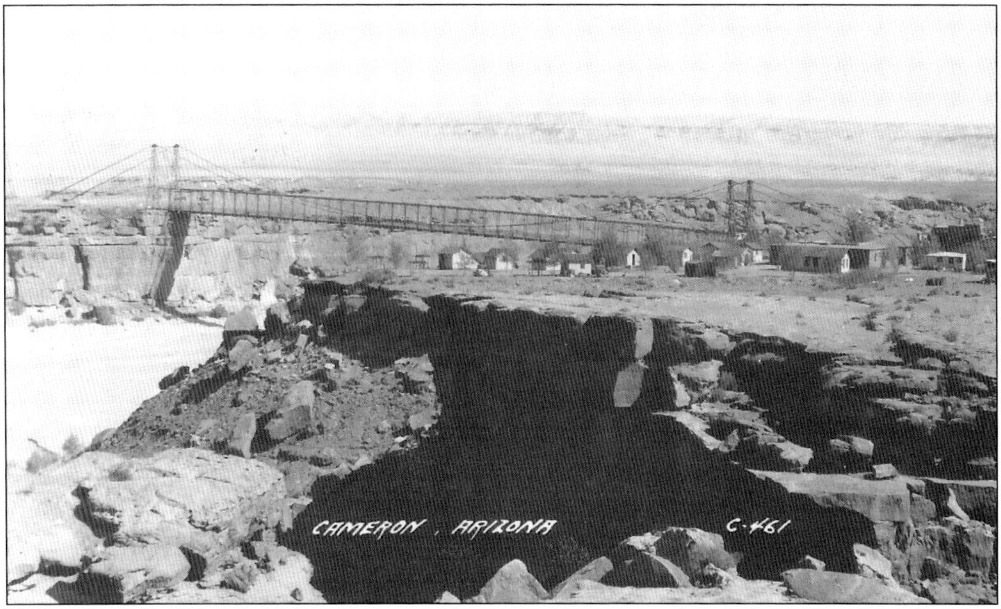

In 1952, Merritt and Winona Holloway took over Rainbow Lodge and Trading Post (below) from Bill and Katherine Wilson, with Barry Goldwater as a nonworking partner. Traveling from Nevada with their three boys, the Holloways stopped at Cameron overnight, expecting to camp behind the store. Jack Richardson would not have them camp out. The Holloways stayed in the motel where Jack and his wife, Betty, treated them like "homefolk." Winona examined the Navajo rugs and the silver and turquoise pawn jewelry in the store. She had never seen the coral jewelry before "in strands and loops in several shades of red." She wrote "these people were traders" and have been at it a long time. She had visions of a similarly successful store when they left the next morning. (Above, courtesy of Lisa Amaral; below, courtesy of Edythe Klopping.)

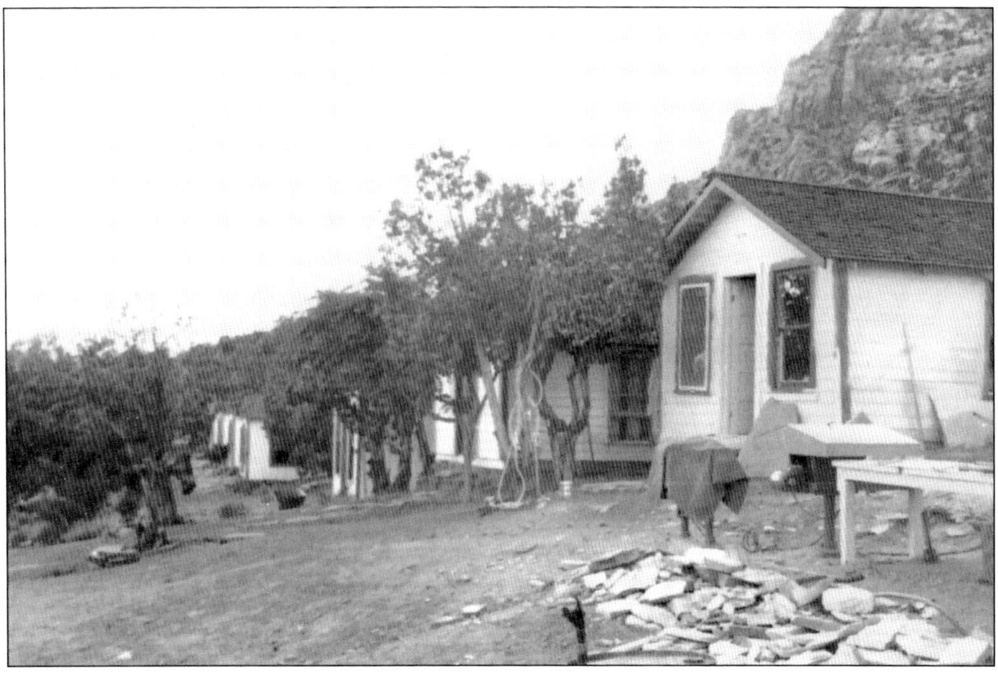

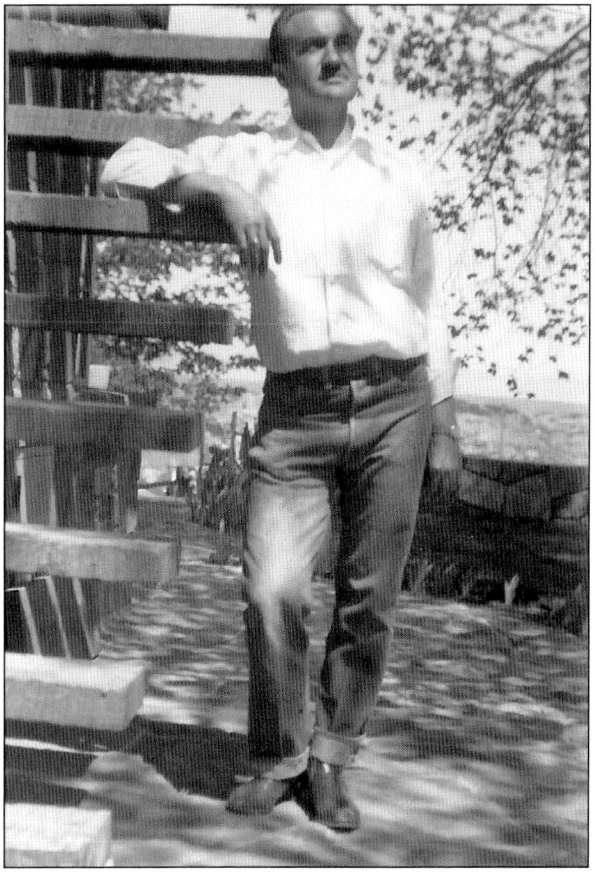

Hubert and Maybel's youngest child, Keith Wilson "Buddy" Richardson, was born in 1919, just three years after Cameron Trading Post was established. Buddy operated Kaibito Trading Post north of Cameron, and he loved everything fast. He kept a boat in San Diego, California, and he owned an airplane that he flew from Kaibito to Cameron and California; he also flew tourists over scenic areas. There was a dirt landing strip across the river from Cameron where he could land his airplane, and old-timers recalled that he was known to have alerted people at the trading post that he was arriving when he flew his airplane under the bridge. (Both, courtesy of Lisa Amaral.)

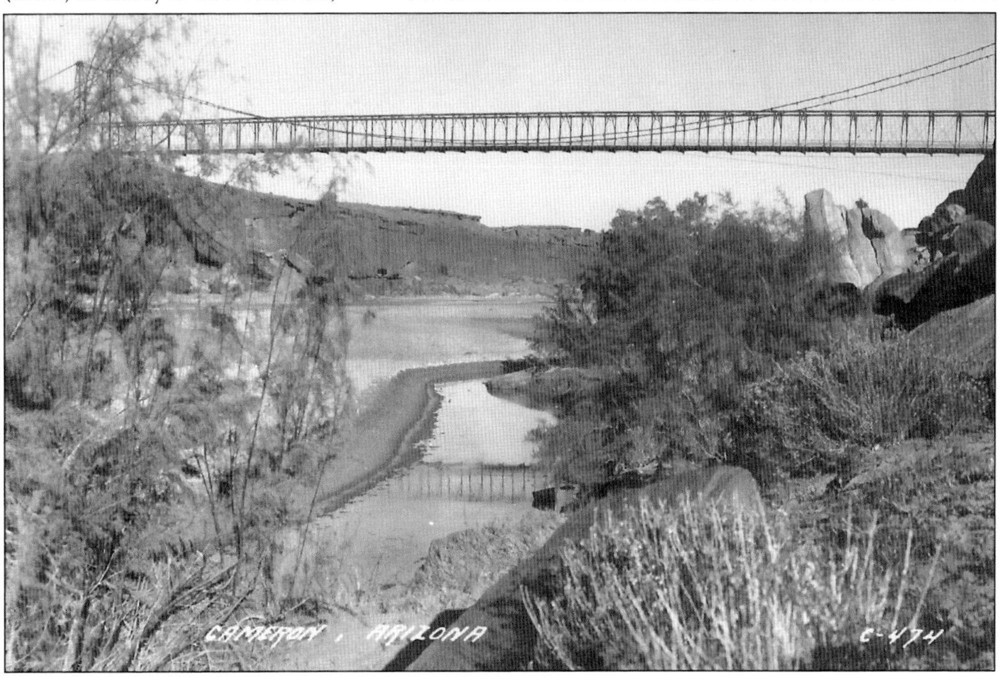

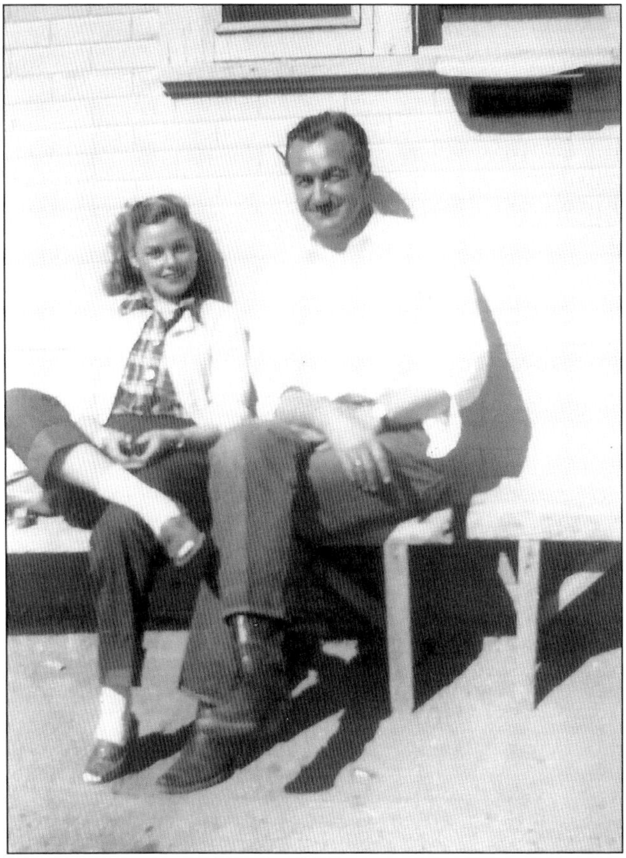

Buddy Richardson and his wife, Hazel, sometimes lived and worked at Cameron. During World War II, Buddy and Hazel managed the trading post at the Navajo Ordnance Depot in Bellmont west of Flagstaff. In the 1950s, Hazel was postmistress at Cameron. They had two daughters, Lisa and Linda. Buddy suffered from osteoporosis and was confined to a wheelchair later in his life. He died in Mesa, Arizona, in 1975 at only 56 years of age. At left, Buddy and Hazel are sitting on a bench in front of Cameron Trading Post. Below is the old sign for the store. The post office was in a stone building next to the store (where the sign now hangs). Today, a new post office serves people from miles around Cameron. Enclosed on the bottom and sides with the Rainbow Man or Yei figure, the fading wooden sign still advertises "Indian Crafts." (Left, courtesy of Lisa Amaral.)

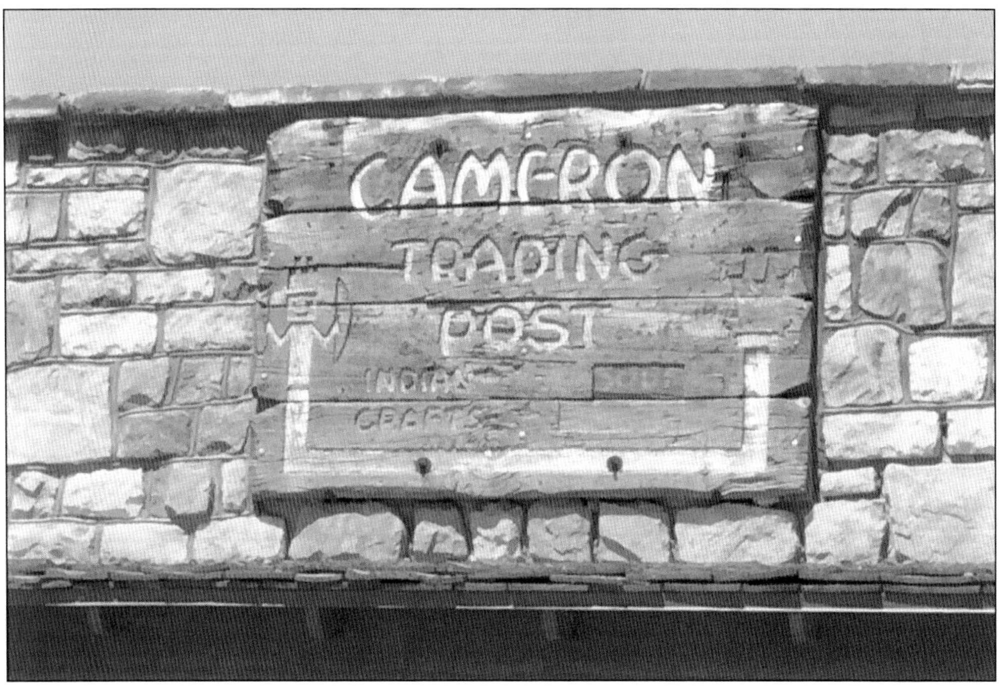

Hubert's granddaughter Lisa Amaral recalled that her family often spent Christmas at Cameron. At right, in this early 1950s photograph, Lisa (left) is sitting with her grandmother Maybel and her sister Linda. In 1955, Lisa's family was living at Cameron. In the Christmas photograph below, Lisa sits next to her grandmother as Linda stands behind her and Hubert stands at the right. That was a difficult year for the Richardsons. In 1955, Jack Richardson died in an automobile accident traveling from Gray Mountain to Cameron, and Lisa contracted polio, one of the first recorded cases in northern Arizona. Her mother, Hazel, was serving as postmistress at Cameron, and before she could take Lisa to Phoenix for treatment, she had to find and swear in her replacement. (Both, courtesy of Lisa Amaral.)

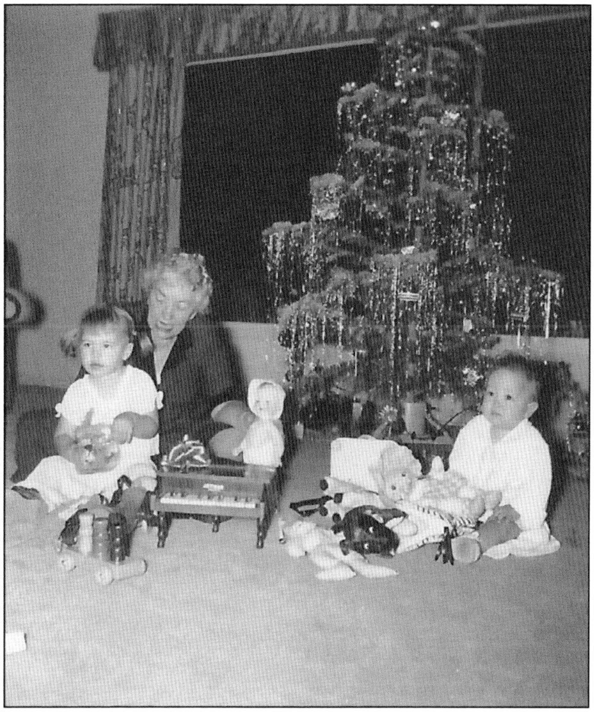

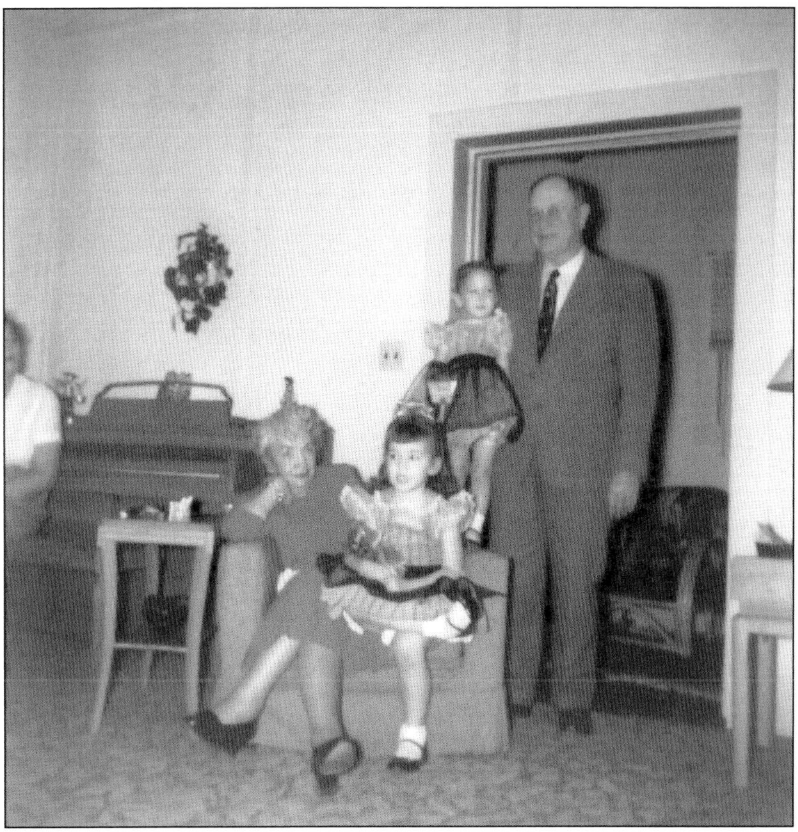

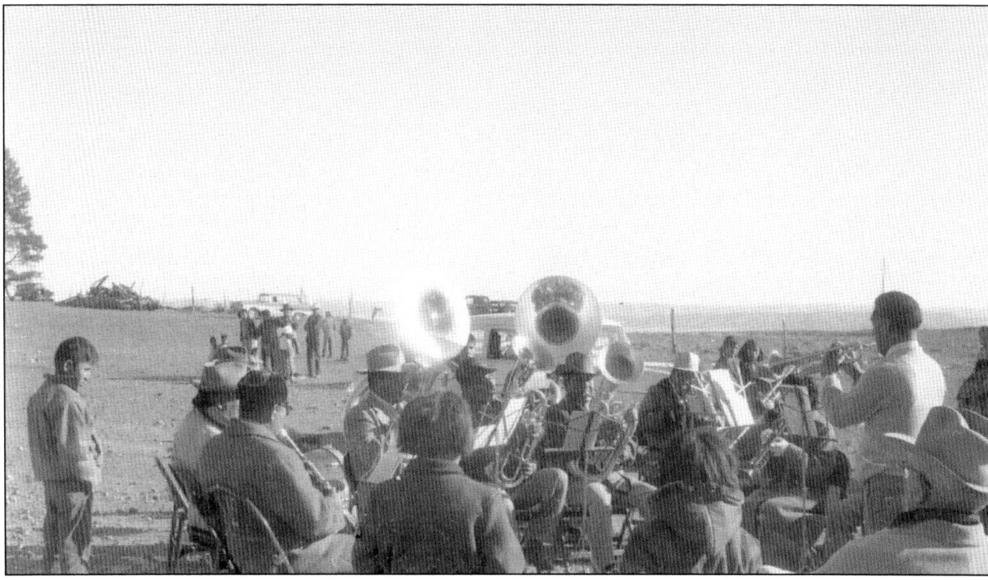

Most trading posts on the Navajo Reservation, including Cameron, hosted Christmas gatherings. There was a huge Christmas party at Buck Rodgers Trading Post in 1957, with a group of local musicians, seen above. Below, Shine Smith, seated and smoking his ever-present cigar, is in the center of the photograph, enjoying the performance. Smith was a defrocked minister who traveled the Navajo Reservation, sometimes helping at trading posts when the owners were away. He lived in a trailer or a tiny cabin Hubert Richardson built for him behind the trading post. Shine also organized huge Christmas parties at various posts. Ads in western magazines solicited gifts for the parties that were often stored at Babbitt warehouses in Flagstaff. The Christmas parties were legendary, sometimes with thousands of Navajos attending. (Both, courtesy of Harvey Leake.)

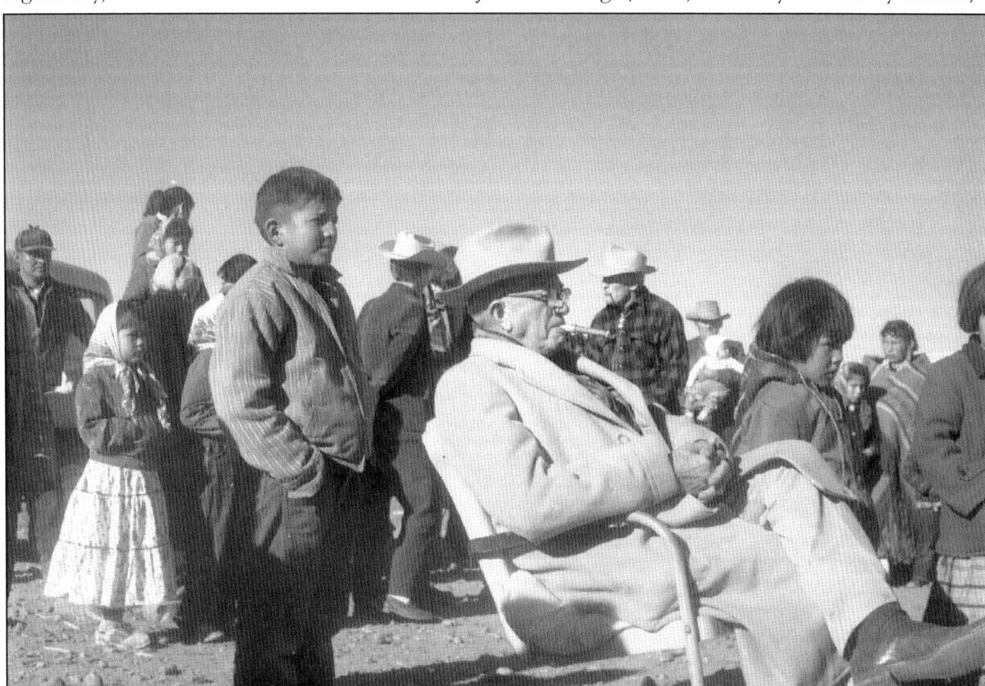

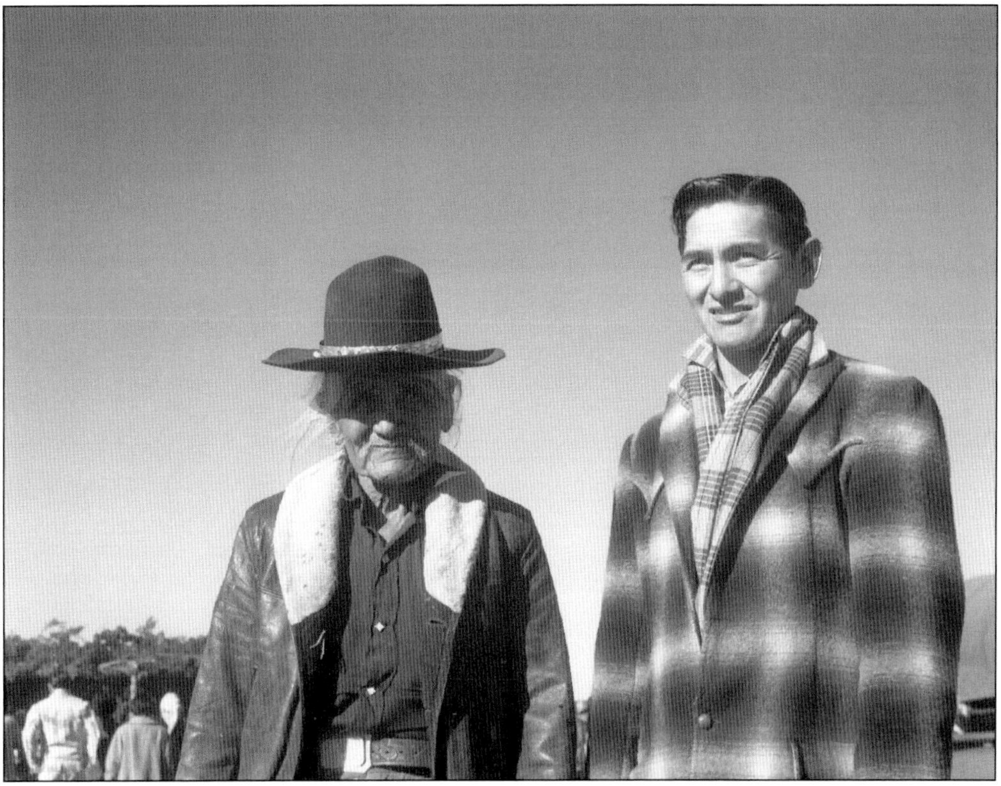

People came from miles away to attend the Christmas parties at the trading posts. Seen above, from left to right, Hosteen Dzi Libéníí, or the Old Man from Gray Mountain, and Eddie Yazzie were among those who traveled to Cameron or Buck Rodgers Trading Post. At right, Emerson Goldtooth, a Navajo tribal policeman, appears to be enjoying the musical performance. (Both, courtesy of Harvey Leake.)

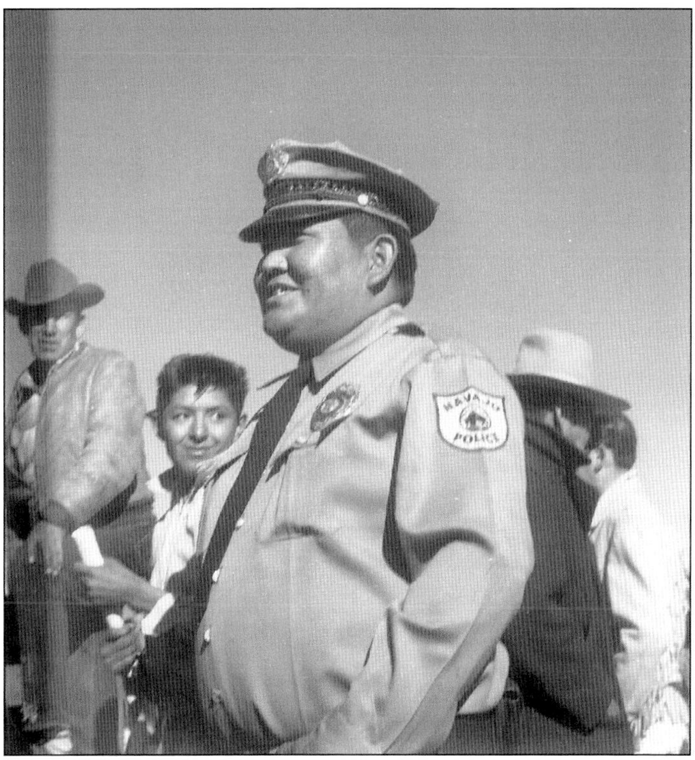

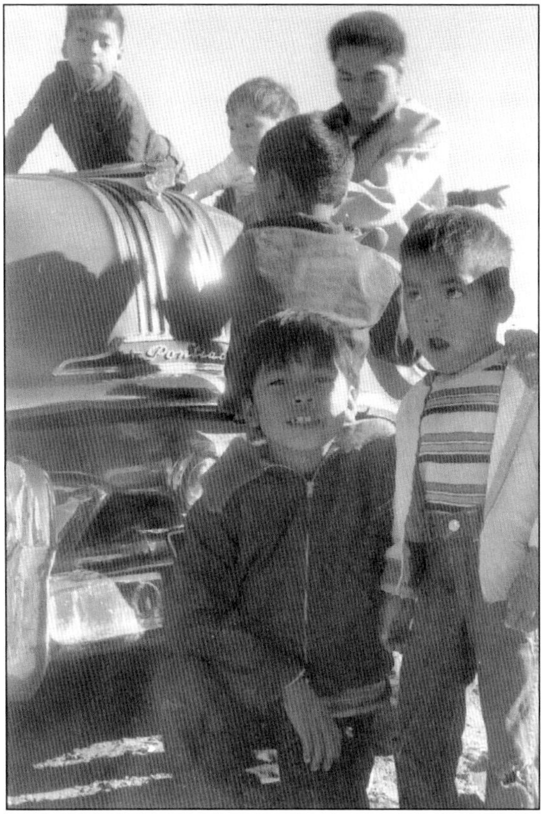

Children loved the Christmas parties at the trading posts, including the group of boys pictured at left. Below, two unidentified women serve stew at the 1957 Christmas party. Traders and Flagstaff businesses contributed to provide the feast for the gathering that could host hundreds or even thousands of people. (Both, courtesy of Harvey Leake.)

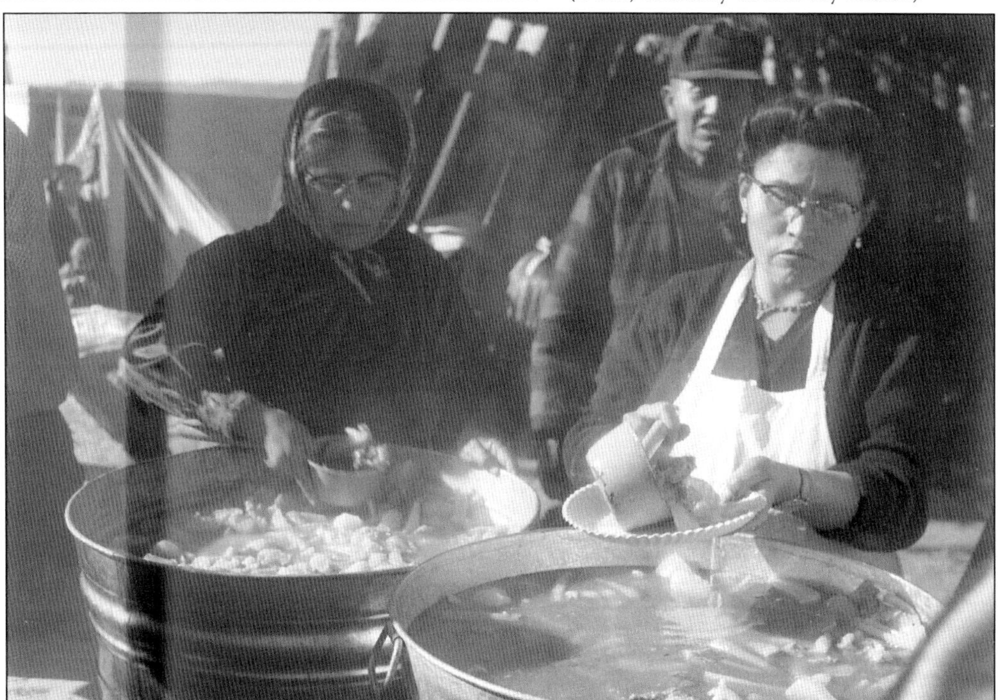

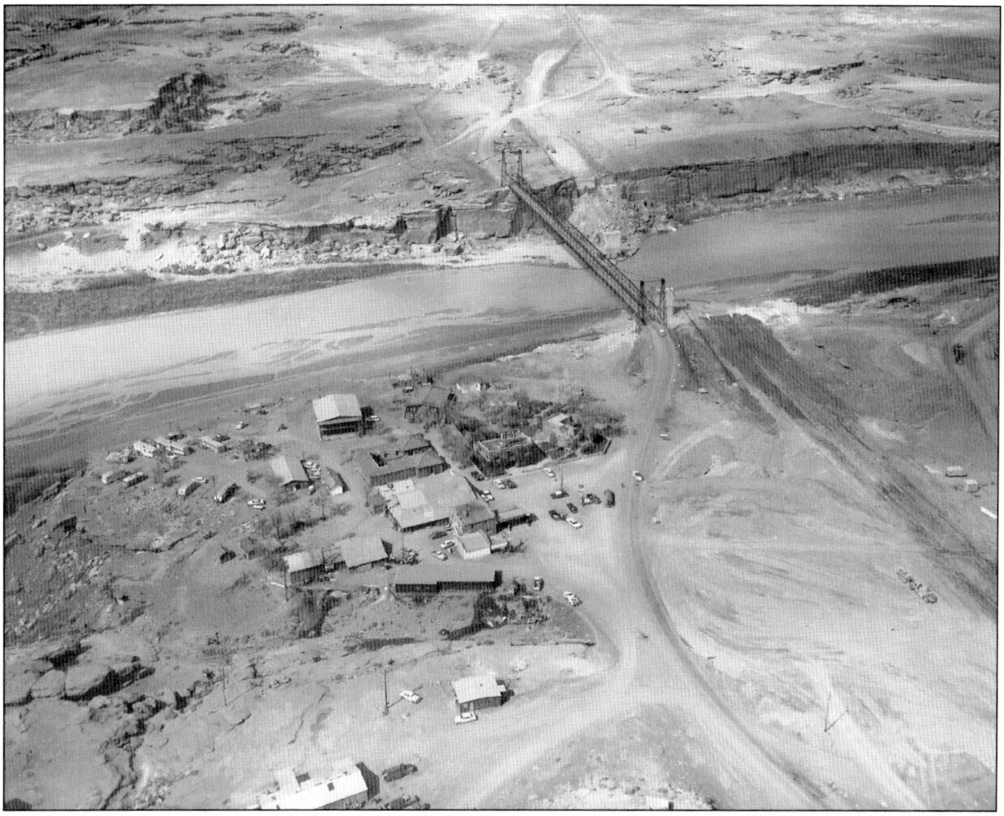

As automobile traffic increased, a newer bridge was deemed necessary at the Cameron crossing over the Little Colorado River. The second bridge was completed in 1959 at a cost of over $500,000. The massive new bridge was constructed using more than 2,500 cubic yards of concrete and 1.2 million pounds of structural steel. Above, in a view looking to the north, construction on the bridge is just beginning. Below, in a view looking to the south, the finished bridge appears to be completed. With the approach to the new bridge, the road has been straightened and no longer curves to the front door of the trading post. The old bridge is now used to carry a natural gas pipeline across the river. (Both, courtesy of Lisa Amaral.)

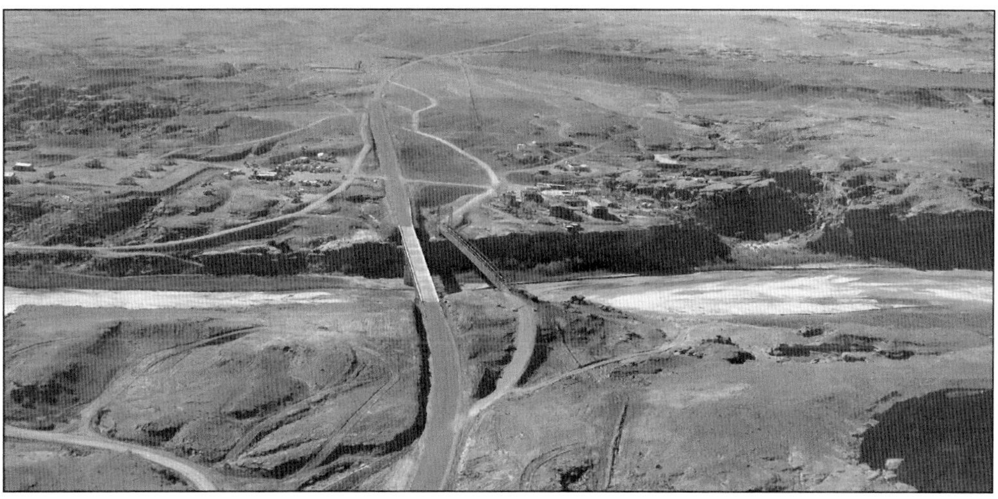

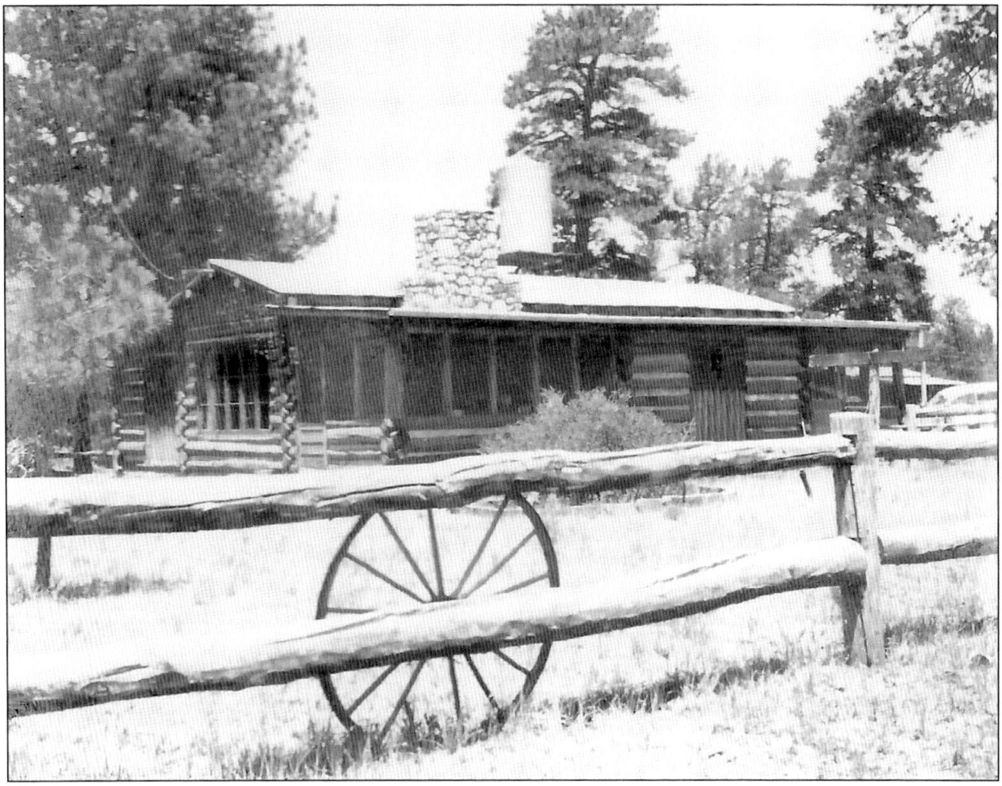

Hubert Richardson owned the 77 Bar, a working cattle ranch west of Cameron and southwest of the Grand Canyon. His granddaughters Lisa Ann and Linda Sue often visited there in the summers. The ranch house is pictured above. Below, Lisa (standing left), Linda (holding the horse's reins), and Hubert stand next to a horse with an unidentified child sitting in the saddle in this early 1960s photograph. (Both, courtesy of Lisa Amaral.)

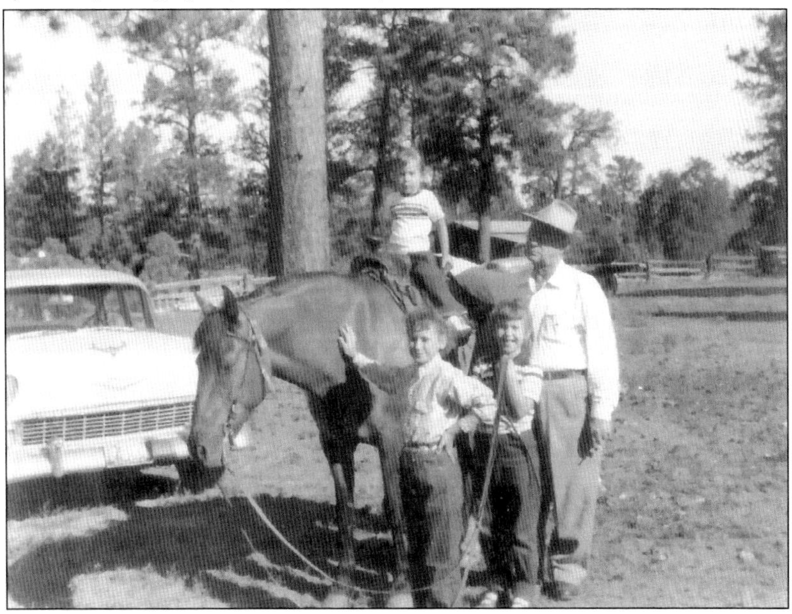

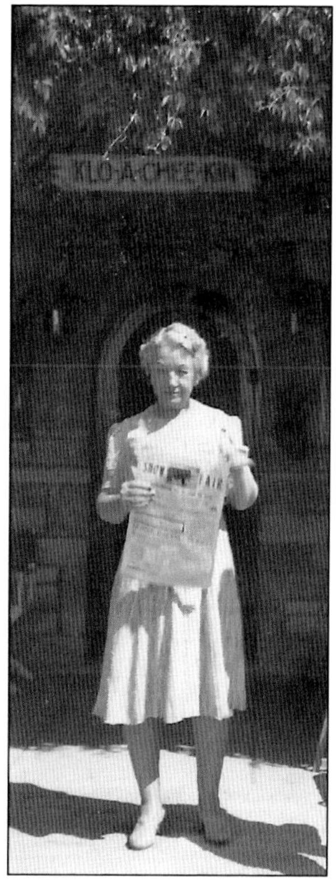

Maybel Richardson, seen at right, died September 6, 1961. She and Hubert had been married 48 years. She had not worked in the trading post with Hubert, but Maybel entertained hundreds of visitors to Cameron over the years, always providing meals, lodging, and warm company for friends and travelers. The garden at Cameron was Maybel's, and under her direction, she created a green and inviting haven in the Painted Desert. She was a quiet woman, and her nephew Bill Richardson recalled that Hubert and Maybel had a wonderful life together. Below, Maybel and Hubert stand at the entrance to the Klo-a-chee-kin Hotel. Evidence of Maybel's love of plants can be seen in the trees, vines, and shrubs that surround the stone building, Maybel's "oasis in the desert." (Both, courtesy of Lisa Amaral.)

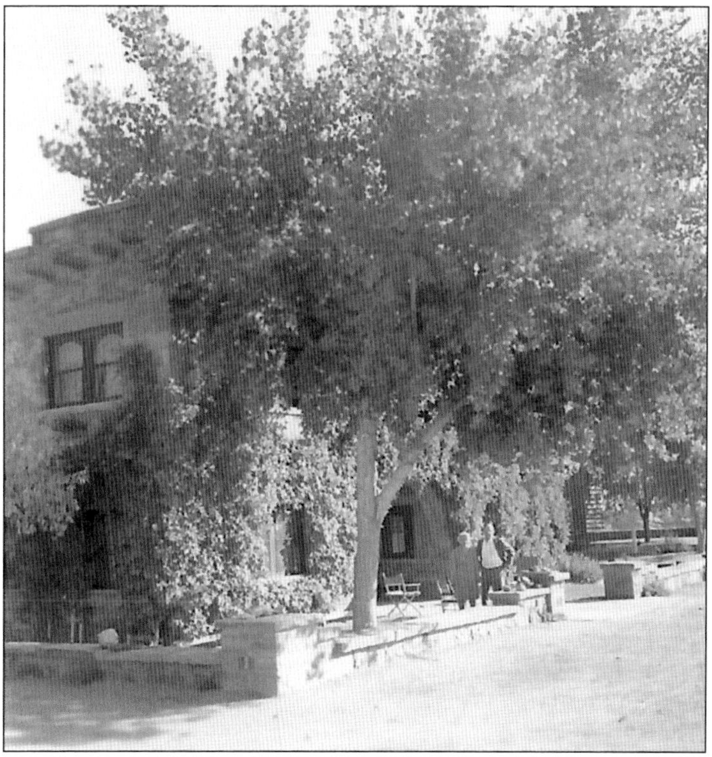

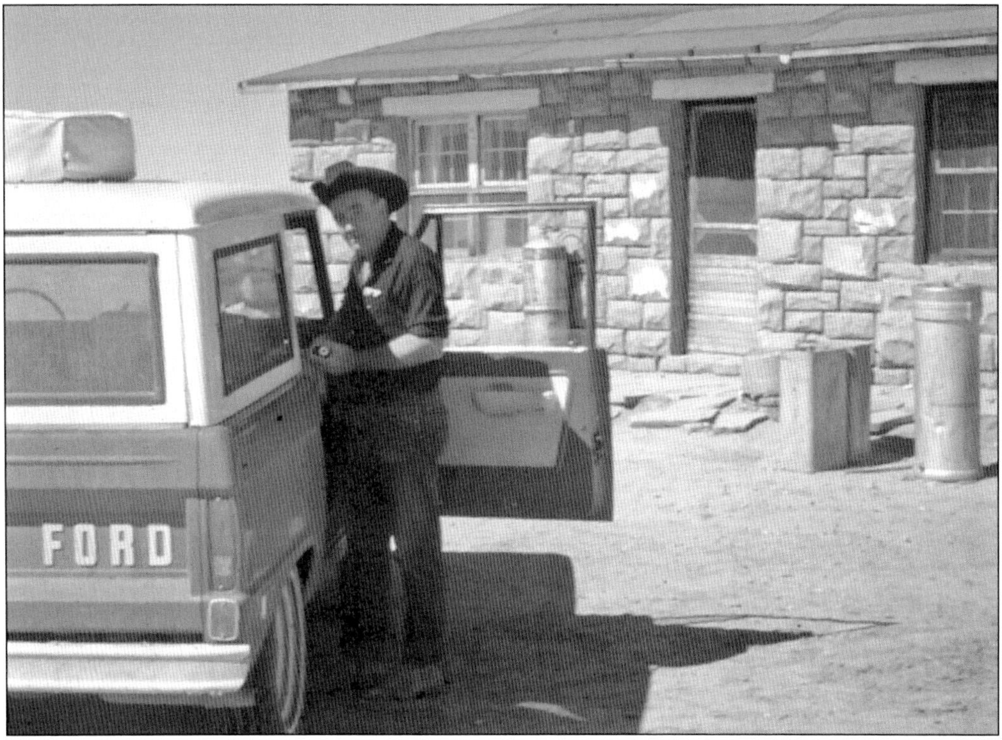

Artist Brownell McGrew (1916–1994), above with his Ford Bronco, visited the Southwest for 30 years, from 1959 to 1989. He photographed and sketched, building a remarkable archive of people and scenes on the Hopi and Navajo Reservations for future paintings, and his trips always began at Cameron Trading Post. There, he reconnected with old friends, and he generally picked up Shine Smith, who traveled the back roads with him, searching out people willing to be models for his paintings. Shine spoke Navajo and Hopi, but usually it took a dollar or two before permission was given for the photograph or sketch. McGrew is known for his detailed and luminous portraits and landscapes, and his work is highly collectible today. Below is McGrew's painting of a Navajo family at Red Lake Trading Post. (Above, courtesy of Byron Hunter; below, courtesy of Abraham Mohler.)

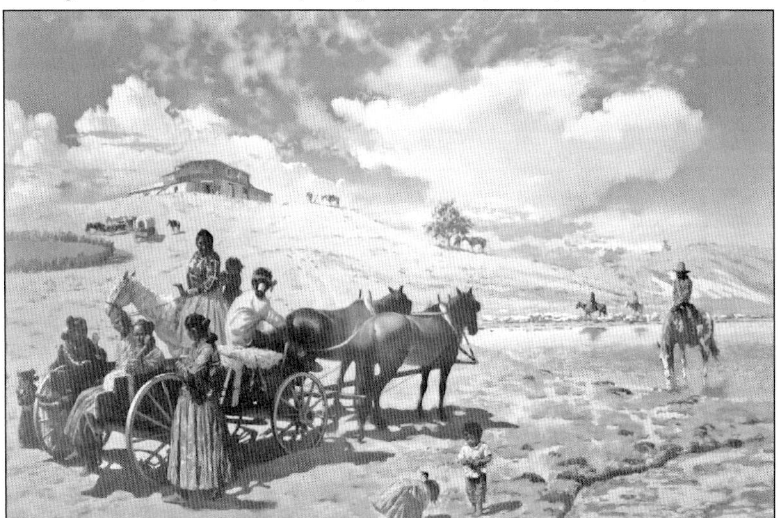

Brownell McGrew sketched this Navajo lady on horseback with her baby wrapped onto her back. This is just one of the thousands of sketches McGrew made of Hopi and Navajo people as well as dozens of trading posts. (Courtesy of the Brownell McGrew family.)

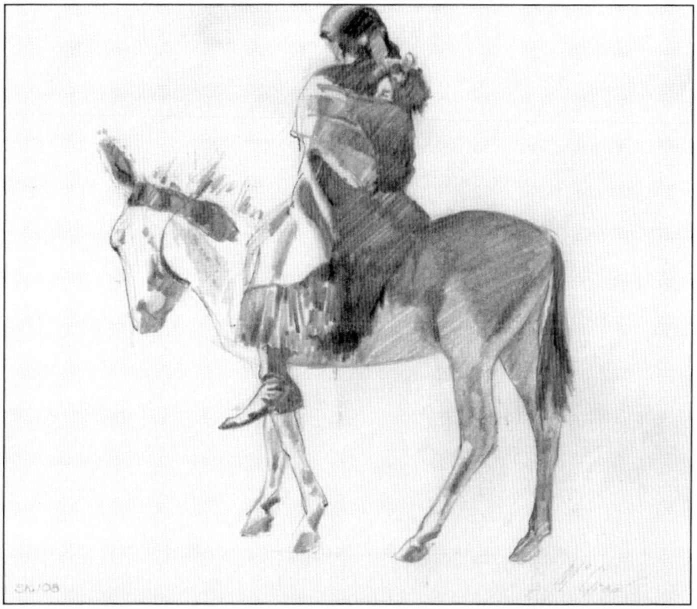

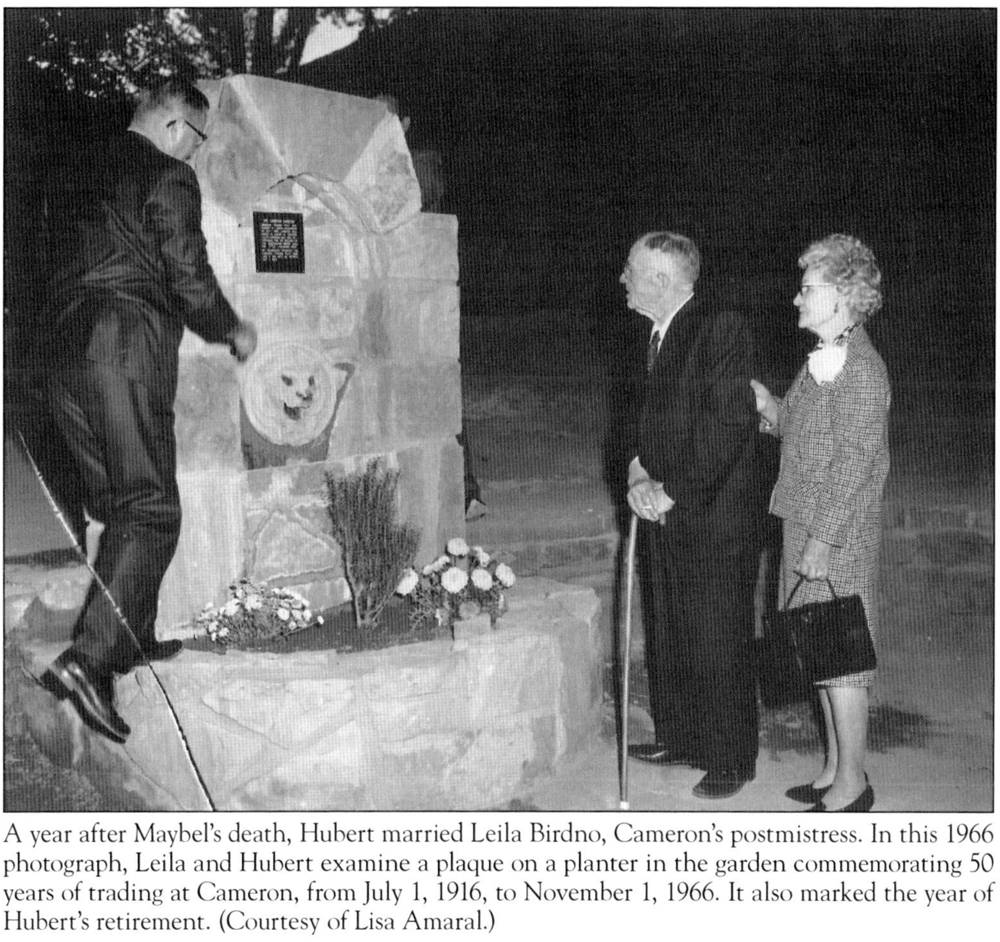

A year after Maybel's death, Hubert married Leila Birdno, Cameron's postmistress. In this 1966 photograph, Leila and Hubert examine a plaque on a planter in the garden commemorating 50 years of trading at Cameron, from July 1, 1916, to November 1, 1966. It also marked the year of Hubert's retirement. (Courtesy of Lisa Amaral.)

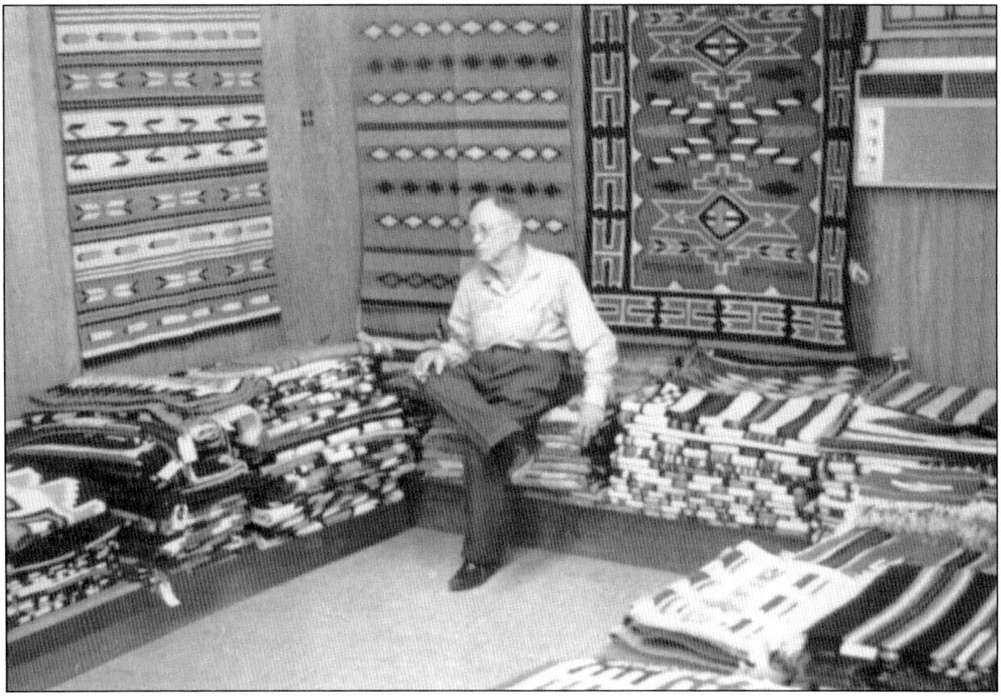

Cameron Trading Post has always carried beautiful Native American arts, everything from silver jewelry, baskets, and pottery to finely woven rugs. Hubert Richardson once remarked that the weavers in the Cameron area were known for their beautifully woven rugs, usually in the Storm Pattern, in reds, blacks, and browns. Above, Hubert sits on a stack of Navajo rugs; below, he is pictured with an unidentified salesperson in the store's gallery area in front of shelves filled with Pueblo pottery. At the right, there are cases lined with silver and turquoise jewelry. (Both, courtesy of Lisa Amaral.)

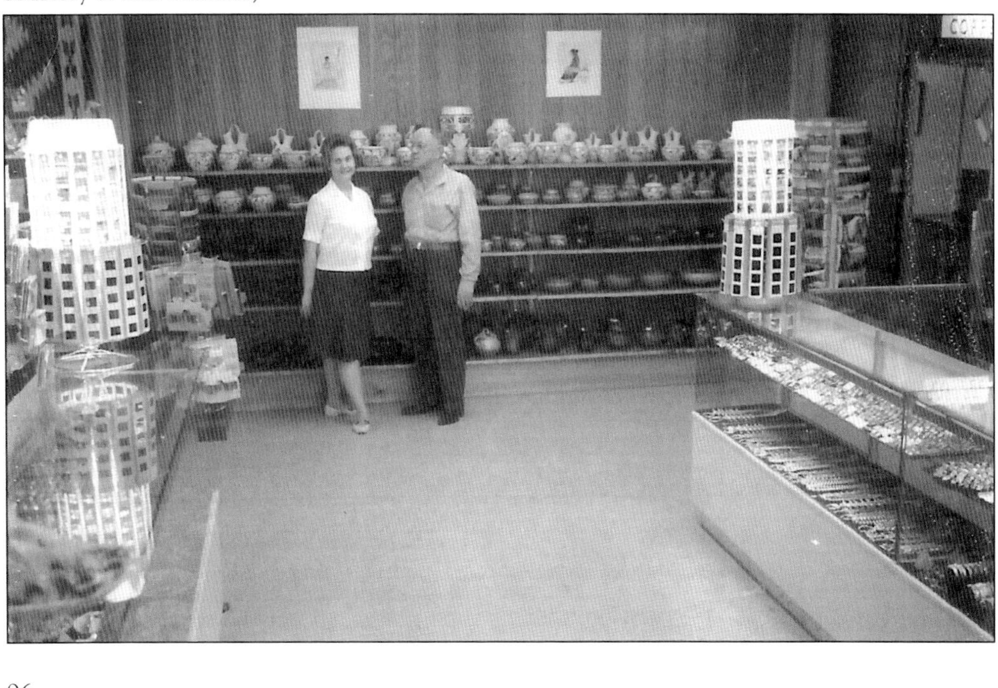

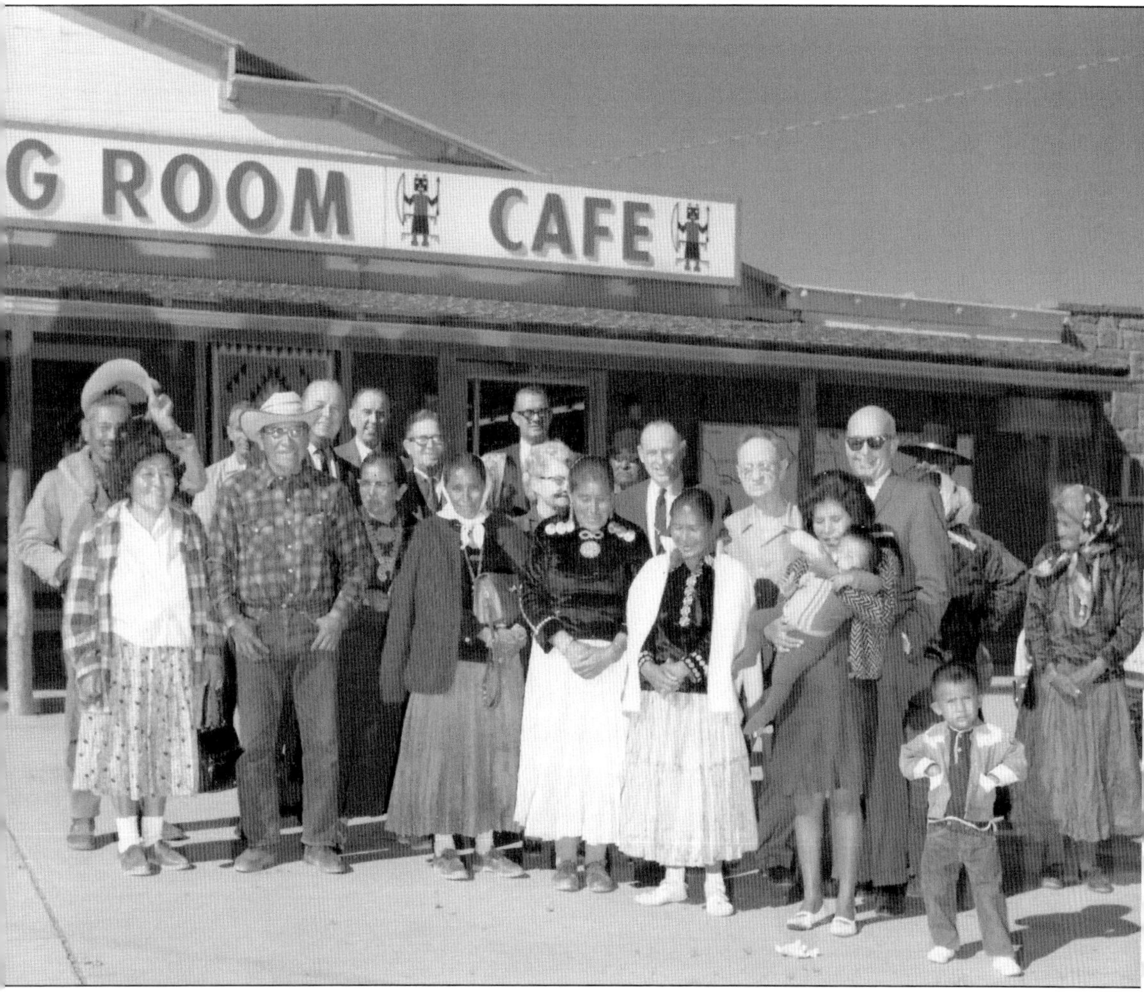

In 1966, Hubert Richardson was 76 years old and had owned Cameron Trading Post for 50 years. His health was failing, his son Jack was dead, Jeannette lived out of the state, and Buddy suffered from ill health. Hubert wanted to retire, and Standard Oil wanted to control the oil business. Through Hubert's lucrative franchise with Standard Oil, he was wholesaling seven million gallons of gasoline a year in northern Arizona. Standard Oil took over the master lease, and the Fred Harvey Company subleased the hotel, restaurant, and store. On November 1, the transfer of the historic store was completed with Hubert handing over the symbolic "key" to the city: a feathered hatchet inscribed with the words "Cameron, Ariz—November 1, 1966." Pictured in the first row are, from left to right, unidentified, Diane Hosteen, unidentified, Nancy Horse, Leila Richardson, Grace Bigman, Grace Yellow Mexican (in the white sweater), Hubert Richardson, Grace Yellow Mexican's daughter and her son, unidentified, and Sally Denetsoh. Those in the second row are unidentified. Hubert said, "I had to quit. It's been a long time. I'm just wore out." (Courtesy of Lisa Amaral.)

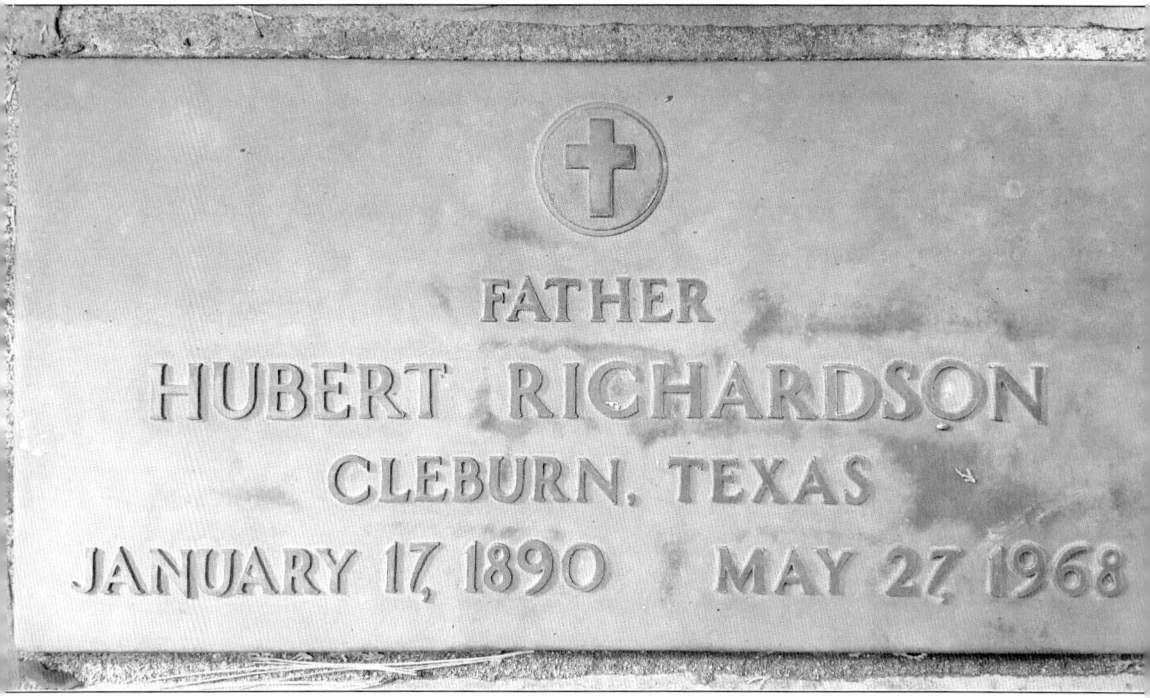

Hubert Richardson died May 27, 1968, less than two years after retiring from Cameron Trading Post. Hubert was buried in the Citizens Cemetery in Flagstaff, Arizona, in a family plot with his first wife, Maybel, son Jack, and daughter Jeannette, who died just eight months later. Stumps of petrified wood, topped with concrete etched with an "R" mark the corners of the plot. A copper penny on Hubert's metal grave marker has tarnished into a turquoise circle; a copper penny on Jack's headstone has a similarly tarnished penny-sized turquoise circle. Lisa Amaral remembered her grandfather as being patient and kind, a remembrance that has been repeated by many Cameron residents who knew him. Hubert spoke Navajo and was said to be fair in all of his dealings, buying wool and rugs, trading for store supplies, and engaging in other transactions with local Navajo customers. Sadly, little memorabilia has survived. Shortly after Hubert's death, Leila packed their possessions, including papers and collections from the store, to move to New Mexico. The moving van crashed, and half a century of history was lost.

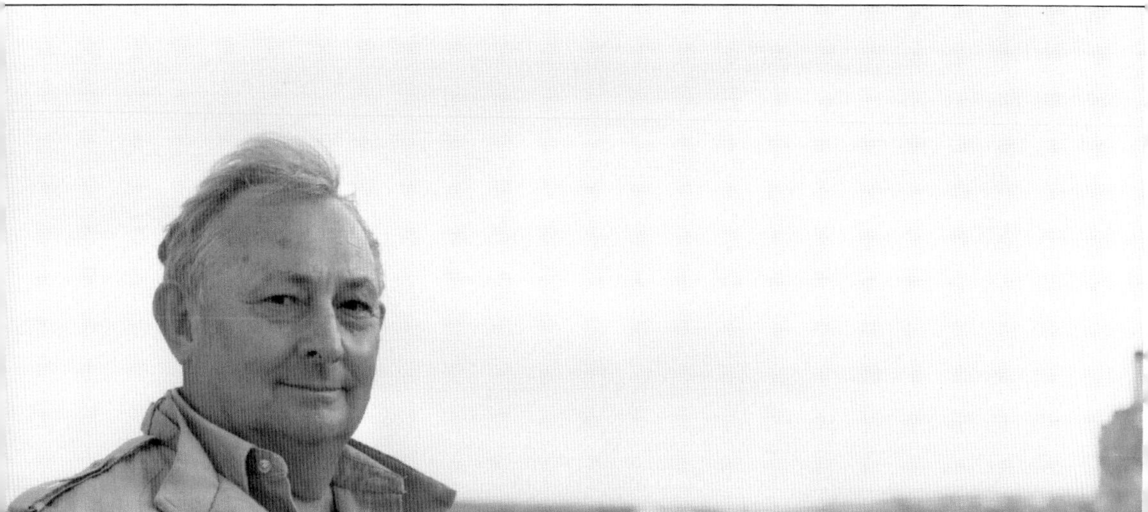

Tony Hillerman (1925–2008), pictured here at Laguna Pueblo, New Mexico, is without question one of the Southwest's most popular and admired authors. The 18 books in his Navajo mystery series span 36 years, with stories of Lt. Joe Leaphorn and Jim Chee of the Navajo Tribal Police. Hillerman made many trips through the Southwest from his Albuquerque, New Mexico, home, and stopped in Cameron to visit local friends. Several scenes from his mysteries *The Dark Wind* and *A Thief of Time* are set at Cameron. In *The First Eagle*, Lt. Joe Leaphorn meets Hopi deputy sheriff Albert "Cowboy" Dashee at Cameron Trading Post. As Leaphorn drives northward, he explains to his companion that the San Francisco Peaks in the distance to the south are "our sacred mountain of the west, you know, made by First Man himself." (Courtesy of Anne Hillerman and the Tony Hillerman Photograph Collection PICT 000-501-0543, Center for Southwest Research, University Libraries, University of New Mexico.)

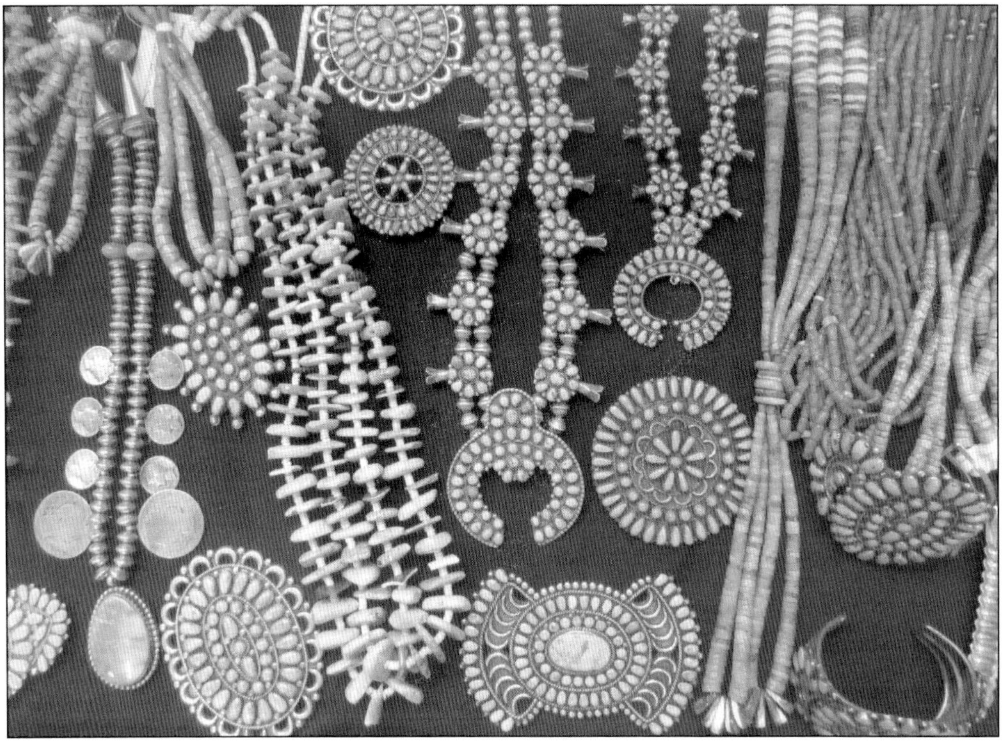

On June 26, 1975, four robbers forced their way into Cameron Trading Post at closing time. Dressed in dark clothing and ski masks, they tied up the manager and forced employee Edward Humetewa to open the walk-in vault. The robbers spent the night emptying the store of pawn items, jewelry, cash, rugs, and other valuables, taking nearly a million dollars in goods and cash. It was the biggest robbery in trading post history, and police speculated that it was the explosion of popularity of Native American jewelry that was the inspiration for the heist. The FBI had a national manhunt, but there were never any convictions, and most of the stolen merchandise was never found. Below, Edward Humetewa worked at Cameron over 50 years. Here, he shares the story of *Cold Bringing Woman* with his grandchildren Brianne and Jerrell Kewenvoyouma in 1994. (Both photographs by Pat Berrett, courtesy of Atkinson Trading Company.)

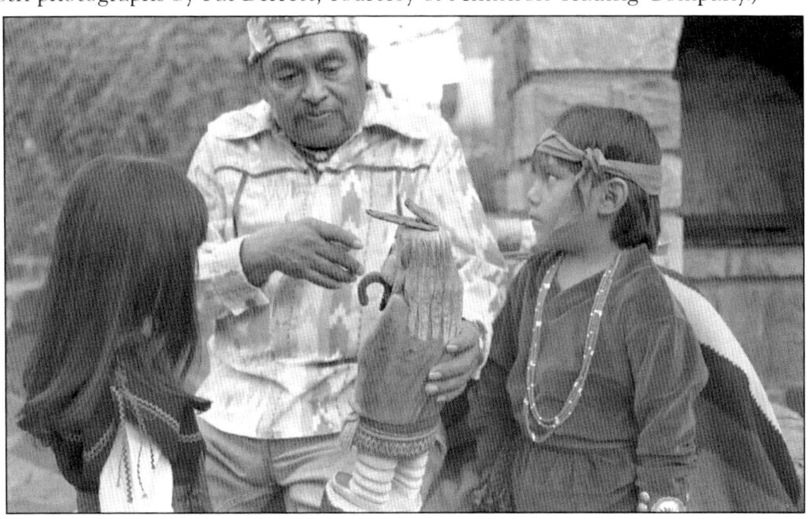

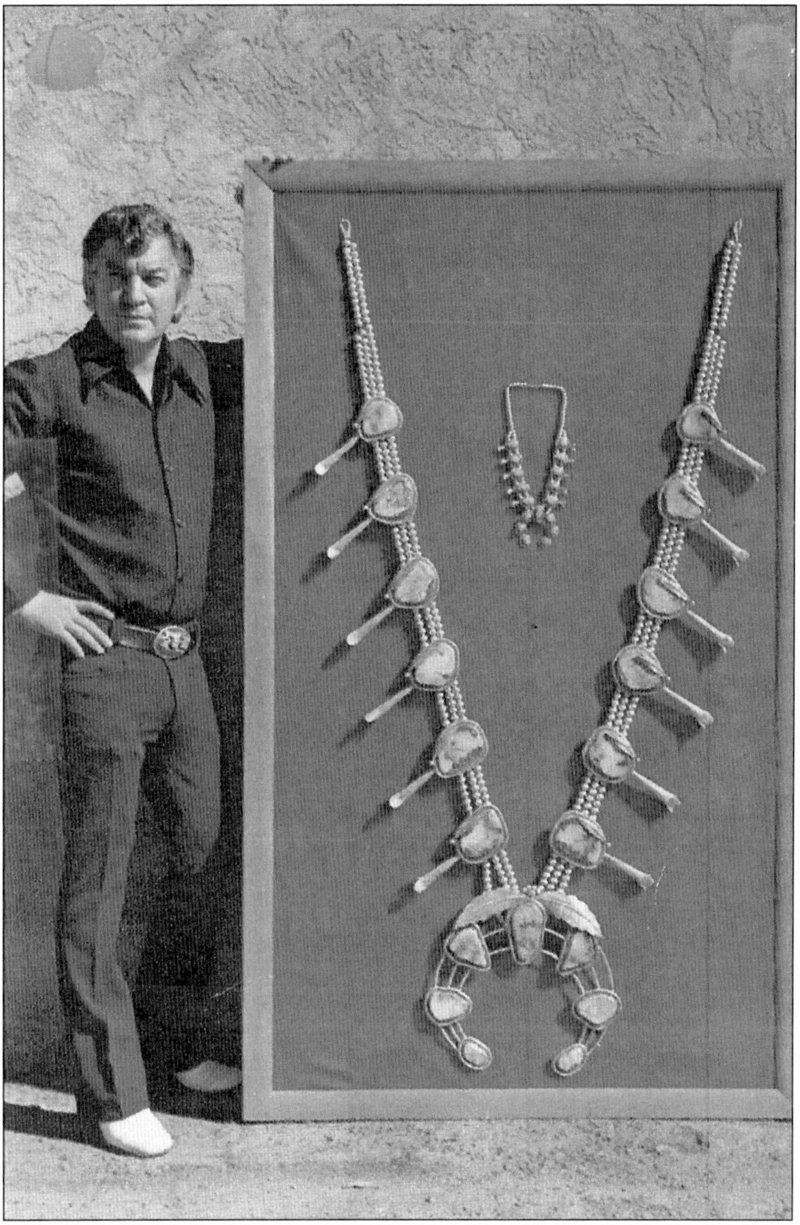

In the 1970s, the world discovered Indian jewelry. Silver and turquoise was in vogue: movie stars wore it, designers featured it in their clothing lines, and the *Wall Street Journal* declared that it was an investment. Business was exploding for jewelry trader Gilbert Ortega, pictured above with the *World's Largest Squash Blossom* in 1976. He bought trading posts and town stores, and when the opportunity came to lease Cameron Trading Post from Standard Oil, he immediately flew to Cameron. There, he saw busloads of tourists shopping at the huge store offering gifts, arts and crafts, souvenirs, groceries, gasoline, wool for the rug weavers, silver for Navajo jewelers, and a fine art gallery with vintage and high-end Indian arts. Ortega leased the store in what he called the biggest deal he ever made. He eventually owned 16 stores, and Cameron was the first to gross over $2 million. Ortega's motto was "Early to bed, early to rise, work like hell, and advertise." (Courtesy of Gayle Ortega.)

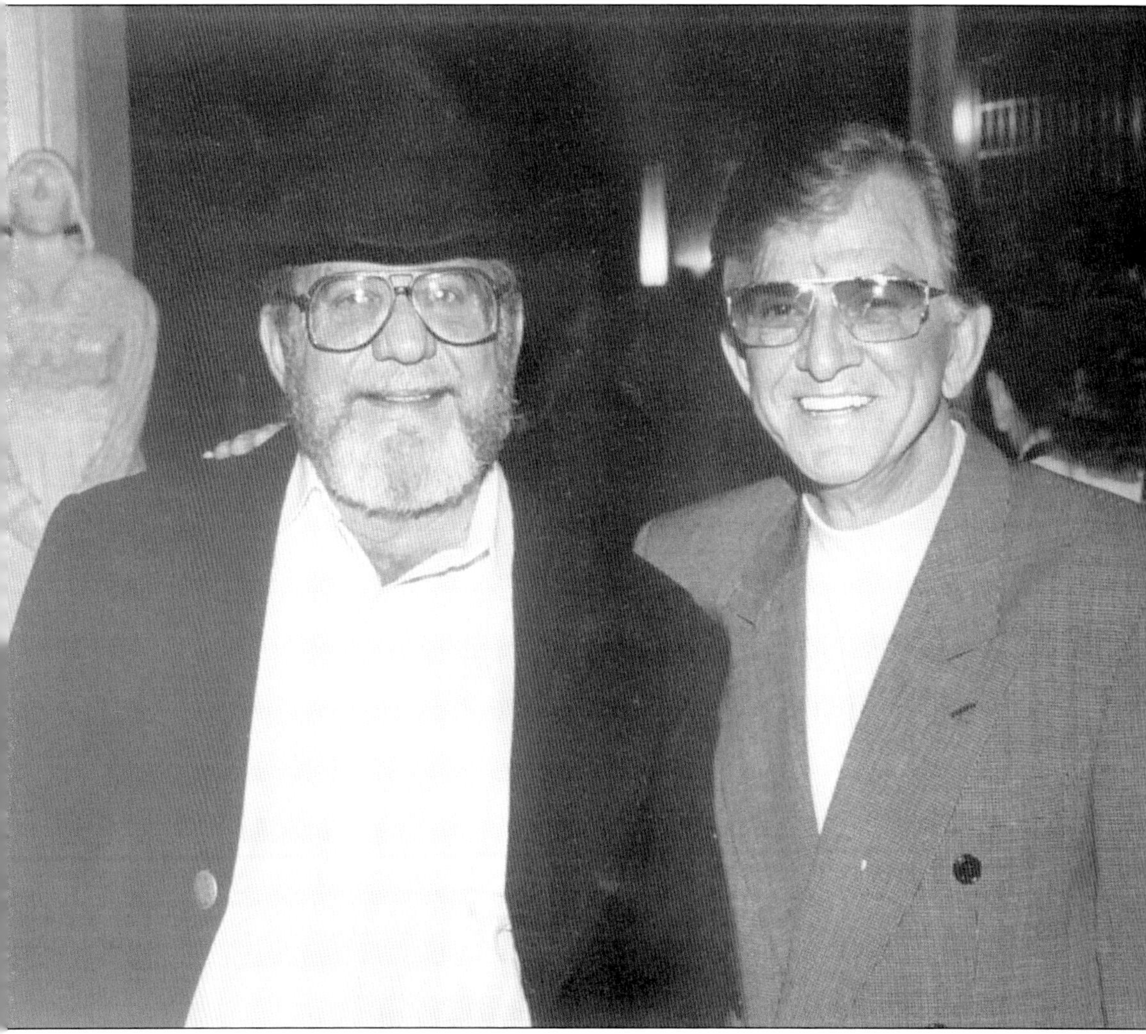

Gilbert Ortega owned Cameron Trading Post for less than a year. He was tired of operating so many stores, and he dreamed of going to Nashville to pursue a recording career. In 1977, Ortega ran into his childhood friend Joe Atkinson in a Gallup, New Mexico, restaurant. They had grown up at nearby trading posts on Route 66—Ortega in Lupton, Arizona, and Joe at Box Canyon Trading Post just over the line in New Mexico. That night at Pal Joey's, Ortega impulsively offered to lease or sell his stores to Atkinson, and the two made notes on cocktail napkins that they each signed. Atkinson offered $5 million for the chain, but Ortega knew Joe wanted Cameron because "he was a smart businessman." Joe got Cameron on a five-year lease with an option to buy. That purchase was completed five years later. Atkinson (left) and Ortega are pictured together at one of Ortega's art auctions in 1995. (Courtesy of Gayle Ortega.)

Shortly after Joe Atkinson took over Cameron Trading Post, he began restoring the historic buildings to their grand, earlier style, to the "feel of the old Cameron." Atkinson, pictured at right, was not a newcomer to Cameron; he is Hubert and Claude "C.D." Richardson's grandnephew, and had visited Cameron over the years. Joe had Maybel Richardson's garden replanted and refurbished the motel and restaurant. He added on to the store and pushed out the area where the restaurant is now located. At right, Joe participates in a round dance with Virgie Kuwanhyoima. Roberto Chaverria was the stonemason who constructed the massive fireplace in the restaurant, pictured below. Chaverria is still at Cameron, and his brother Pancho is in charge of the well and water delivery. (Right, photograph by Pat Berrett; both, courtesy of Atkinson Trading Company.)

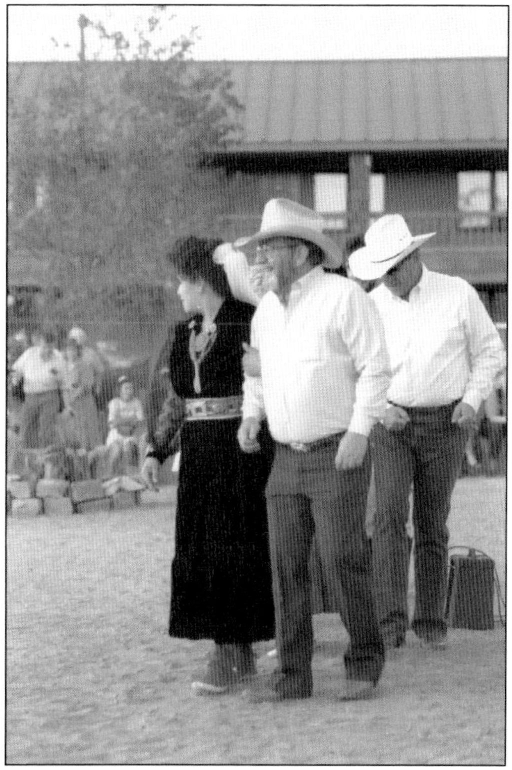

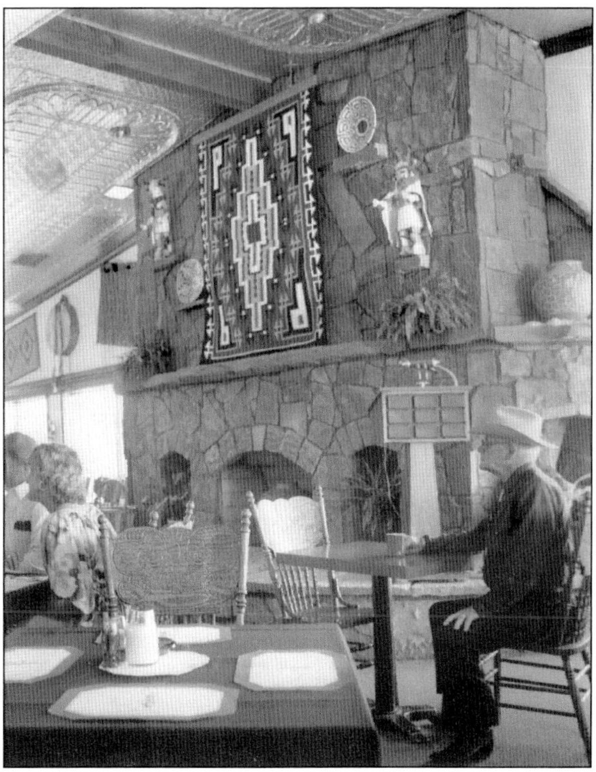

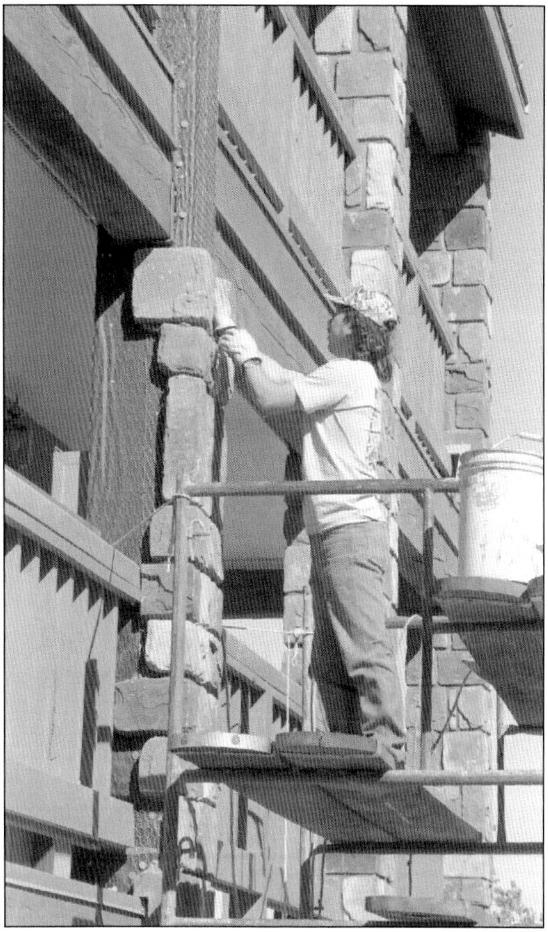

Over the years, other buildings have been added to the trading post complex, including motel buildings that serve the growing traffic. The Apache building was added in 1993, and in 1994, the Navajo building was torn down and rebuilt. At left, Hubaldo Chavarria completes the stonework on the Navajo building. Joe Atkinson noted that anytime a building was added or remodeled, the work was not complete until a Navajo medicine man came out to do a blessing ceremony, as seen below. A boy and girl represent First Man and First Woman. The medicine man recounts stories and recites special prayers. Standing at the right are John Lee Robbins (left), Monica Worker (center), and Bruce Williams, the medicine man, in 1993. (Both photographs by Pat Berrett, courtesy of Atkinson Trading Company.)

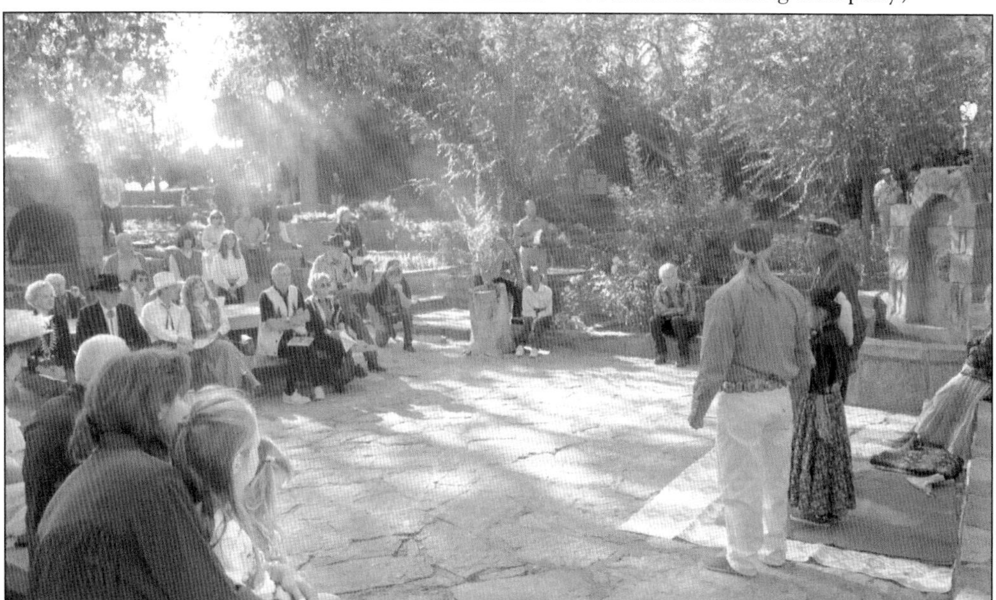

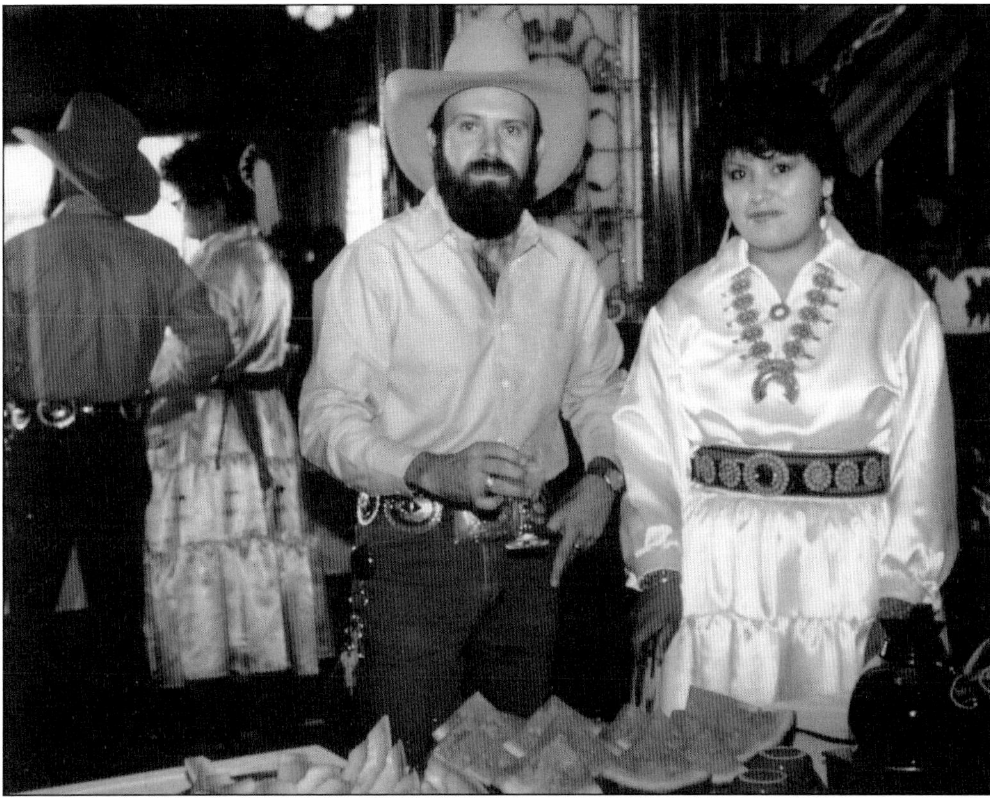

Joe Atkinson hired Leonard "Lenny" Mora to manage Cameron Trading Post. He was a good manager, and as Joe recalled, he spoke several languages—"Spanish, English, Italian, French, German, and pretty darn good Navajo." Above are Mora and Virgie Kuwanhyoima; at right, Martha Semallie dishes food at a gathering at Cameron Trading Post about 1985. (Both photographs by Pat Berrett, courtesy of Atkinson Trading Company.)

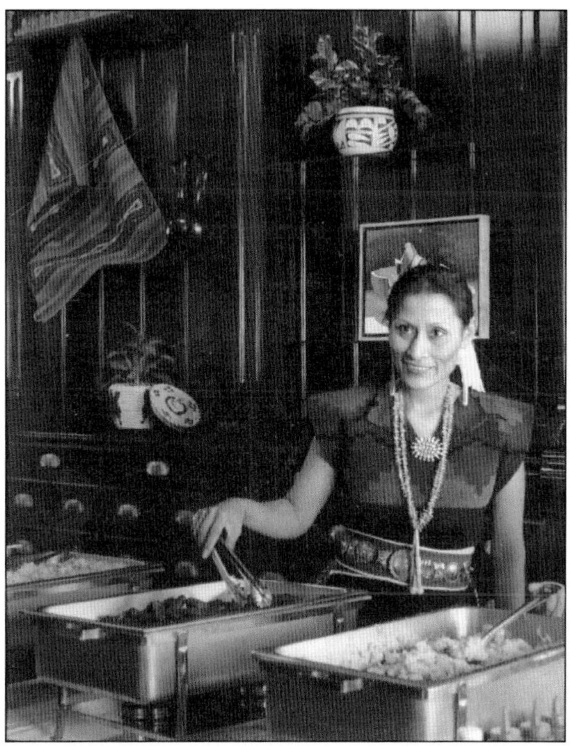

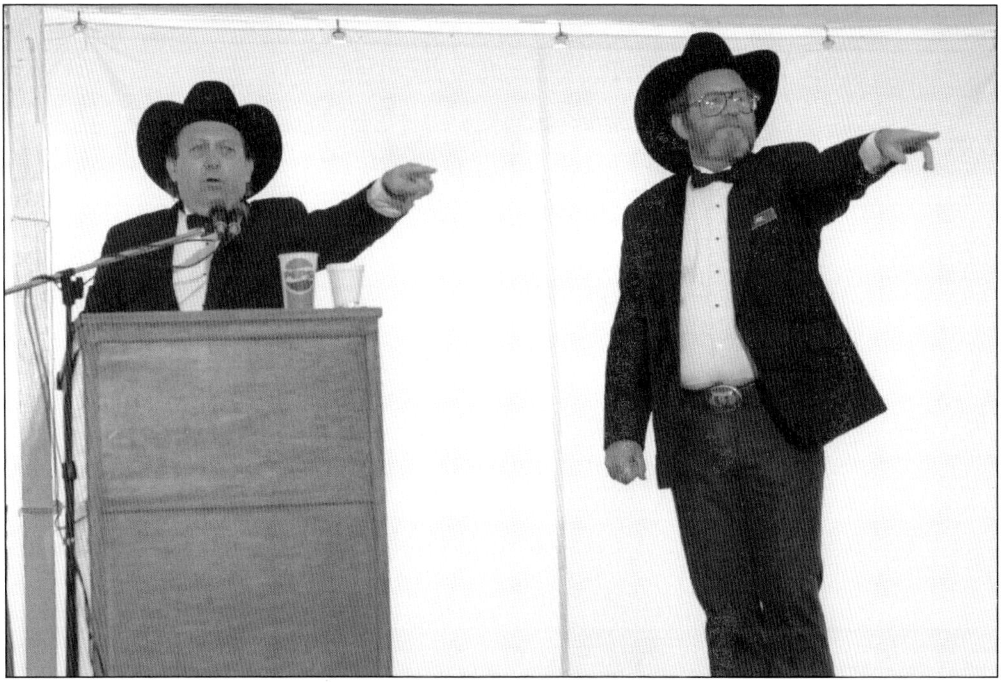

In 1986, Joe Atkinson began holding annual auctions on Columbus Day weekend in October. These auctions continued until 1996, when the last auction was held. Several of the catalogs feature photographs of Cameron employees wearing or holding auction items. Other images picture local Cameron people: children, weavers, silversmiths, and ranchers. Above, Tommy Elkins is the auctioneer and Joe is the auction spotter at the right. Below, Tinitia Kewenveoyouma, granddaughter of longtime employee Edward Humetewa, holds a turquoise nugget necklace in the 1995 auction. (Both photographs by Pat Berrett, courtesy of Atkinson Trading Company.)

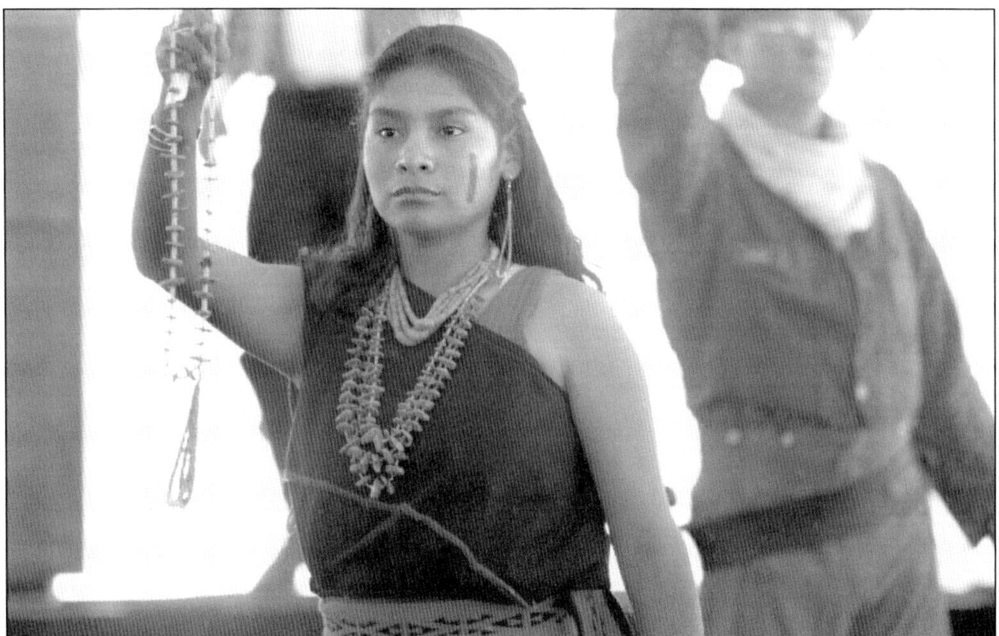

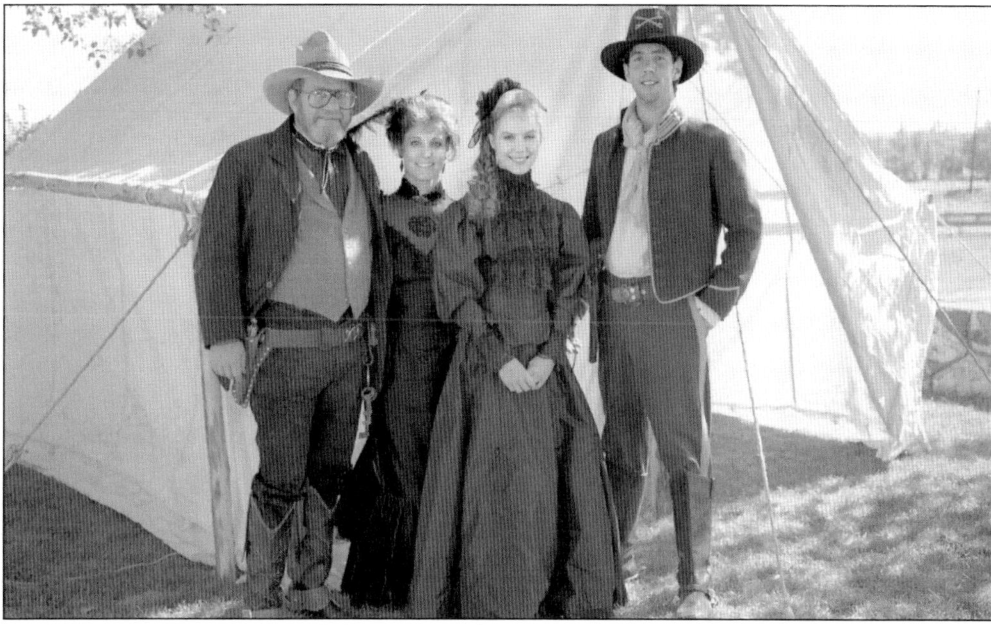

As the auctions went on, people began attending in vintage clothing, and there was always one day during the three-day event where everyone was in costume. Above, from left to right, Joe, Jeanell, Shauna, and Josh Atkinson all wear Old West clothing, about 1995. The desperadoes below, from left to right, are Roberto Chavarria, Joe Atkinson, Josh Atkinson, and Leonard Mora. (Both photographs by Pat Berrett, courtesy of Atkinson Trading Company.)

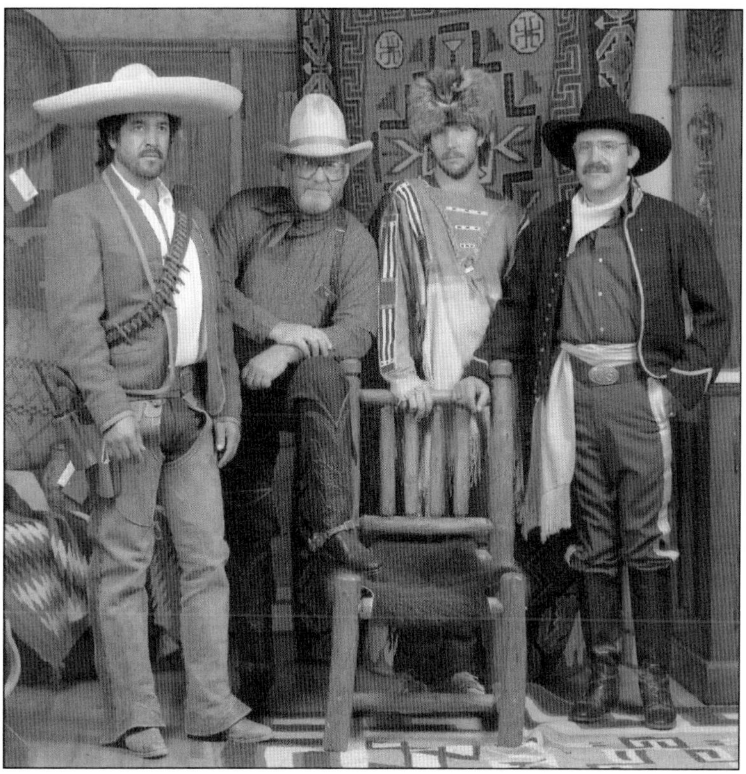

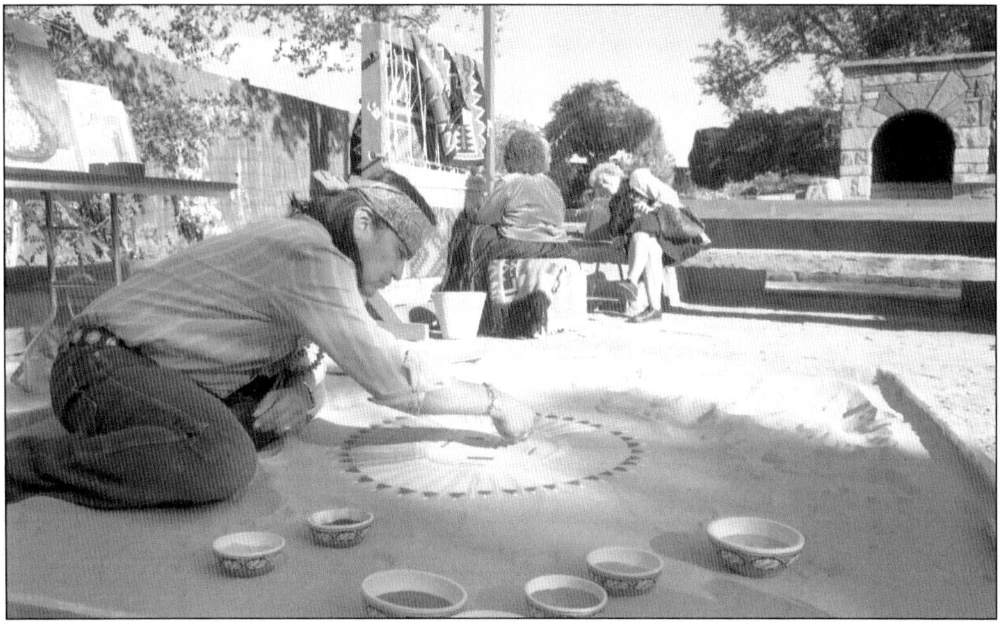

Native American artists were often invited to demonstrate their work, such as weaving and basketmaking, at the annual auctions and other events at Cameron. Navajo artist Eugene Joe (Baatsoslani) is creating a sandpainting. These intricate sandpaintings are made with colored sand and pulverized minerals, and they are most often created for Navajo ceremonies. Jean Mann is the weaver who has captivated a tourist beyond Joe. (Photograph by Pat Berrett, courtesy of Atkinson Trading Company.)

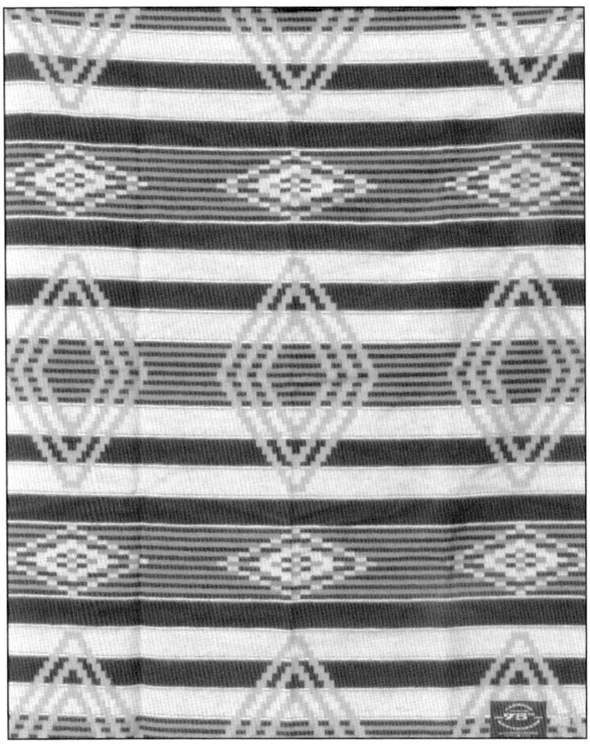

In 1991, on the occasion of its 75th anniversary, Cameron Trading Post commissioned the Pendleton Woolen Mills in Pendleton, Oregon, to create a commemorative Pendleton wool blanket that was available for collectors. The blanket is a reversible design based on an old Navajo chief's blanket. The special commemorative blue Pendleton tag is visible on the lower-right edge of the blanket. (Courtesy of Atkinson Trading Company.)

In 1936, Mildred Reynolds purchased an unknown number of rugs from Cameron Trading Post through Hubert and Jack Richardson for her custom-built home in California. The colors and patterns of the Navajo rugs blended beautifully with the home constructed of local redwood. The family has saved the original receipt from the purchase, seen at right. "J.R." would have been Jack Richardson, and Jeanette was his 19-year-old sister. The note asking about the price listed versus the price quoted is the first clue that Jeanette worked in the store. She left Cameron shortly afterward when she married. The Storm Pattern rug pictured below was purchased at Cameron Trading Post in 2003. The Storm Pattern is said to have originated at Cameron and features lightning bolts connecting the winds in the four corners with a storm house placed at the center. (Right, anonymous at owner's request.)

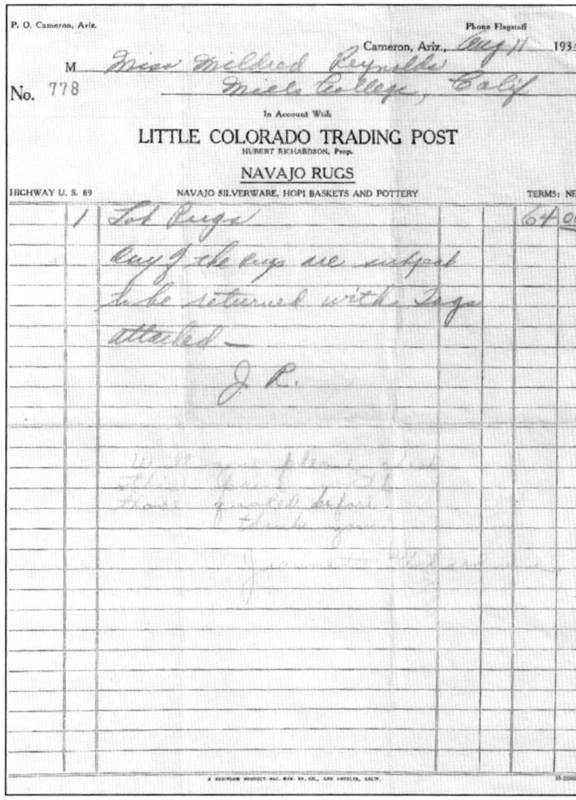
P. O. Cameron, Ariz. Phone Flagstaff

Cameron, Ariz., Aug 11 193[illegible]

M Miss Mildred Reynolds

No. 778 Mills College, Calif

In Account With

LITTLE COLORADO TRADING POST

HUBERT RICHARDSON, Prop.

NAVAJO RUGS

HIGHWAY U. S. 89 NAVAJO SILVERWARE, HOPI BASKETS AND POTTERY TERMS: NET

1	Lot Rugs	64.00
	Any of the rugs are subject to be returned with Tags attached —	
	J. R.	

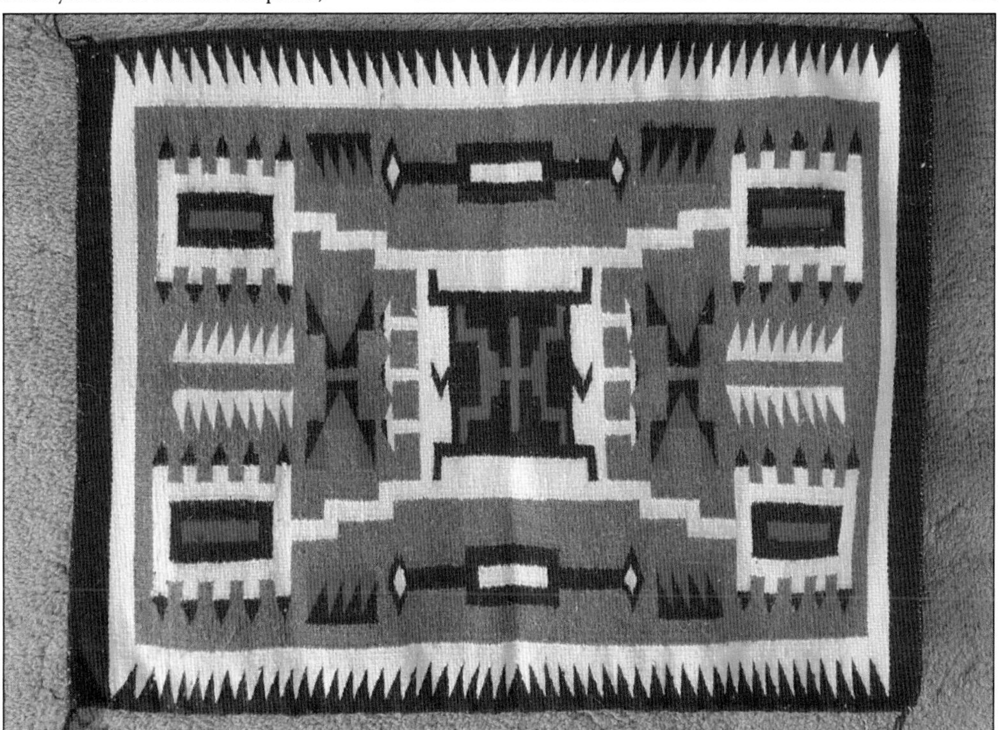

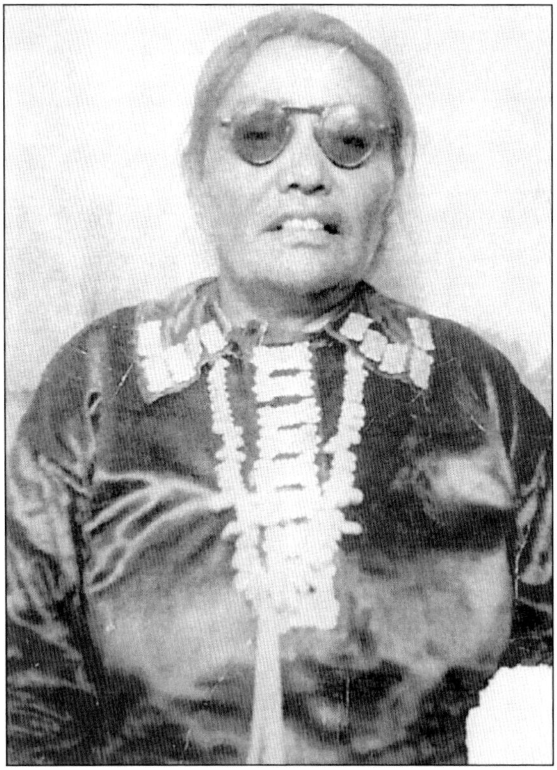

Zohnie Santa Fe, seen at left, was a weaver who traded at Cameron Trading Post. Below, she stands at the left holding her large weaving that features diamonds across the center and zigzags or possibly lightning on each end; her daughter Lillie Dugi is at the right. Hubert Richardson went to Zohnie and asked her to make the rug with the diamonds and zigzags in a particular size because he wanted two identical rugs for the hotel. (Both, courtesy of Lillie Dugi.)

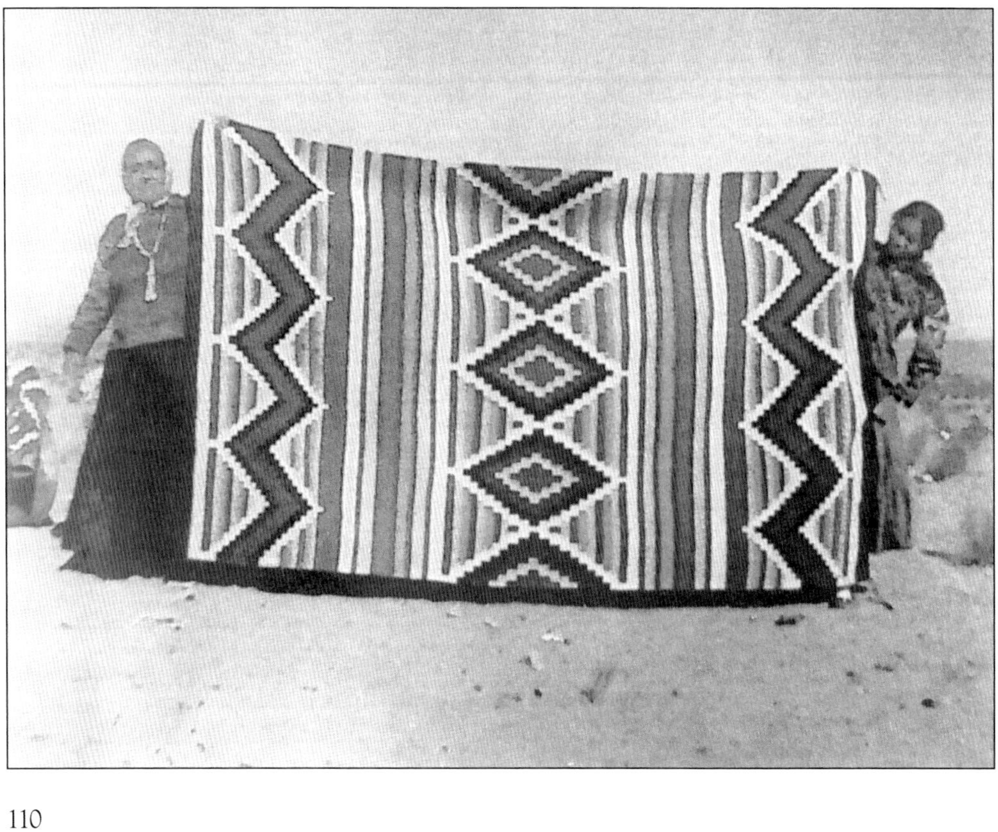

Jean Mann worked at Cameron as the resident weaver for many years. After she retired, she often worked at a bead stand on Highway 64 west of Cameron at the Little Colorado River Gorge where she sold beaded jewelry and small weavings. (Courtesy of Jean Mann.)

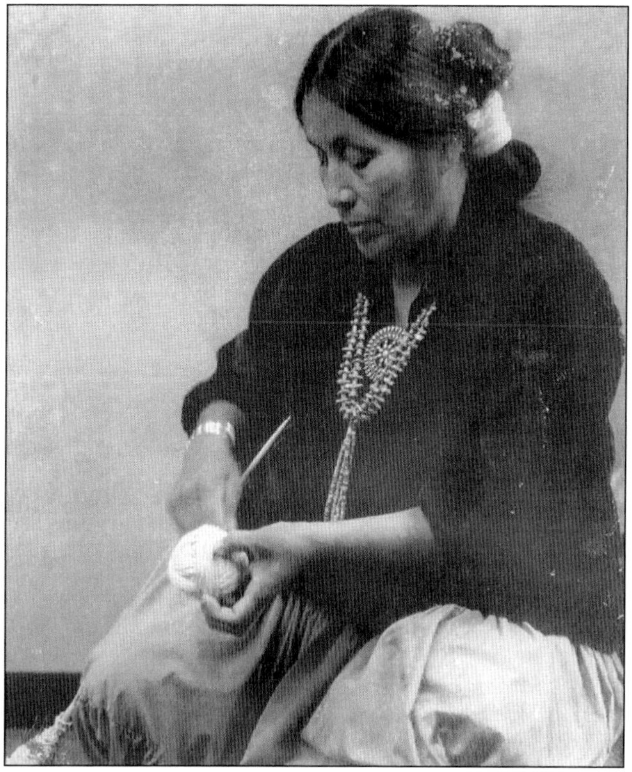

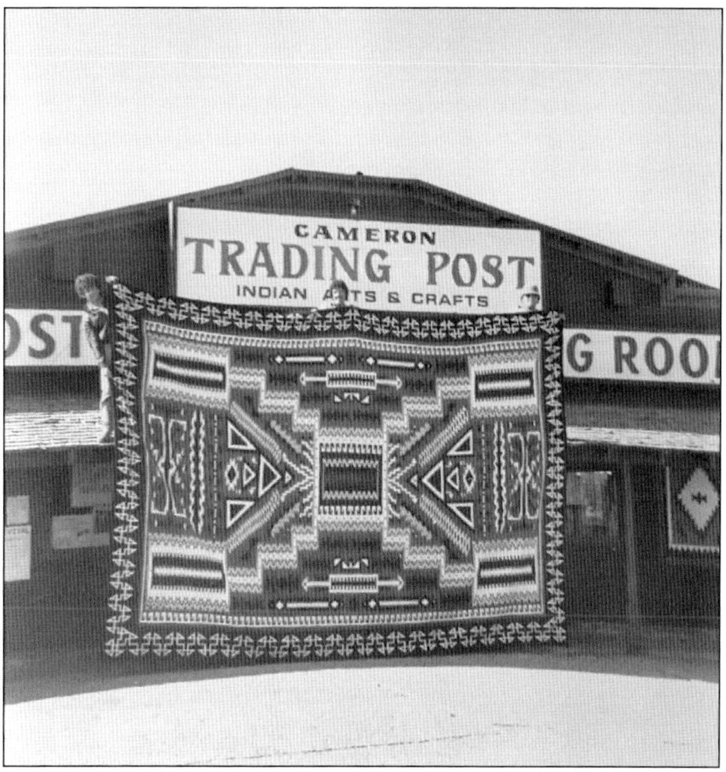

The exceptionally large and elaborate weaving by Lena Chief is a complex variation of a Storm Pattern rug. Because of its size, it is displayed in front of the trading post and held by three people standing on the roof of the porch—from left to right, Robert Chavarria, unidentified, and Edward Humetewa. (Courtesy of Andrew Kerley.)

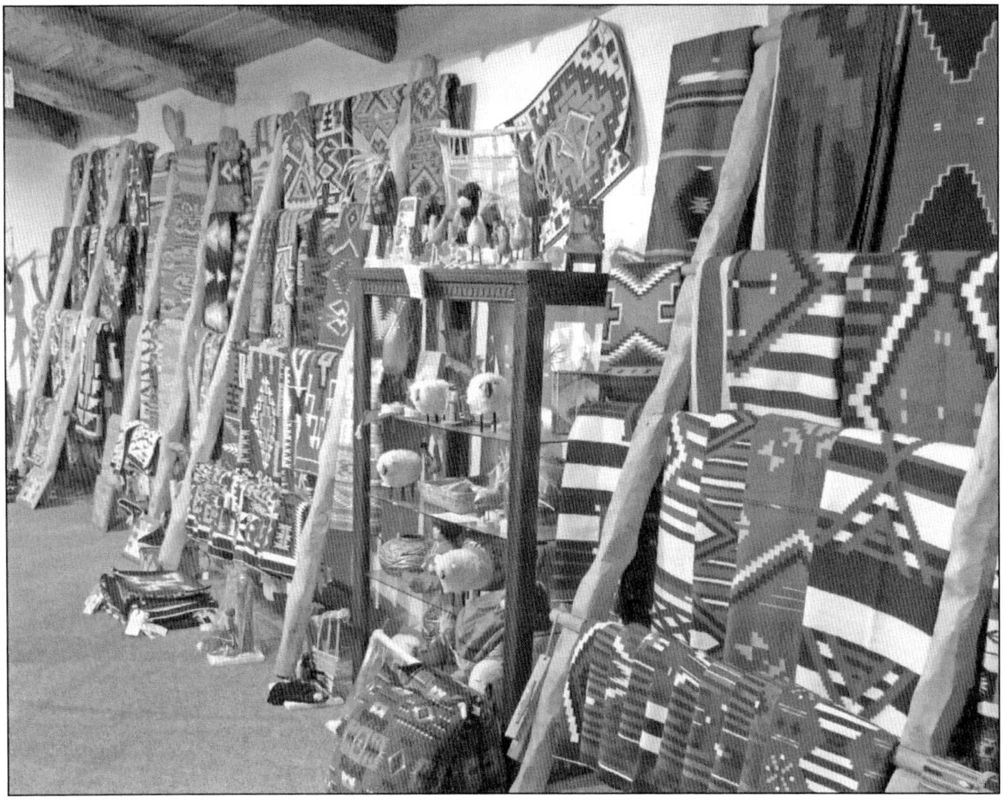

The rug gallery in the main store, pictured above, features fine contemporary weavings in several styles. A visitor can purchase a weaving at Cameron knowing with certainty that it is genuinely made by a Navajo weaver. Pictorial weavings, such as the small, wall-hanging pieces seen below, are also popular. The talented Cameron weavers create images with hogans, herds of sheep, pickup trucks, American flags, and trains. The weavers also design pieces with holiday themes, such as the Christmas scene at the right featuring hogans, a snowman, and Santa Claus and his reindeer flying across the sky. The word on the weaving at the left, *yah-ta-hey*, is a common Navajo greeting.

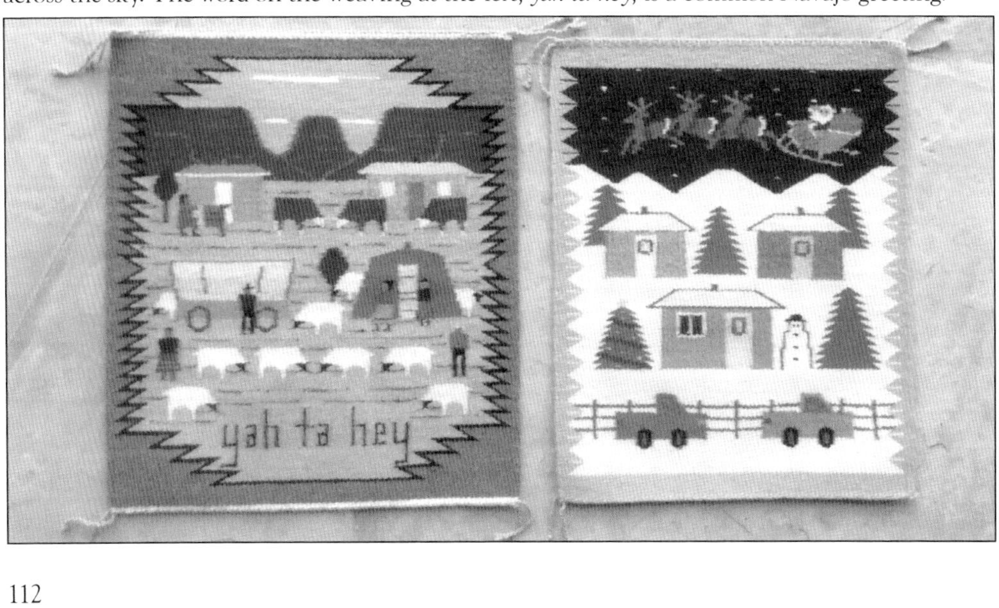

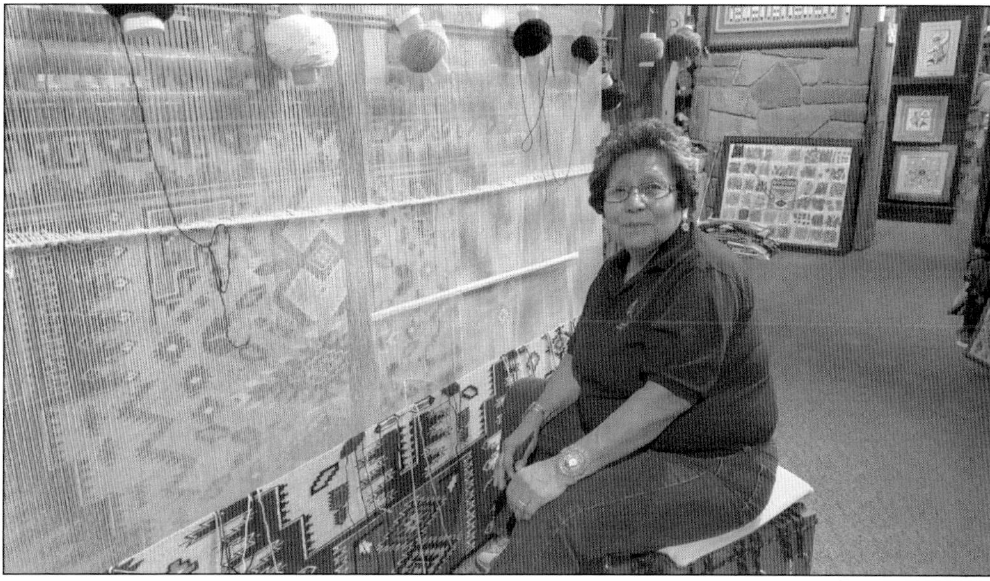

Elsie Glander was born in the Gray Mountain area and raised near Cameron. She is a member of the Honey Comb Cliff Dweller Clan. Elsie began weaving at the family's summer hogan near Gray Mountain when she was 9 years old; her mother set up Elsie's own loom when she was 13, and Elsie said, "I finally got the whole skill. Now, they call me the famous weaver." Most of Elsie's rugs are geometrics or Storm Pattern, and she is known for her large rugs, often measuring 9 feet by 12 feet. Elsie purchases commercial yarns that she washes and re-spins to give her rugs a finer texture. She has been the weaver at Cameron since 1997, and her rugs have been sold to collectors around the world. Elsie always includes a small flaw in the rug's design, saying that is her "signature and the identification of my work."

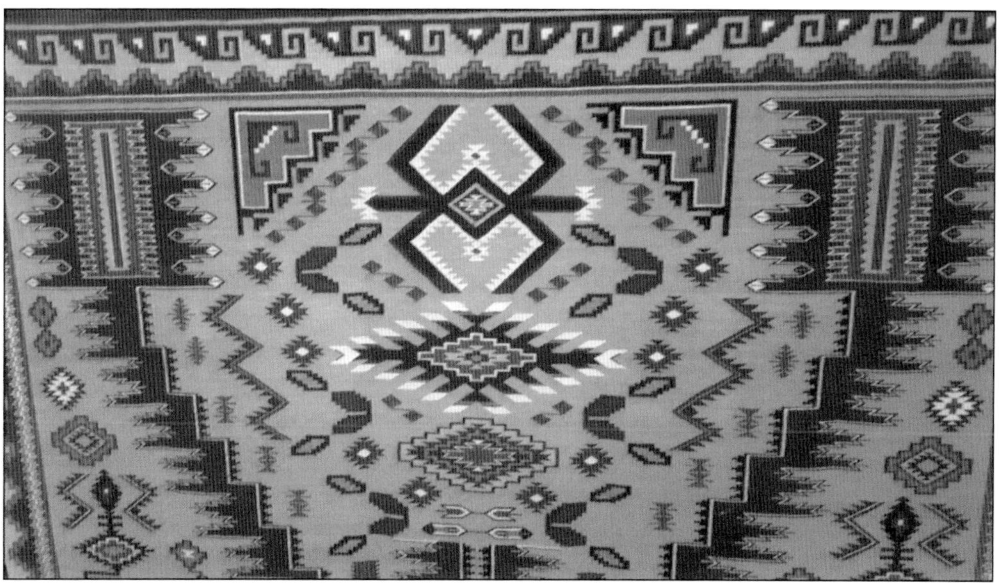

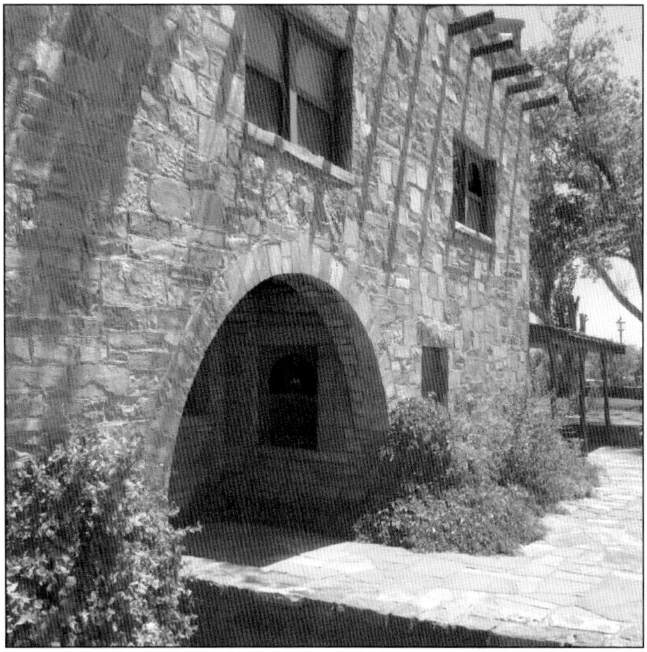

The 1928 Klo-a-chee-kin Hotel next to the trading post store is now a fine art gallery. While beautiful rugs, jewelry, pottery, and baskets are available in the main store, the gallery displays high-end, historical Native American artworks. The gallery features vintage silver and turquoise jewelry, Hopi pottery, including pieces by Nampeyo and her family, historic baskets, and many fine weavings. The c. 1875 Navajo Late Classic Serape, below, has zigzag bands and "Spider Woman" crosses. The price on this magnificent weaving was nearly $100,000. A visit to the Cameron gallery is much like a tour through a major museum.

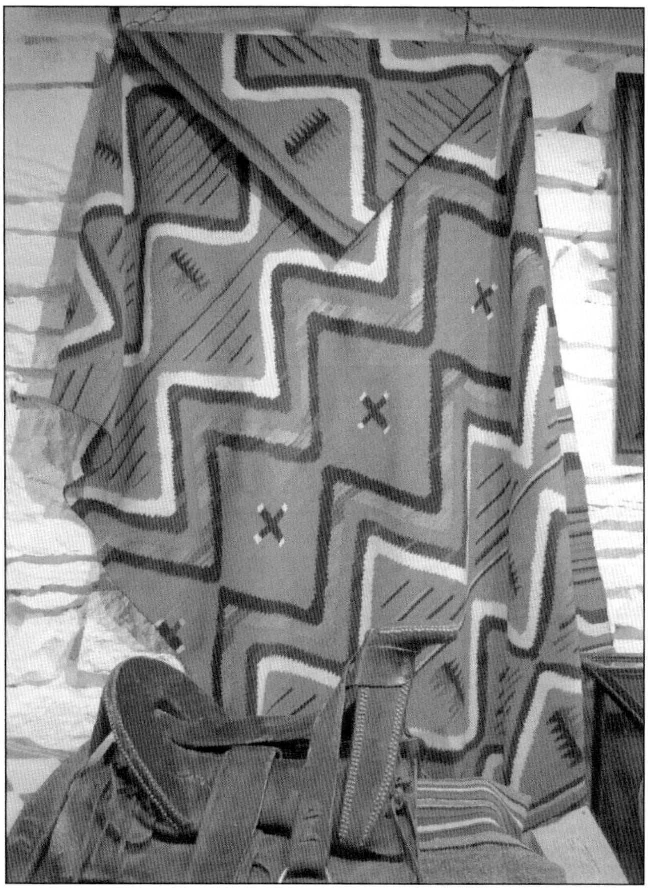

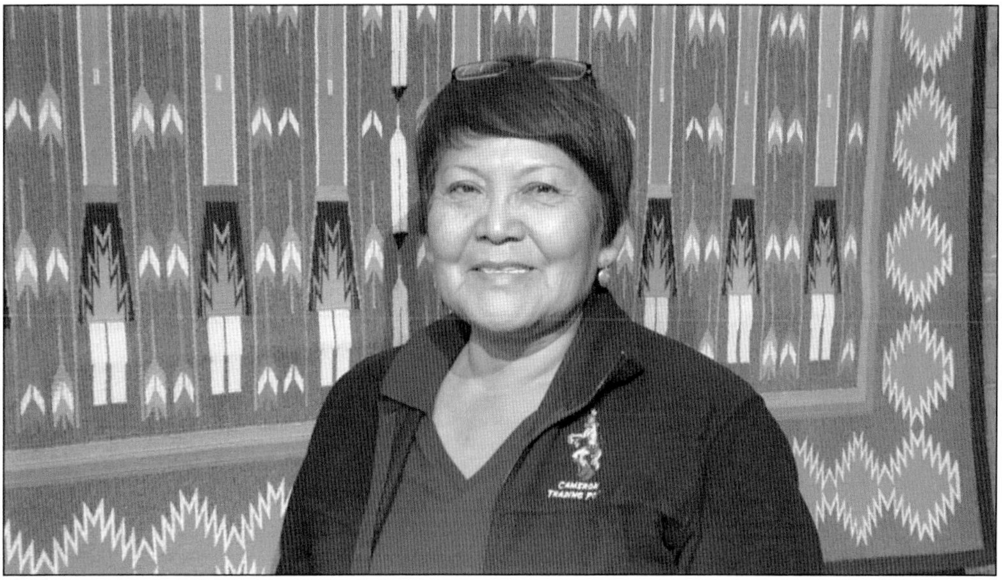

Caroline Wilson is a second-generation employee at Cameron. Her mother, Julia Johnson, had 10 children, whom she supported by working in the motel. Caroline remembers going to the trading post as a girl and informally helping her mother make up beds in the motel. She recalled that her reward was always a glass of lemonade. Today, Caroline works in Cameron's fine art gallery, the old 1928 original hotel building. Below is a gallery display with a vintage Apache fringed leather dress, a Yei rug, bronze sculpture, a Tohono O'odham lidded basket, and a historic pot.

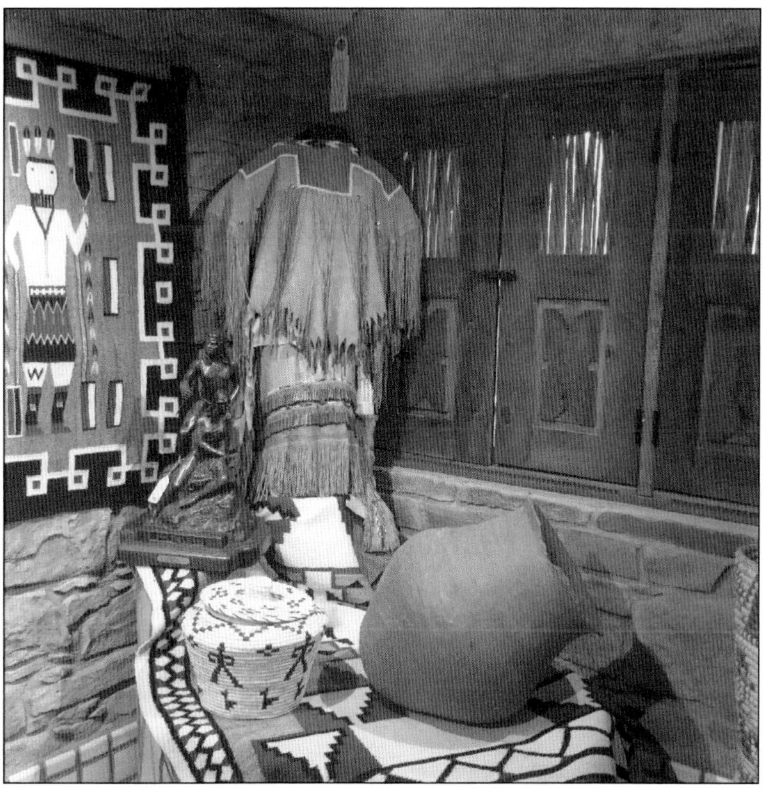

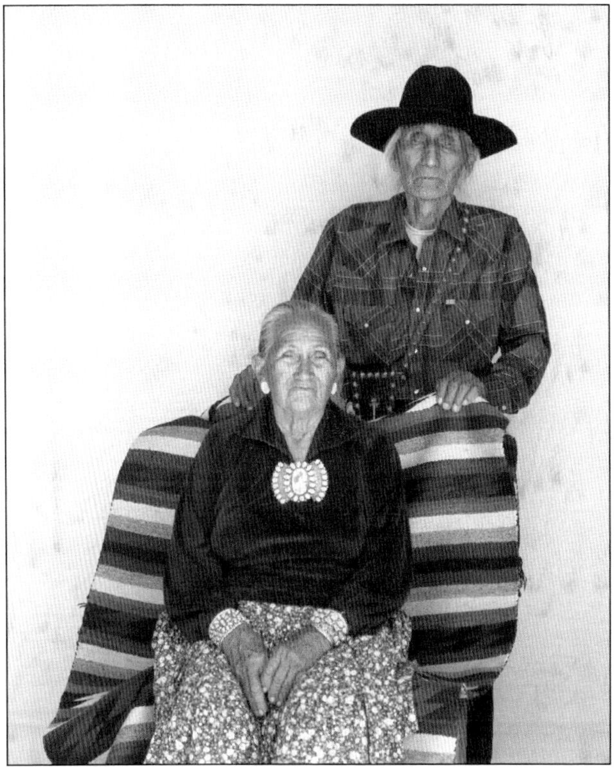

Kenneth Dugi (1908–1994) and his wife, Belle, are featured on the cover of the 1993 auction catalog. Kenneth was born in Hidden Springs, 23 miles north of Cameron, into the Tall House Clan, or Clan Kiiya'aanii. The Dugis raised cattle and sheep, and they had eight children. At his death, it was said that "Kenneth will be remembered as a man who embodied the spirit and dignity of the Navajo People." (Photograph by Pat Berrett, courtesy of Atkinson Trading Company.)

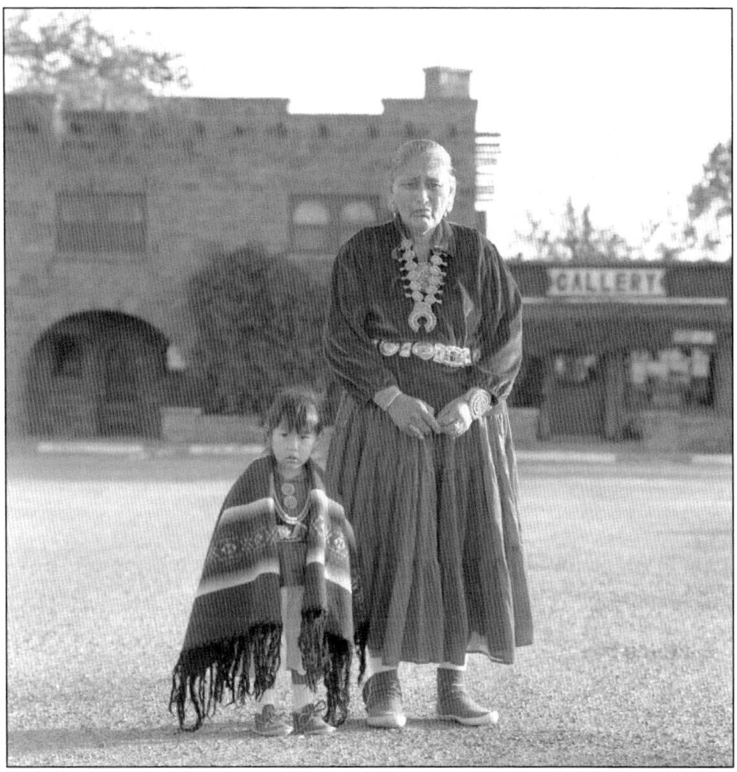

Nora Robbins visited Cameron Trading Post with her granddaughter Rena Robbins in the early 1990s. They are standing in front of the gallery, which is attached to the original 1928 Klo-a-chee-kin Hotel at the left. (Photograph by Pat Berrett, courtesy of Atkinson Trading Company.)

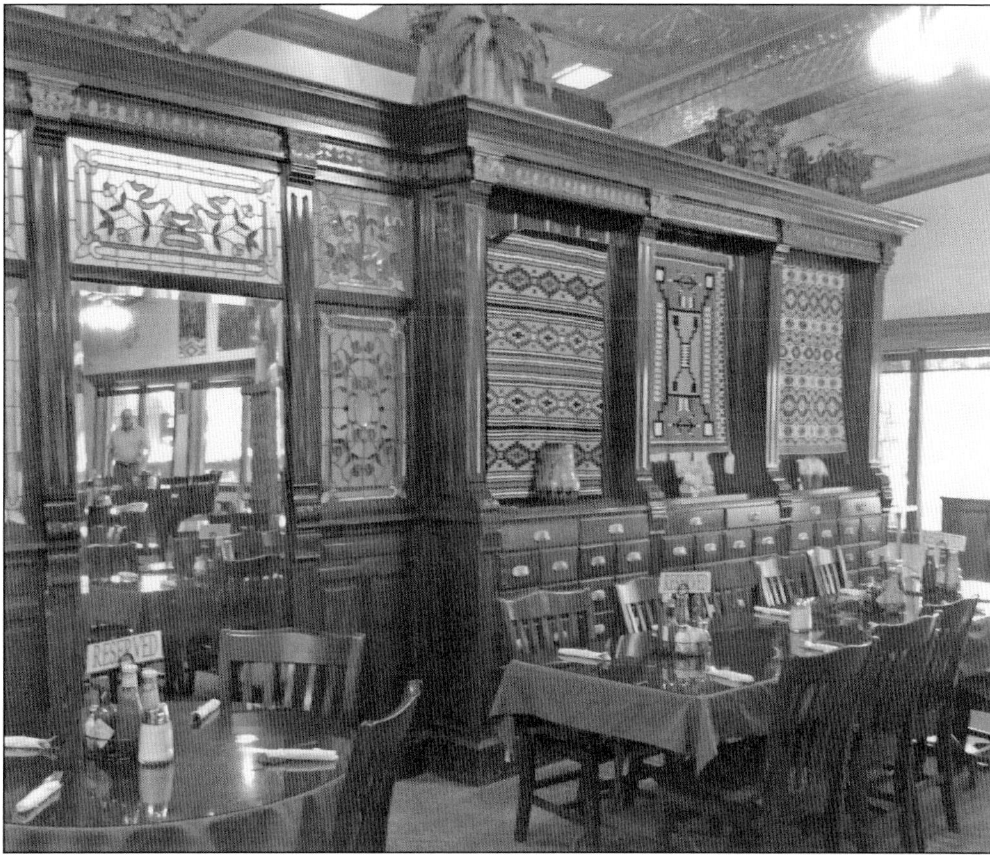

There are two kitchens at the Cameron restaurant, on opposite sides of the dining room. Tour buses and vans stop at Cameron daily, so the restaurant is always prepared to serve large groups. Picture windows in the restaurant look out into the gorge of the Little Colorado River. Angel Walker was a third-generation Cameron employee, known for her cheerful greetings and friendly smile. Below, Angel serves a Navajo taco, likely the most popular entree on the restaurant menu. It is described as being as large as a hubcap. According to restaurant manager Treva Walker, Cameron routinely purchases 500 pounds of pinto beans a week, fry bread is made daily, and flour is purchased in 50 pound bags, 80 bags each month. In the summer, the restaurant serves between 600 and 1,000 meals a day, and "everybody comes at once."

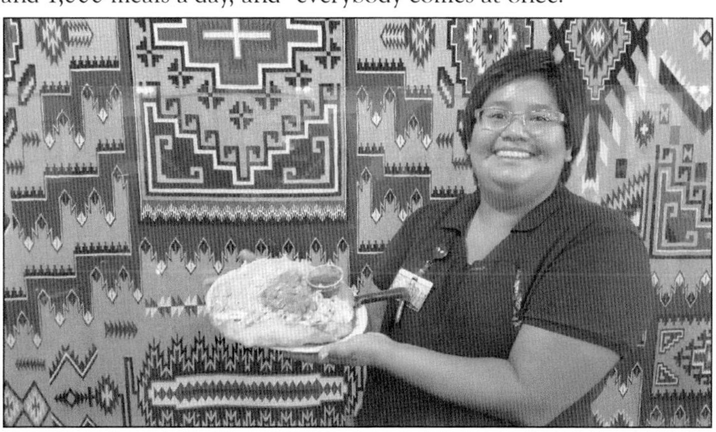

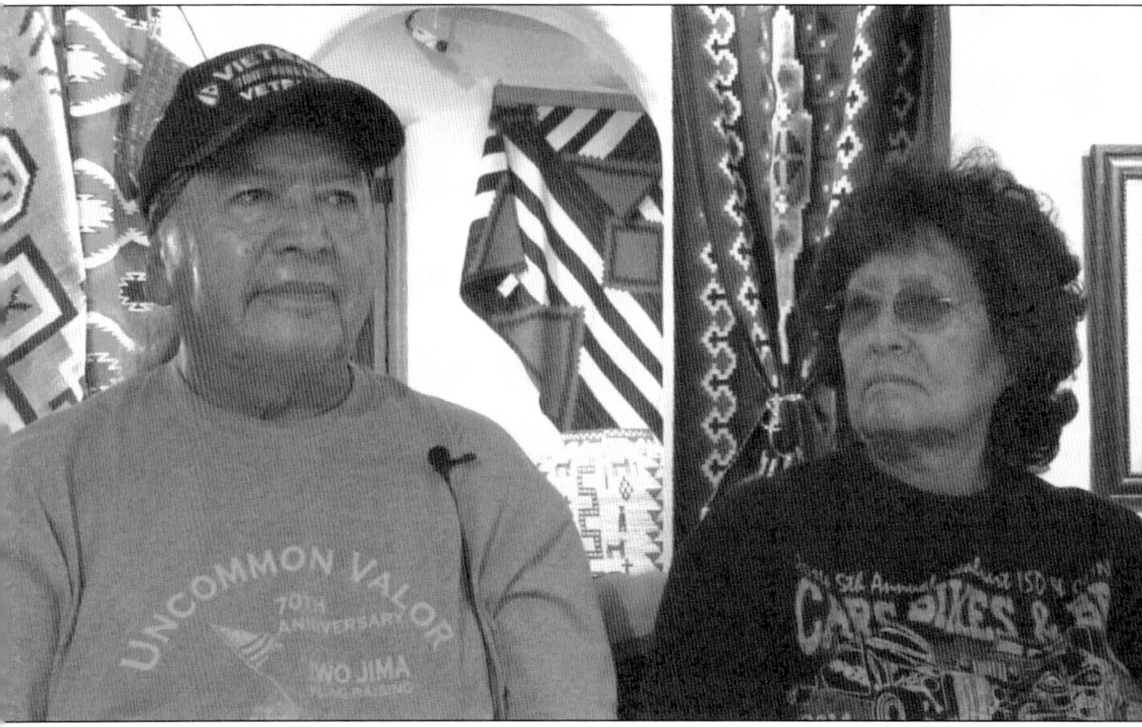

Tex and Helyn Walker live southwest of Cameron Trading Post. They have no electricity, and they haul water for their home once a week. One of Tex's grandfathers was Charlie Huskon, an early Cameron resident. Charlie was a prospector and also worked for Hubert Richardson. In the early years, it took a week to go to Flagstaff by wagon to get supplies and return. Later, Charlie drove the freighting truck. Tex recalled that as a boy, he and his friends would climb onto the bridge cables to swing or slide down. There were steel girders under the bridge, and they would run across them and play "not it." He also remembers that the men would gather wild tobacco that grew at Gray Mountain to smoke. Later, tobacco came in a block and a slice would be cut off and placed in paper or a rolled corn husk to make a cigarette. Cheese came in long rolls, and slices could be cut and wrapped for customers. Tex and Helyn also remember a vintage, hand-turned coffee grinder. Whole coffee beans were shipped to the trading post. (Courtesy of Atkinson Trading Company.)

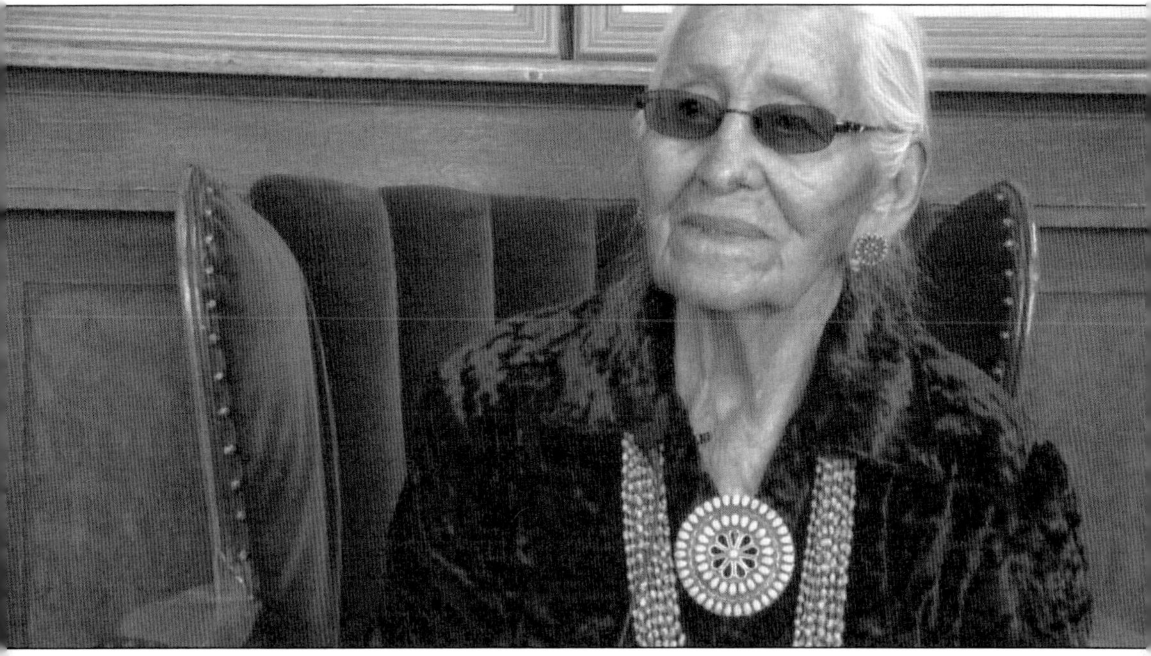

Betty Huskon was born in 1924, and she married Max Huskon when she was 19 and Max was working for Hubert Richardson. She remembered that in those early years, just a few automobiles came through Cameron. Betty wove rugs that she traded at the post, and if she needed money, Hubert would give her an advance, but he was never in a hurry to be repaid: "He was kind." Even though Hubert was 34 years older than Betty, she called him son, and he called her "Shimá," translated as "mother." They had an affectionate and joking relationship. Betty recalled living at Bodaway Gap, where she helped her grandfather who was a silversmith; she pumped the bellows to heat the fire that melted the silver. As a girl, when Betty's uncle bought a Model T with a chicken wire bed, she loved to ride in the back, even though she shared the space with sheep and chickens. Her father-in-law's image was painted above the entrance to the trading post (and can be seen in the cover image). Betty never attended school, and she speaks only Navajo. (Courtesy of Atkinson Trading Company.)

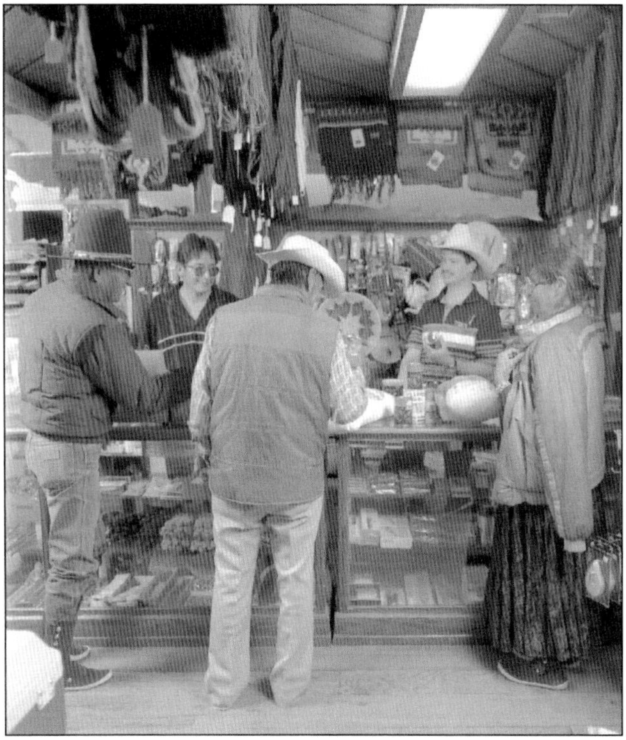

One author wrote in 1962 that Cameron was a tourist haven on Highway 89, and the boom in visitors backed "Hubert Richardson into a glass-and-wood partitioned office." The boom never slowed down; today, visitors can purchase souvenirs and trinkets or high-end collectibles. At left, local customers (from left to right) Ross Williams, Pete Roy Boone, and Rose Boone are served by (from left to right behind the counter) Jimmy Jensen and Mike Davis in 1991. Below, colorful hanks of wool hang above the grocery store counters, offering a rainbow variety of yarns for the local weavers. Nora Clark is at the counter, being helped by Edward Humetewa and Irvin Benally. (Both photographs by Pat Berrett, courtesy of Atkinson Trading Company.)

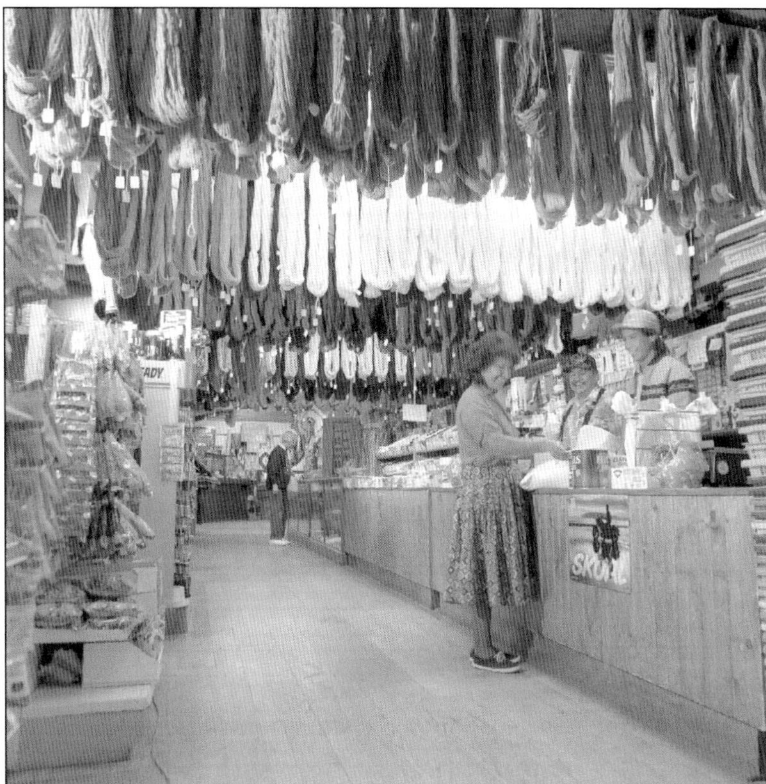

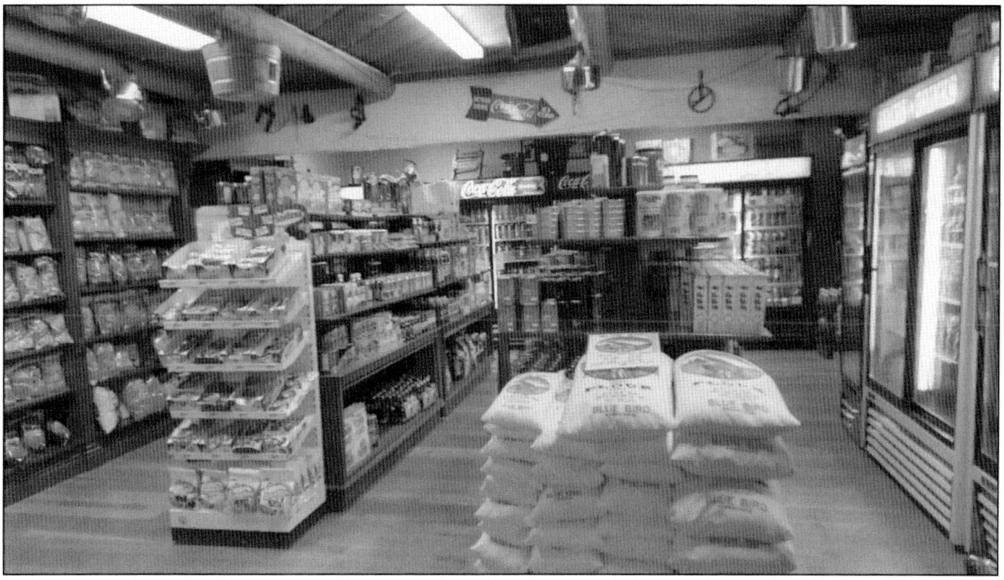

The market at Cameron offers a variety of dry goods, food, and snacks—everything from suckers and bins of candy to 25-pound bags of Blue Bird Flour. There are also cases with beading supplies as well as skins and pelts, which are used for crafts and also in ceremonies.

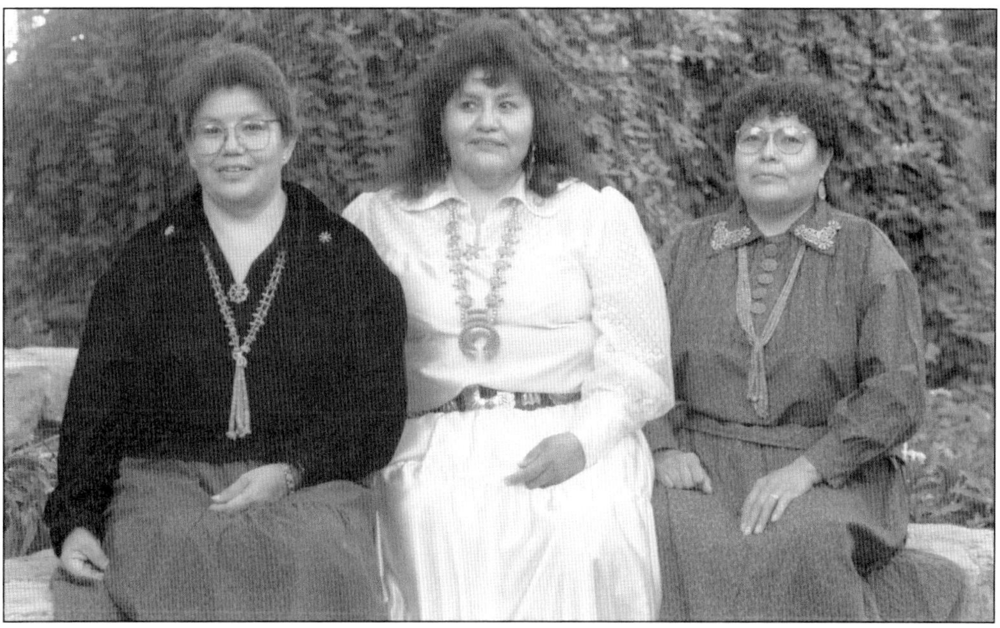

Three longtime Cameron employees are, from left to right, Susie Colorado, her sister Della Chief, and Susie Yazzie. Colorado started at Cameron Trading Post in 1973, when it was managed by Fred Harvey. Chief began working in the trading post in the 1960s. When Joe acquired Cameron in 1977, she would remind him not to lose sight of Cameron traditions. Yazzie now works in the office; she started in 1980. (Photograph by Pat Berrett, courtesy of Atkinson Trading Company.)

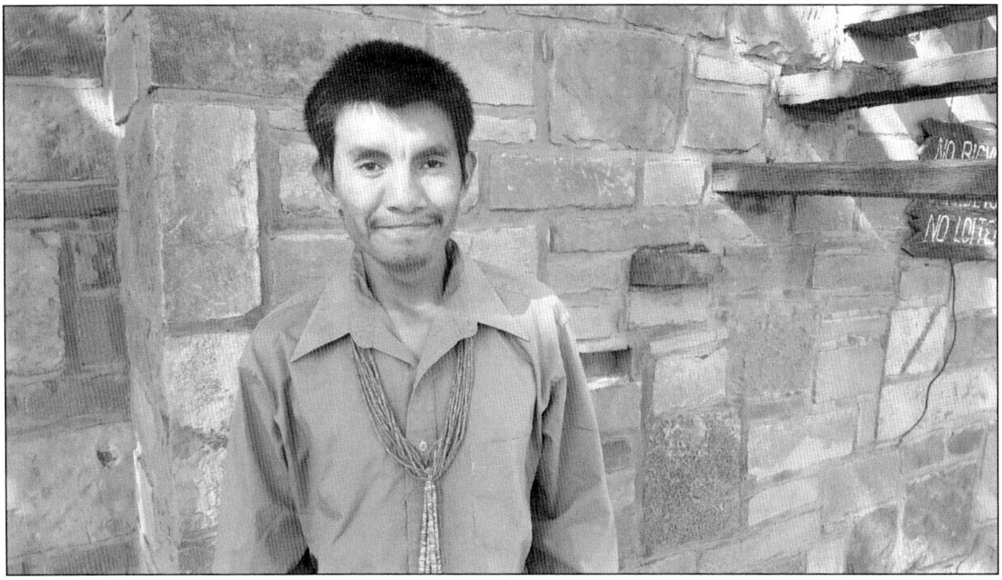

Leland Jones grew up at Cameron and has worked at Cameron Trading Post for 10 years. Below, Leland is holding a vintage Coca-Cola advertising sign. Carved in wood, the sign includes stylized kachina figures. It has hung in the trading post for decades. Leland's parents and grandparents lived near Cameron and also in the Wupatki area. Leland says that history inspires him, and he always tries to interest young people in the local history. Leland has given his time, knowledge, and support to this book project; it never could have been done without his innumerable contributions. Many thanks to you, Leland. Ahéhee'.

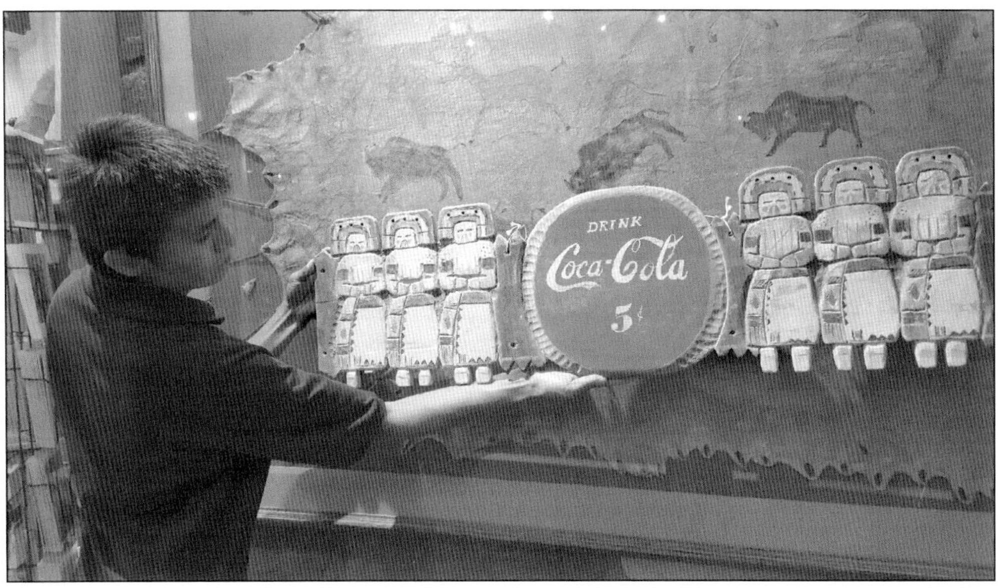

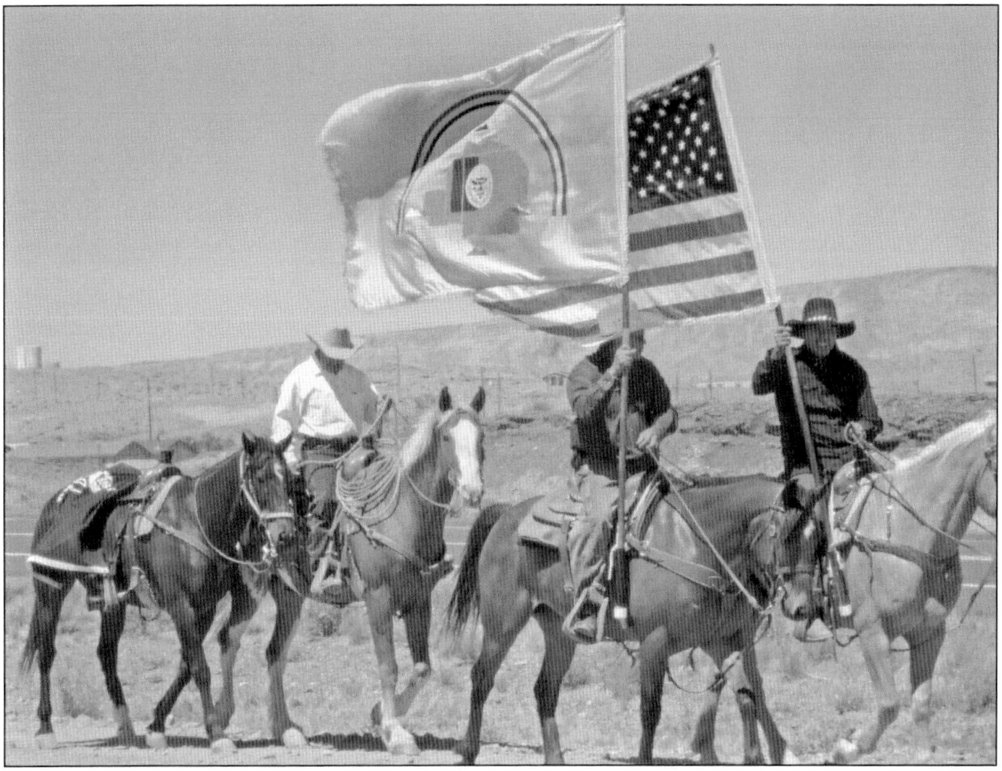

The Cameron Veterans Organization is known to have the largest number of veterans on the Navajo Reservation, and the local people have a strong tradition of military service. One local man, Jimmie Preston, was a code talker in World War II. In 2010, a welcome-home ceremony was held for Nat Lee, who was killed in an ambush in Vietnam. In the 1970s, Lee's flag and medals were lost in a fire. For the ceremony, replacement medals and a flag were presented to his family. There was a Blessingway Ceremony and a riderless horse (with military boots turned backwards in the stirrups) to welcome home his spirit and let him know that he was not forgotten. Above are, from left to right, Pastor Jones, unidentified, and Tristan Gordy. Pictured below is the Color Guard for the Native American Veterans of the Vietnam War. (Both, courtesy of Leland Jones.)

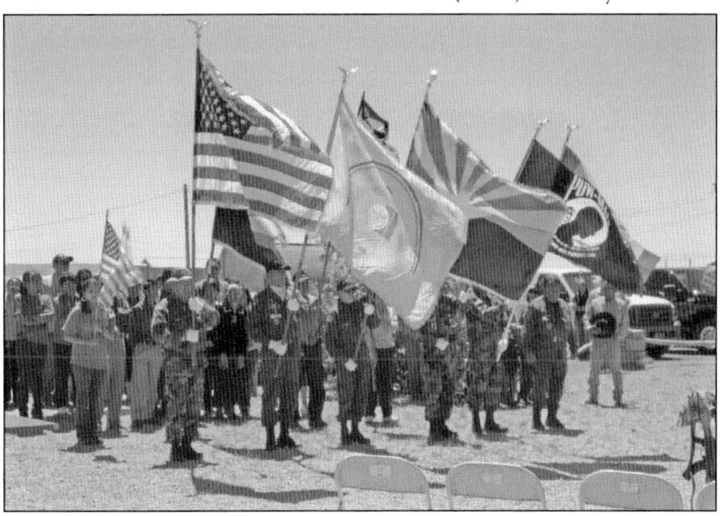

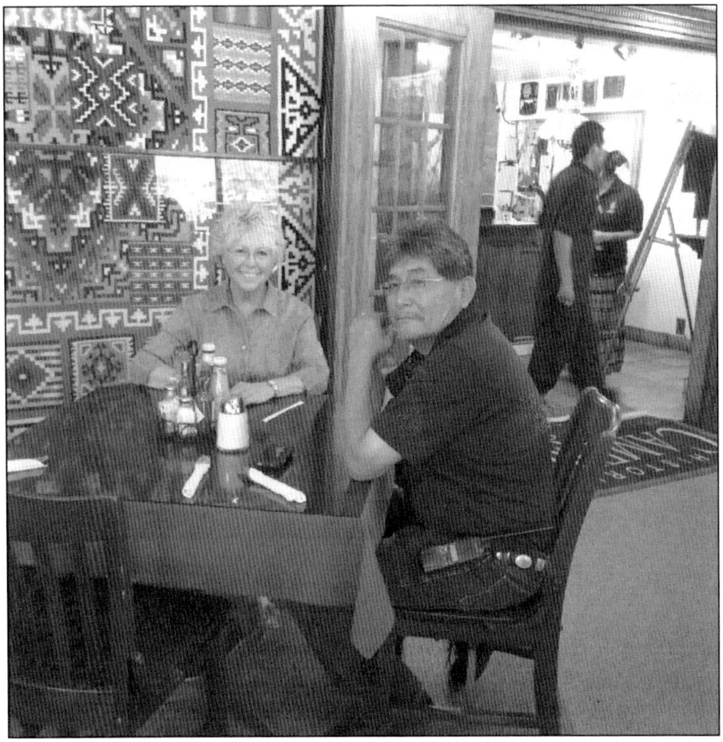

Jimmy Jensen has worked at Cameron Trading Post for more than 30 years. He worked with Joe Atkinson on the remodeling of the buildings. Jensen, pictured with the author, is a descendant of Peshlakai Etsidi, the famous early silversmith. Jensen also worked in silver, and some of his pieces are in museum collections. Now, he oversees much of the maintenance and operations of Cameron Trading Post.

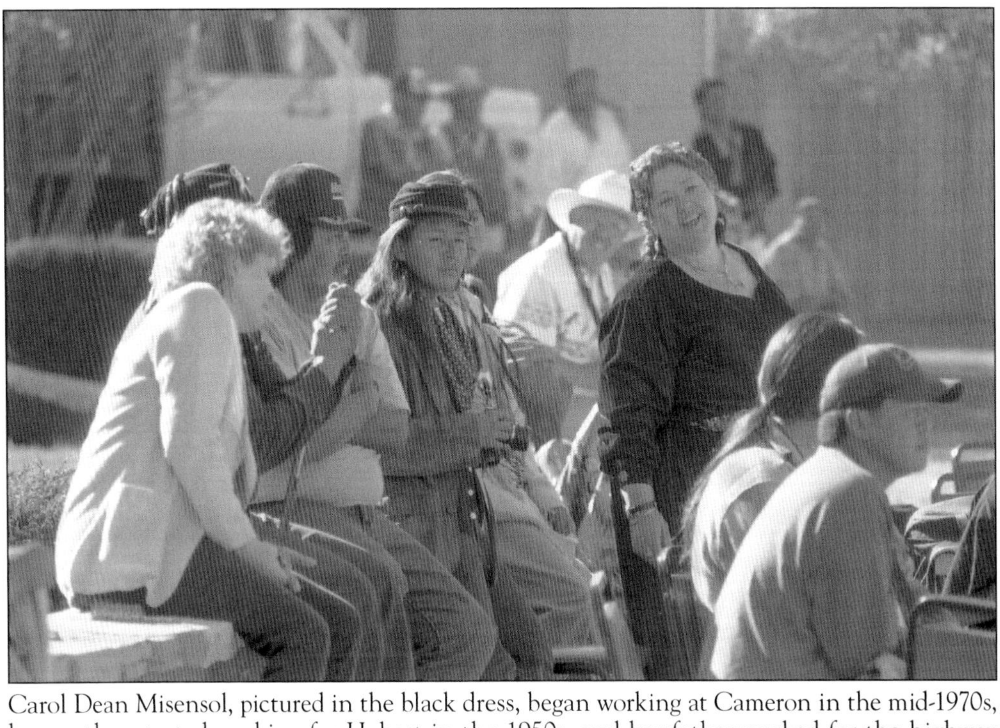

Carol Dean Misensol, pictured in the black dress, began working at Cameron in the mid-1970s, her mother started working for Hubert in the 1950s, and her father worked for the highway department; they lived at the ADOT camp. Carol Dean was the manager of the curio shop until her death in 2014. (Photograph by Pat Berrett, courtesy of Atkinson Trading Company.)

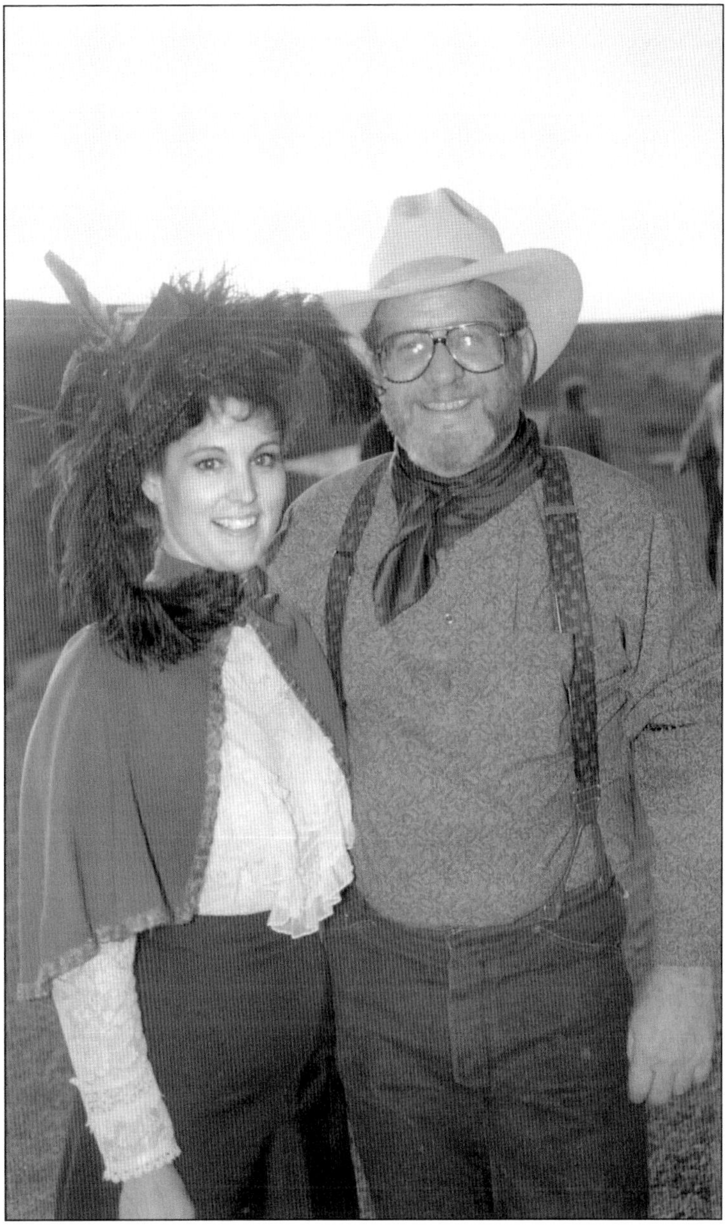

After owning Cameron Trading Post for nearly four decades, Joe Atkinson was quoted as saying that at Cameron, "we are like a large family. We share traditions, celebrations, and daily life." Christmas parties for local families are a longtime tradition at Cameron. About 500 to 600 dinners are served, and Santa Claus arrives to hand out toys and gifts to children. On a different day, there is an employee party with a gift exchange, and the employee of the year is named. Reflecting on the last decades of Cameron Trading Post, Joe commented, "The most important aspects of the trading post have changed very little in the last century. We're still the locals' sounding board for legal, governmental, and other very practical, everyday matters. We continue to be a family, sharing holidays, traditional ceremonies, birthdays, weddings, etc." Joe and his wife, Jeanell, are dressed in period costume for one of the 1990s auctions. (Photograph by Pat Berrett, courtesy of Atkinson Trading Company.)

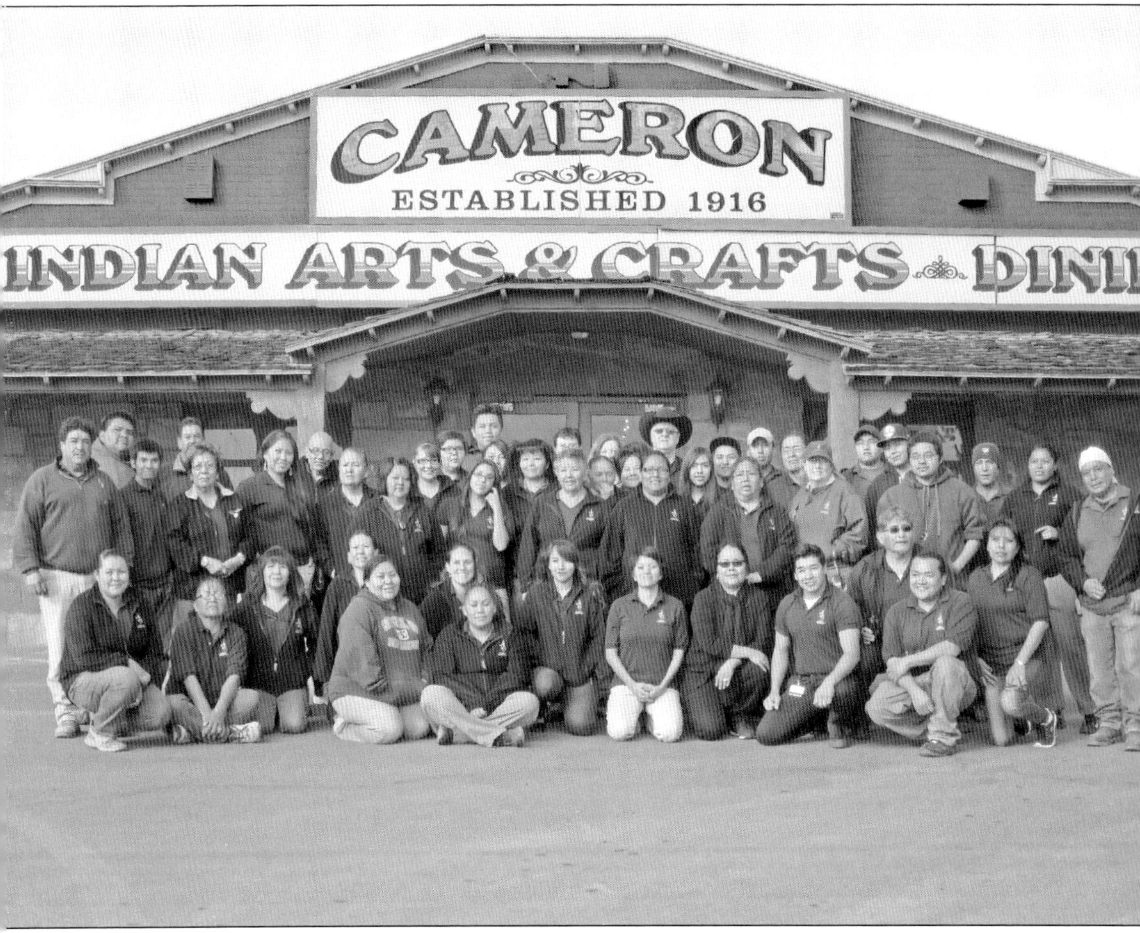

Cameron Trading Post employs many people who keep all of the facilities operating smoothly—working in the store, gas station, gallery, and behind the scenes in maintenance and facilities support. Many of the employees have a long employment history at Cameron Trading Post, and many are also the sons and daughters and grandchildren of earlier generations of people who worked at the post. With the 2016 Centennial Celebration, Cameron employees and nearby residents look forward to the next 100 years. Owner Joe Atkinson says that "what makes Cameron special is not only the fine weavings, baskets and beadwork—it's the ambiance. Here you're not just told about the people, their traditions, and what trading post life is like—you experience it. This gives works of art meaning and brings them to life." (Courtesy of Atkinson Trading Company.)

Bibliography

Bezunartea, Patricia. *Gilbert Ortega: The Story of the Man Behind the Name*. Scottsdale, AZ: Gilbert Ortega Family Publications, 2007.

Bird, Roland T. *Bones for Barnum Brown: Adventures of a Dinosaur Hunter*. Fort Worth: Texas Christian University Press, 1985.

Eddington, Patrick and Susan Makov. *Trading Post Guidebook: Where to find the Trading Posts, Galleries, Auctions, Artists, and Museums of the Four Corners Region*. Flagstaff, AZ: Northland Publishing Company, 1995.

Hall, Sharlot M. *Sharlot Hall on the Arizona Strip: A Diary of a Journey Through Northern Arizona in 1911*. Flagstaff, AZ: Northland Press, 1975.

Hegemann, Elizabeth Compton. *Navajo Trading Days*. Albuquerque: University of New Mexico Press, 1963.

Hillerman, Anne. *Tony Hillerman's Landscape On the Road with Chee and Leaphorn*. New York: HarperCollins Publishers, 2009.

Kosik, Fran. *Native Roads: The Complete Motoring Guide to the Navajo and Hopi Nations*. Flagstaff, AZ: Creative Solutions Publishing, 1996.

LaFarge, Oliver. *Raw Material*. Cambridge, MA: Riverside Press, 1945.

Mangum, Richard and Sherry Mangum. "The Amazing Trackless Train and the Lost Town of Bobsburg." *Plateau Journal* 5 (2):36-41, 2001.

McClintock, James H. *Mormon Settlement in Arizona*. Tucson: University of Arizona Press, 1985.

McNeill, Joe. *Arizona's Little Hollywood: Sedona and Northern Arizona's Forgotten Film History 1923–1973*. Sedona, AZ: Northedge & Sons, 2010.

McNitt, Frank. *The Indian Traders*. Norman: University of Oklahoma Press, 1962.

Richardson, Gladwell. *Navajo Trader*. Tucson: University of Arizona Press, 1991.

Thybony, Scott and David Edwards. *The Painted Desert Land of Wind and Stone*. Tucson: University of Arizona Press, 2006.

Westerlund, John S. *Arizona's War Town: Flagstaff, Navajo Ordnance Depot, and World War II*. Tucson: University of Arizona Press, 2003.